Antitrust

BY MARK A. LEMLEY
University of California, Berkeley

CHRISTOPHER LESLIE
Chicago-Kent College of Law

Tenth Edition

THOMSON
BAR/BRI

EDITORIAL OFFICES: 111 W. Jackson Blvd., 7th Floor, Chicago, IL 60604
REGIONAL OFFICES: Chicago, Dallas, Los Angeles, New York, Washington, D.C.

PROJECT EDITOR
Erin Johnson Remotigue, B.A., J.D.
Attorney At Law

SERIES EDITOR
Elizabeth L. Snyder, B.A., J.D.
Attorney At Law

QUALITY CONTROL EDITOR
Sanetta M. Hister

Summary of Contents

Text Correlation Chart

Gilbert Law Summary ANTITRUST	Areeda, Kaplow, Edlin *Antitrust Analysis* 2004 (6th ed.)	Pitofsky, Goldschmid, Wood *Trade Regulation* 2003 (5th ed.) 2004 Supp.	Sullivan, Hovenkamp *Antitrust Law, Policy and Procedure* 2003 (5th ed.) 2004 Supp.
I. RESTRAINTS OF TRADE—AT COMMON LAW			
A. Contracts in Restraint of Trade	Page 33	Page 23-35	Page 21-22
B. Common Law Monopolies and Combinations in Restraint of Trade	32-34	23-69	18-26
II. THE FEDERAL ANTITRUST LAWS—IN GENERAL			
A. Background	34-42	35-69	23-29
B. Summary of Principal Statutes Regulating Competitive Behavior	42-45, 847-880	Appendix 1-35	26-41, 1087-1095; Supp. 1
C. Antitrust Jurisdiction	97-102	120-125, 1171-1277; Supp. 49-65	77-92, 827-828; Supp. 6-8
D. Antitrust Remedies	45-80	70-117; Supp. 16-17	65-161, 169-184, 230-234; Supp. 5-10
III. MONOPOLIZATION			
A. Monopolization by a Single Firm	367-525	128-196, 722-832, 847-931; Supp. 19-47	557, 593-731; Supp. 19-32
B. Attempts to Monopolize	525-532	832-847	746-790; Supp. 32
C. Conspiracy to Monopolize			788
IV. COLLABORATION AMONG COMPETITORS—HORIZONTAL RESTRAINTS			
A. Introduction	113-114	51-67, 197-328	30-41, 187-292, 360-379; Supp. 1, 11-15
B. Price Fixing Among Competitors	114-202	197-297	190-292; Supp. 11-14
C. Division of Markets	143-149	297-328	360-379; Supp. 15
D. Group Boycotts and Concerted Refusals to Deal	273-302	329-378	379-425
E. Joint Ventures by Competitors	196-202, 259-261, 284-288, 783-784	378-410, 1081-1091; Supp. 18	360-364
F. Disseminating Information Among Competitors	244-261, 274	586-613	214-236; Supp. 12
G. What Constitutes an "Agreement," "Combination," or "Conspiracy" Among Competitors	202-242, 261-272, 572-573	490-586, 613-618	292-359, 447-448, 917; Supp. 14-15
V. VERTICAL RESTRAINTS			
A. Introduction	533-535	620-624	427-429
B. Resale Price Maintenance by Sellers	91-92, 341-343, 535-587	624-648, 679-720	429-475
C. Exclusive Distributorships and Customer and Territorial Restrictions	552-587	648-720, 931-935	330-332, 476-497; Supp. 17
D. Tying Arrangements	587-653	876-931	510-588; Supp. 18

Gilbert Law Summary ANTITRUST	Areeda, Kaplow, Edlin *Antitrust Analysis* 2004 (6th ed.)	Pitofsky, Goldschmid, Wood *Trade Regulation* 2003 (5th ed.) 2004 Supp.	Sullivan, Hovenkamp *Antitrust Law, Policy and Procedure* 2003 (5th ed.) 2004 Supp.
E. Exclusive Dealing—Requirements Contracts	653-668	931-962; Supp. 48	498-510
VI. MERGERS AND ACQUISITIONS			
A. Clayton Act Section 7	44, 678-687	964-971	827-828
B. Judicial Interpretation of Section 7	683-684	971-1168	828-916; Supp. 33
C. Horizontal Mergers	687-762	971-1081	818-885; Supp. 33
D. Vertical Mergers	762-775	1127-1168	793-818
E. Conglomerate Mergers	775-799	1081-1127	885-908
F. Joint Ventures	783-784	1081-1091	903-904
G. Department of Justice Merger Guidelines	499-503, 710-738, 770-773, 787-788	975-977, 1034-1062, 1115-1118, 1156-1160	815-818, 849-885, 905-907; Supp. 33
H. Pre-Merger Notification	684-687		
VII. PRICE DISCRIMINATION—THE ROBINSON-PATMAN ACT			
A. Economic Analysis of Price Discrimination	801	1278-1283	925-933; Supp. 35-37
B. Elements of a Prima Facie Robinson-Patman Violation	98, 802-821	1284-1321	933-952; Supp. 37
C. Defenses to a Prima Facie Violation of Robinson-Patman Act	821-833	1321-1342	952-965
D. Prohibitions on Indirect Price Concessions	838-846	1343-1350	947-950
E. Buyer's Inducement or Receipt of a Discriminatory Price	833-838	1350-1358	966-971
F. Exemptions	803-804	1283	932-933; Supp. 35-37
G. Damages	804	1289-1290	114, 944-947
VIII. "UNFAIR METHODS OF COMPETITION"			
A. Federal Trade Commission Act Section 5	55, 98, 855-858	73-76	39-41; Supp. 1
B. Anticompetitive Practices Covered by Section 5	55, 98, 269-272	73-76, 884, 938-939, 1357-1358	587-588
C. Section 5 as Source of Rule-Making Power	57-58		70
D. FTC Remedies	55-58	90-96	69-70
IX. INTELLECTUAL PROPERTY RIGHTS AND THEIR ANTITRUST IMPLICATIONS			
A. Economic Justifications for Patents	102-106		
B. The Patent System	106-111, 352-354		
C. Copyrights	103		
D. Relationship of Intellectual Property to Antitrust Laws	311-316, 340-366, 479-483, 594-597	812-831	363-364, 706-736
X. EXEMPTIONS FROM THE ANTITRUST LAWS			
A. Background	80-81	117-126	

Gilbert Law Summary ANTITRUST	Areeda, Kaplow, Edlin *Antitrust Analysis* 2004 (6th ed.)	Pitofsky, Goldschmid, Wood *Trade Regulation* 2003 (5th ed.) 2004 Supp.	Sullivan, Hovenkamp *Antitrust Law, Policy and Procedure* 2003 (5th ed.) 2004 Supp.
B. Agricultural Organizations	87	126	998-999
C. Interstate Water, Motor, Rail, and Air Carriers	81-85	119-120, 735-736	
D. Export Trade Associations	101-102		994-995
E. Bank Mergers	87	978-990	836-840
F. Insurance	88	126	995-998
G. Stock Exchanges	84-85	119	980-985; Supp. 39
H. Labor Unions	23, 85-86	125-126	990-994; Supp. 41-43
I. Professional Baseball	87	348	999; Supp. 43-44
J. "State Action" Exemption	87-97	302-303, 450-488	1025-1059; Supp. 46-47
K. Concerted Action by Competitors Designed to Influence Governmental Action	302-340	410-450, 1184-1193, 1272-1273	999-1025
L. Rejection of "Learned Profession" Exemption	159-172, 295-300	225-227, 230-233, 362-377, 453-457	210-214, 236-241, 397-398, 405-414

Capsule Summary

monopoly is ownership of so large a part of the market supply or output of a commodity as to *stifle competition* and give effective control over prices, distribution, and other aspects of commerce. A *combination in restraint of trade* is a concerted action among competitors that tends to *create a monopoly* or otherwise endanger competition.

2. Early Common Law §33

In the 17th century, English courts began to strike down monopolies, and in 1623, the Statute of Monopolies was enacted, prohibiting monopoly grants by the Crown. Early English cases did not deal with monopolies created by private agreement since most were created by public grant.

3. Later Common Law—"Rule of Reason" Approach §39

Combinations and agreements that restrain trade were not unlawful per se. They were valid if *reasonable* and if they did not create a monopoly or otherwise endanger the public interest. An exception existed for "distress industries"—an entire industry threatened with financial ruin.

II. THE FEDERAL ANTITRUST LAWS—IN GENERAL

A. BACKGROUND §43

In the last half of the 19th century, as America became an industrialized society, the common law was thought to be ineffective at stemming the growth of industrial monopolies, trusts, and cartels that were gaining power sufficient to restrict output, raise prices, and engage in predatory practices. In response, Congress enacted the Sherman Act in 1890, which went far beyond the common law by establishing *absolute prohibitions* enforceable by *private damage actions* and by the equity power of the federal courts to *restrain* violations.

B. SUMMARY OF PRINCIPAL STATUTES REGULATING COMPETITIVE BEHAVIOR

1. Federal Statutes of General Application

a. Sherman Act §54

This Act prohibits unreasonable agreements in restraint of trade and monopolizing, attempts to monopolize, and combinations or conspiracies to monopolize in interstate commerce. Civil and criminal penalties are provided.

b. Clayton Act §55

Enacted in 1914 to tighten further the legal standards of the Sherman Act, the Clayton Act prohibits tie-in sales, exclusive dealing arrangements, and mergers where the effect may be substantially to lessen competition or tend to create a monopoly in any line of commerce. The Clayton Act generally exempts labor unions and agricultural associations from both acts and also provides that a private party can recover *treble damages* for violations of both acts.

c. Federal Trade Commission Act §56

Also enacted in 1914, this Act created the Federal Trade Commission, which is empowered to enforce section 5 of the Act prohibiting unfair methods of competition in or affecting commerce and unfair or deceptive acts or practices in or affecting commerce. The FTC also enforces the Clayton and Sherman Acts.

d. Amendments to antitrust laws §62

The Robinson-Patman Act was enacted in 1936 for the purpose of prohibiting certain price discriminations. The Celler-Kefauver Act of 1950 tightened anti-merger and asset acquisition provisions of the Clayton Act. The Hart-Scott-Rodino Improvements Act of 1976 expanded the Department of Justice's investigatory powers, required pre-merger notification for certain mergers, and established parens patriae procedures whereby state attorneys general may sue to recover damages caused by antitrust violations affecting consumers.

2. Federal Statutes Covering Specific Industries §66

Other statutes have also been passed to regulate specific industries and/or exempt industries from antitrust coverage, *e.g.*, the Federal Aviation Act.

C. ANTITRUST JURISDICTION

1. "Interstate Commerce" Requirement

a. Sherman Act §67

The "interstate commerce" requirement is satisfied when an activity has a **substantial economic** effect on interstate commerce—even if the business or activity is intrastate (*e.g.*, a charitable activity may have sufficient effect). Note, however, that in **criminal** prosecutions, the government must allege a **demonstrable nexus** between the defendants' activity and interstate commerce.

b. Clayton Act §75

Originally applicable only to corporations engaged in interstate commerce, the Clayton Act now applies to **persons** engaged in commerce or in any activity **affecting** commerce.

c. Robinson-Patman Act §76

This Act has more stringent requirements: The discriminating seller must be engaged in interstate commerce **and** at least one of the two alleged discriminatory sales must be across state lines.

2. "Foreign Commerce" §79

The Sherman Act also applies to extra-territorial activities that **were intended to, and actually do, cause anticompetitive effects** in the United States. Some limitations, however, are recognized (*e.g.*, when activities are required by foreign law or when antitrust law enforcement may conflict with international laws).

D. ANTITRUST REMEDIES

1. Criminal Sanctions

a. Statutory violations §83

Violation of section 1 or 2 of the Sherman Act is a felony, punishable by fines up to $350,000 or imprisonment up to three years, or both.

Corporations can be fined up to $10 million. Alternatively, the government may recover twice the defendant's pecuniary gain or twice the victims' loss. A *criminal* conviction requires proof of criminal intent (*i.e., **knowledge*** of probable effect) and anticompetitive effect. There are *no* criminal sanctions for violations of the Clayton Act or FTC Act, although certain intentional price discrimination *is* criminal under the Robinson-Patman Act.

(1) Corporate violations   §88
Individual directors, officers, and agents who authorized or committed criminal acts may be guilty of misdemeanors, punishable by a $5,000 fine, one year in jail, or both.

b. Enforcement   §89
The criminal provisions are enforced by the Antitrust Division of the Department of Justice, which is authorized to use civil investigative demands to acquire probative material and subsequently to convene a grand jury. As a practical matter, criminal proceedings are usually instituted only when there is strong evidence of a ***per se violation*** of the antitrust laws or egregious predatory conduct.

2. Equitable Relief   §93
Both the government and private parties can obtain equitable relief including injunctions, divestiture, and cancellation of contracts. Remedies are *cumulative; i.e.,* private and public suits can be pursued simultaneously.

3. Action for Damages   §98
Section 4 of the Clayton Act permits injured persons to sue for treble damages, costs, and attorneys' fees that are incurred as a result of antitrust violations.

a. Who may sue   §99
"Persons" who may sue under section 4 include foreign governments (no treble damages), state attorneys general as parens patriae, private individuals or companies whose "business" or "property" has been injured. "Property" includes the monetary loss suffered by *consumers* who are the victims of price fixing or other anticompetitive activities.

(1) Plaintiff must suffer "antitrust injury"   §107
Plaintiff's injury must *directly result* from defendant's action and he must be able to prove "antitrust injury," defined as an injury of the type the antitrust laws were intended to prevent, and which flows from that which makes the defendant's conduct unlawful.

(a) Standing requirements   §113
Even if a plaintiff proves an antitrust injury, standing to sue may be denied for other jurisprudential reasons (*e.g.,* injury is too remote or plaintiff is not a direct purchaser).

(2) "Direct" vs. "indirect" purchasers   §114
Only direct purchasers may sue for damages. Thus, indirect purchasers further down the distribution chain from the price fixing or antitrust violation may not sue for damages that were allegedly "passed on" to them.

b. Damages—types and amount
Plaintiffs can recover lost profits, increased costs, and/or the decrease in value of an investment. Awards are upheld if based on a just and reasonable estimate determined from relevant data.

c. Defenses
A defendant might attempt to prove that the cause of action is beyond the four-year **statute of limitations** for private damage actions. The four-year period, which runs from the date the **damage is suffered**, may be delayed by fraudulent concealment. The statute is tolled by institution of government proceedings. A defendant may **not**, however, defend against a damage claim on the grounds that plaintiff had "unclean hands" by once participating in the illegal activity himself or that the plaintiff had "passed on" any overcharges or damages to others further down the line of distribution. Both of these defenses have been rejected.

d. Effect of government judgment
If the government has already obtained a final judgment against an antitrust violator, private antitrust plaintiffs may use that final judgment as **prima facie evidence** against the defendant in a subsequent treble damage action. However, government-negotiated **consent decrees** or **nolo contendere** pleas do **not** qualify as final judgments for this purpose.

e. No right to contribution
Antitrust defendants are **not** entitled to contribution from co-conspirators.

4. Consent Decrees
Often the government and defendant settle by a consent decree. The court must determine if such decrees are in the public interest.

5. Federal Trade Commission Remedies
The FTC has **exclusive authority** to enforce section 5 of the FTC Act and concurrent authority to enforce certain sections of the Clayton Act. Remedies include issuance of cease and desist orders, injunctive relief, civil penalties for violations of cease and desist orders, and restitution.

III. MONOPOLIZATION

A. MONOPOLIZATION BY A SINGLE FIRM
Firms with monopoly power are able to reduce output and raise prices and thereby earn higher (monopoly) profits than would be earned in a competitive market structure.

1. Definition of "Monopolizing"
The Sherman Act does not outlaw monopolies (which can be **innocently** acquired or maintained) as such, but rather the **act of monopolizing**. This requires proof of: (i) **possession** of monopoly power in a **relevant market and** (ii) the **willful acquisition or maintenance** of that power.

2. Monopoly Power in a Relevant Market §144

The relevant market, *i.e.*, the area of effective competition for the defendant, must be measured and defined in order to assess monopoly power. This inquiry requires definition of the relevant **geographic** market and the relevant **product** market.

a. Relevant product market §145

This is determined by consumer preferences and by the extent to which consumers find other goods or services reasonably interchangeable. Thus, if other goods are thought by consumers to be interchangeable, the goods will generally be included in the relevant product market. Relevant market definition is a difficult area of the law, often involving competing economic testimony in a particular case.

(1) Single-brand markets §148

The Supreme Court has held that a single brand or service can be a relevant market, although this theory is controversial.

b. Relevant geographic market §149

This is the area in which competing sellers sell or consumers **practically** turn to for substitute goods. There may be submarkets within a general geographic market.

c. Proving monopoly power §153

Monopoly power is the power to **control prices or exclude competition** in a relevant market. Firms in monopoly or oligopoly market structures possess some degree of market power, as compared to firms in competitive market structures, where firms do not have the power to reduce output or raise prices.

(1) Measuring "market power" §158

Market share that an alleged monopolist has **presently** captured is the prime factor examined by courts, although it is not the sole determinant. Generally, a market share in excess of 70% is strongly suggestive of monopoly power, whereas a market share below 40% is insufficient. Market shares between 40% and 70% may or may not be sufficient, depending on the facts of individual cases.

(a) Other factors §160

A second determinant of market power is whether there are **significant barriers** to new firms that wish to enter the market. A 100% market share was held to **not** constitute a monopoly where no barriers existed. Also, a lack of **future market potential** such that a company will not continue to dominate the market precludes the finding of a monopoly.

3. "Purposeful Act" Requirement—Prohibited Market Behavior §168

Because the mere possession of monopoly power alone is insufficient to constitute a violation of section 2 of the Sherman Act, some additional act or conduct is required before a violation will be found. This additional purposeful act will be found if the defendant monopolist has engaged in predatory or coercive conduct otherwise violating section 1 of the Sherman Act or in other *purposeful and intentional* conduct aimed at *acquiring, maintaining, or exercising monopoly power*.

a. **Caution** §170
Deliberate or purposeful acts do *not* include monopoly power resulting from *superior skill, foresight, or industry* or that which is *thrust upon* a person because of market conditions (natural monopolies). Note that *specific intent* to monopolize is *not* required. *A need not intend to monopolize to be found guilty*

b. **Examples of anticompetitive conduct** §173
Violations can occur in particular cases from *exclusionary conduct* that eliminates competition, *predatory pricing* (*below-cost pricing* where defendant has a *dangerous probability of recouping* the money it lost on such pricing), foreclosing distribution channels, bundled rebates, or the anticompetitive denial of *access to an "essential facility."* (Note that the Court has never recognized the essential facilities doctrine. Although a refusal to deal with competitors is not precluded conduct, a firm with monopoly power cannot cancel existing deals based on its monopoly market share.)

4. **Monopsony Power** §188
Section 2 of the Sherman Act also applies to monopoly power exercised on the side of *buyers* ("monopsony power").

5. **Defense—"Innocently Acquired" or "Natural" Monopolies** §189
Monopoly power innocently acquired (*e.g.*, by superior skill or natural advantage) does *not* violate section 2. However, if subsequent to the acquisition, a defendant acts in an anticompetitive, predatory, or exclusionary manner, a violation may occur.

B. **ATTEMPTS TO MONOPOLIZE** §192
Section 2 of the Sherman Act also condemns *attempts* to monopolize. A plaintiff must prove that a defendant has engaged in *predatory or anticompetitive conduct* with a *specific intent* to monopolize, and a *dangerous probability of achieving monopoly power*. Note, however, that aggressive competition is *not* illegal.

C. **CONSPIRACY TO MONOPOLIZE** §197
Conspiracy to monopolize violates section 2 of the Sherman Act and section 1, which prohibits conspiracies in restraint of trade. A section 2 conspiracy violation requires proof that the involved parties were *"consciously committed"* to the anticompetitive scheme.

IV. **COLLABORATION AMONG COMPETITORS—HORIZONTAL RESTRAINTS**

A. **INTRODUCTION**

1. **Horizontal Restraints** §199
Antitrust laws, primarily section 1 of the Sherman Act, place limits on collaboration among *competing firms*, *i.e.*, horizontal restraints. Unilateral action does not result in a violation; there must be an *agreement or concerted*

action between competitors that unreasonably restrains trade and has an *effect on interstate commerce*.

2. **Rule of Reason vs. Per Se Violations**

    a. **Rule of reason test** §202

The literal language of the Sherman Act would appear to condemn every agreement in restraint of trade. Early cases, however, interpreted this language to condemn *only unreasonable restraints* of trade, thus creating a rule of reason. The rule requires a *case-by-case determination* of the reasonableness of any agreement, *i.e.*, whether the agreement *promotes or suppresses competition*.

    (1) **Factors considered in rule of reason test** §204

In assessing the impact on competition, the court will evaluate the structure of the industry, facts peculiar to the firm's operation in that industry, the history and duration of the restraint, the reasons why the restraint was adopted, and the effects on the competitive market, including price and output.

    b. **Per se violations** §205

Certain agreements among competitors are unreasonable as a matter of law—*i.e.*, *illegal per se*. When an agreement or conduct is classified as *illegal per se*, lengthy analysis and balancing generally are not permitted at trial. Per se rules reduce the time and cost of trial, are easier to administer by courts, and provide businesses with "bright line" standards for conduct. Prime examples are horizontal price fixing and market division, as well as certain tie-ins and boycotts (discussed *infra*).

    c. **Characterization** §206

Characterizing conduct is a critical step. A court initially must determine whether the conduct or effect falls within a *per se* category. If not, and the *purpose or effect is unclear*, or the defendant can demonstrate that the agreement either makes the market *more competitive* or *increases efficiency* through integration, then a rule of reason analysis is applied, balancing the anticompetitive harms and the procompetitive benefits.

    d. **"Quick look" rule of reason** §209

An intermediate standard (*i.e.,* "quick look" analysis) is applied where per se condemnation is inappropriate, yet no detailed industry analysis (*i.e.,* rule of reason analysis) is necessary to demonstrate the anticompetitive nature of an *inherently suspect restraint*. However, a quick look analysis is inappropriate if the defendants have a plausible procompetitive justification for their concerted action.

B. **PRICE FIXING AMONG COMPETITORS**

1. **Per Se Violation** §211

Any combination or agreement that has the purpose or effect of raising, depressing, fixing, pegging, or stabilizing the price of a commodity in interstate or foreign commerce is *per se illegal*.

2. No Justification Permitted §212

Justifications to the effect that the horizontal price fixing agreement was reasonable or was entered into to end "ruinous competition" are banned. The only *exception* is a credible argument that a particular agreement makes a market function *more competitively* or creates integrative efficiencies, thus requiring a rule of reason analysis.

3. Exception for Regulated Industries §214

An exception to price fixing prohibitions exists for certain *government regulated industries* (e.g., railroads).

4. Sufficient Proof §215

A plaintiff must prove *either an unlawful purpose or an anticompetitive effect*. It is unnecessary to establish market power to set or influence prices.

No market power analysis required

5. What Constitutes "Price Fixing" §216

An *expansive* interpretation of price fixing includes fixing *minimum or maximum* prices, using common "*list prices*," *production or purchase price limits*, and the *elimination of competitive bidding* or *short-term credit*.

C. DIVISION OF MARKETS §225

Any *direct or indirect* agreement among competitors to divide the market for a *particular product, territory, or customers* is *illegal per se*, since it gives each participant an effective monopoly in his share of the market. *No justifications* or defenses are recognized. However, "areas of primary responsibility" have been allowed.

D. GROUP BOYCOTTS AND CONCERTED REFUSALS TO DEAL

1. In General §230

A *group of competitors* may not agree to cease dealing with a person or firm outside of the group, deal only on certain terms, or coerce suppliers or customers not to deal with the boycotted competitor. Such agreements result in a combination in restraint of trade.

2. Per Se vs. Rule of Reason §231

Supreme Court decisions on the treatment of group boycotts under section 1 have resulted in confusion regarding which rule is applicable. Early cases appeared to establish the rule that horizontal group boycotts were illegal per se. However, some cases applied the rule of reason and, at least in one case, the quick look rule was applied. The most recent Supreme Court pronouncement on the subject reaffirms the *illegal per se rule*. For this reason, courts may be reluctant to find a "boycott" exists.

3. Self-Regulation by Industries §235

It is unlawful for trade associations or competitors to use boycotts or unreasonable restraints to enforce standards of conduct within the industry. However, courts are more likely to uphold association rules in industries subject to *extensive government regulation* (e.g., the stock exchange).

4. Political Boycotts §237

Boycotts motivated by political purposes are usually beyond the jurisdiction of the Sherman Act and may also be protected speech under the *Noerr-Pennington* doctrine.

E. JOINT VENTURES BY COMPETITORS §238

A joint venture (an undertaking by two or more business entities for some limited purpose) is *illegal per se* if the *purpose* of the combination is illegal per se. However, if the purpose and effect produces *integrative efficiencies*, the venture is judged by the *rule of reason*. A rule of reason analysis requires a *balancing of the anticompetitive effects* of the joint activities *against any legitimate interest* thereby served.

1. Industry Structure Important §246

The effects of joint activities may vary depending upon the economic structure of the industry. Thus, joint activities in generally competitive industries may be tolerated more than similar activities in concentrated or oligopolistic industries.

F. DISSEMINATING INFORMATION AMONG COMPETITORS §248

Competitors often exchange information through a trade association. It is necessary to determine whether an exchange of information helps to perfect the market or create efficiencies, *or* whether it is monopolistic and anticompetitive.

1. Exchange of Information on Prices §249

Exchange of price information is *very suspect* and likely to violate section 1. Factors that strongly indicate unlawful activity include exchange of information concerning current or future prices and identification of the parties involved, or in the context of a highly concentrated or oligopolistic market structure.

2. Exchange of Information Other Than Price §250

Exchange of information other than price will be condemned only if it is aimed at *lessening competition*, policing a cartel, or *facilitating interdependent pricing*.

G. WHAT CONSTITUTES AN "AGREEMENT," "COMBINATION," OR "CONSPIRACY" AMONG COMPETITORS §251

Finding an "agreement" is critical to a section 1 violation since that provision of the Sherman Act condemns "contracts, combinations . . . or conspiracies" in restraint of trade (*e.g.,* price fixing, market division, group boycotts, etc.). Often only circumstantial evidence is available.

1. Conscious Parallelism Among Competitors §252

Conscious parallelism is a process not unlawful in itself, by which firms in a concentrated market effectively have shared market power and economic interests and set their prices at a profit-maximizing, supracompetitive level. A party must know of its competitors' actions and decide to act in conformity with them.

2. Interdependent Conscious Parallelism Among Competitors

a. Circumstantial evidence of agreement §254

Where an agreement cannot be proved by direct evidence, circumstantial evidence may show an agreement. Consciously parallel interdependent action may be sufficient evidence of agreement in certain circumstances. Agreement may be inferred when parties undertake parallel actions that are truly *interdependent* in that benefits accrue to the parties only if *all* participate and there is no other rational explanation for the parties' taking such actions independently.

b.   Mere conscious parallelism not sufficient   §255

Mere conscious parallelism that has *independent business justification* is not sufficient to conclusively establish an agreement.

c.   Plus factors   §256

In order to prove the existence of an agreement, a plaintiff must prove, in addition to conscious parallelism, plus factors (*e.g.,* communications among defendants, economic motive, radical departure from previous business practices, etc.).

d.   FTC Act   §257

The FTC has also employed the concept of interdependent conscious parallelism in its enforcement of section 5, which bans *unfair methods of competition* but does *not* require any contract, combination, or conspiracy. The FTC must still establish anticompetitive purpose and a lack of competitive justification.

3.   Expanding Concept of "Combination"   §259

In addition to contracts and conspiracies, combinations in restraint of trade violate section 1 of the Sherman Act. Some cases have *expanded the concept of "combinations"* to include group action that is not included in the terms "contracts" and "conspiracies," *e.g.*, *acquiescence* by a group of retailers.

4.   Intra-Corporate Conspiracy   §260

A corporation cannot conspire with itself or its employees, nor can employees conspire with each other, absent independent parties. However, anticompetitive activities within one entity may still be an illegal attempt to monopolize.

5.   Inter-Corporate Conspiracies   §261

A conspiracy *can* exist between or among separate but related entities (*e.g.*, partially-owned subsidiaries). However, a conspiracy *cannot* be found between a corporation and its *wholly-owned subsidiary*.

a.   Interlocking directorates   §263

This situation may not establish a conspiracy under section 1, but it may violate *section 8 of the Clayton Act*. The involved corporations must be *direct competitors* and each firm must have capital aggregating *more than $10 million*. Enforcement of section 8 has been lax.

V.   VERTICAL RESTRAINTS

A.   INTRODUCTION

1.   Definition of "Vertical" Restraints   §267

Vertical restraints refer to agreements and conduct among participants at *various levels of production and distribution* (e.g., manufacturers and wholesalers or wholesalers and retailers). (Horizontal restraints involve relationships between firms on the same level.) Vertical restraints are analyzed under sections 1 and possibly 2 (monopolization) of the Sherman Act, and section 3 of the Clayton Act.

product unless the customer also agrees to buy another (the "tied") product from the seller. The buyer is thus coerced and the suppliers of the tied product are foreclosed.

a. Requirements §292

For an illegal tie: (i) there must be **separate** tied and tying products; (ii) the sale must be **conditional** on the arrangement **or due to coercion or force;** (iii) the seller must have sufficient **economic power in the tying product** to appreciably restrain competition in the **tied** product; and (iv) the arrangement must affect a **more than insubstantial dollar amount** of commerce in the tied product market.

2. Statutory Prohibitions §297

Clayton Act section 3 prohibits tying of **goods or commodities** where the **effect may be to substantially lessen competition**. Sherman Act section 1 prohibits unlawful tying of services, intangibles, or real property. Although at one time different statutory standards were applied, now they have converged. FTC Act section 5 also covers tie-ins illegal under either the Clayton or Sherman Acts.

3. Tying Usually Illegal Per Se §304

To prove a violation, plaintiff must show that the above requirements are met, *i.e.,* separate tying and tied products, market power, etc. *But note:* "Illegal per se" as used here **differs** from the rule applied to horizontal price fixing agreements. In tying cases, an illegal per se analysis requires a **detailed inquiry** into market definitions and the existence of market power, a procedure not used in other "per se" cases.

a. Standards of proof §306

In determining whether products are **separate**, courts consider the **character of demand** for the items; *i.e.,* there must be separate demand for the individual products. The trend in evaluating **market power** is examination of the **defendants' power to force consumers to make choices** they would not make in a competitive market.

4. Defenses §311

Defendant may argue that a tie is necessary because defendant is starting a **new business** with a highly uncertain future or that the tie is necessary for **quality control protection of goodwill**, although the quality control argument seldom succeeds. Courts have refused to apply the per se rule to prevent the chilling of efficient innovation. Instead, tying arrangements are evaluated under the rule of reason.

E. EXCLUSIVE DEALING—REQUIREMENTS CONTRACTS §315

Exclusive dealing agreements or arrangements will survive scrutiny, provided they do not involve a **substantial dollar volume of the market** (quantitative substantiality test) or they do not **foreclose a substantial share of the market** from other competitors.

1. Rule of Reason §318

Under either section 1 of the Sherman Act or section 3 of the Clayton Act, exclusive dealing arrangements are subject to a rule of reason analysis. Note that *de facto exclusive dealing* may be found even where there is no express contract for exclusive dealing.

VI. MERGERS AND ACQUISITIONS

A. CLAYTON ACT SECTION 7 §320

Section 7 prohibits horizontal, vertical, and conglomerate mergers and also mergers by acquisition of assets or stock, where the effect of the acquisition *may* be to *substantially lessen competition* or tend to create a monopoly. Note that both parties must be *engaged in commerce*. Section 7, as amended, has made section 1 of the Sherman Act irrelevant in application to mergers.

B. JUDICIAL INTERPRETATION OF SECTION 7 §326

Three key phrases are central to the courts' application of section 7: "line of commerce," "section of the country," and "may be substantially to lessen competition."

1. Market Definition—"Line of Commerce" §327

Section 7 requires the same product market analysis as used for monopolization under the Sherman Act (*i.e.*, line of commerce), with emphasis on *interchangeability of products*.

2. Market Definition—"Section of the Country" §329

The Supreme Court has interpreted "section of the country" to mean the *relevant geographic market*, *i.e.*, area where merger will have both an *immediate and direct* effect on competition. Note that there may be *more than one* relevant market.

a. Limitation §331

However, the Court in more recent cases has apparently narrowed the relevant geographical market to the localized area where the acquired firm had significant direct competition, *i.e.,* where it actually marketed its goods or services.

3. Anticompetitive Effects—"May Be Substantially to Lessen Competition" §332

Designed to have a *preventative* effect, section 7 attempts to halt anticompetitive effects *before* they happen. It applies whenever a proposed merger indicates a tendency toward monopoly or a *reasonable likelihood* of a substantial lessening of competition is shown. There *must* be a *probability*, not a mere possibility, of such an effect.

4. Justifications for Mergers §336

Limited exceptions have been created to protect mergers whose *net effect is pro-competitive*. Exceptions are possible in the following circumstances: *small companies* wish to merge to compete more effectively against dominant firms (this defense unlikely to succeed); a *failing company* and a competitor propose to merge and no other purchaser is available; defendant can show that the merger *will not in fact injure competition* or would result in *increased economic efficiencies*, thus benefiting competition and consumers. *Post-acquisition* evidence *may be admissible* when it is *not* in control of the merged companies and shows fundamental changes in the industry.

C. HORIZONTAL MERGERS §343

Horizontal mergers are mergers between competitors, *i.e.*, companies performing similar functions involving comparable goods or services.

1. **Bright Line Rules vs. Totality of Circumstances** §344

    Courts have attempted to establish bright line rules for ***presumptive illegality*** based primarily on ***market concentrations and market shares*** of the merging firms. Generally, the more concentrated the market and the larger the market share of the parties, the more likely the merger will be deemed illegal. However, the modern trend is to evaluate cases on the ***totality of their circumstances***. Horizontal mergers are usually considered the most odious type of merger because of their direct anticompetitive effect.

    a. **Mitigating factors** §346

        Even in cases of presumptive illegality, courts consider certain mitigating factors (*e.g.,* homogeneity of products, barriers to entry, certain efficiencies created by merger).

2. **Mergers That Eliminate Perceived Potential Entrant** §349

    A merger may violate section 7 because it eliminates a potential competitor perceived to be "waiting in the wings" to enter the acquired company's market. Theoretically, the mere presence of the "waiting" firm causes the firms already in the market to be more competitive in pricing and output practices. Hence, a merger would destroy these pro-competitive advantages.

    a. **Evidence required** §351

        A prima facie case is shown by evidence that the ***acquiring firm*** had the ***necessary means to enter***, the existing firms were ***influenced by the potential entry***, and the ***number of potential entrants*** was not so numerous as to make insignificant the elimination of the acquiring firm.

3. ***Brown Shoe* Analysis** §352

    In *Brown Shoe Co.*, the Court not only examined market share evidence, but also considered ***economic and historical factors*** that indicated a ***trend toward concentration***. The ***lack of any affirmative justification*** was also stressed.

4. **"Presumptive Illegality" Test** §353

    Under *Philadelphia National Bank*, a merger that produces a firm ***controlling an undue percentage share*** of the relevant market ***and*** that results in a ***significant increase in concentration*** in that industry is presumed illegal unless the defendant is able to show that the merger is not likely to have anticompetitive effects.

    a. **Undue percentage share** §354

        Once again, relevant market definition is significant. *Philadelphia National Bank* held that a ***30%*** market share was excessive. But lesser percentage shares may also be sufficient. However, market share ***is only one factor*** considered.

    b. **Significant increase in concentration** §355

        Since one purpose of section 7 is to halt the rising tide of concentration in American business, the increase in concentration caused by a merger is a significant piece of information in evaluating the merger's legality. In *Philadelphia National Bank*, an increase in concentration by 33% was considered significant.

c. Totality of circumstances §356

Some lower courts (and the Department of Justice ("DOJ") Horizontal Merger Guidelines) have noted that market concentration and market share data alone are **not** determinative, and that other evidence of anticompetitive effects is necessary to sustain a ruling of illegality.

5. Burdens of Proof §358

Once a prima facie case (sufficient market share/concentration ratios) has been made, the **defendant** must rebut the prima facie case or must prove that it is entitled to a recognized defense (*e.g.*, failing company).

6. Effects of Guidelines §359

The Horizontal Merger Guidelines (discussed *infra*) are more lenient toward mergers than the rules applied by the Supreme Court. The Guidelines measure market concentration differently and follow the totality of circumstances approach to establish illegality.

D. VERTICAL MERGERS §360

Vertical mergers are mergers between companies in a supplier-customer relationship. While they do not increase market power in the manner of a horizontal merger, they nevertheless may have the effect of foreclosing competitors or increasing entry barriers for competitors.

1. Application of Section 7 §361

Courts analyze vertical mergers by defining the relevant **geographic and product markets**, measuring the **market share,** determining the **extent of the market foreclosure** caused by the merger, and considering **economic and historical factors** peculiar to the case, including **trends toward concentration,** barriers to new entry, and the **nature and purpose** of the merger.

a. Recent trends §362

Modern courts tend to apply a rule of reason analysis that examines whether the vertical merger will have **significant anticompetitive effects** in either the upstream or downstream market.

E. CONGLOMERATE MERGERS §364

Conglomerate mergers include all types of mergers that are **not horizontal or vertical**. The term is also applied to product or market extension mergers that do not fit within horizontal or vertical market definitions.

1. Application of Section 7 §365

Under section 7, challenges may be mounted to mergers that lessen or eliminate potential competition (of a **perceived potential entrant or an actual potential entrant**), **make powerful firms more powerful** by giving them an unfair advantage, or significantly increase the **potential for reciprocity** between the merged firms. Some anticompetitive effect must be possible for section 7 to apply.

F. JOINT VENTURES §370

A joint venture is created when two entities combine their resources to create a new product, distribution network, etc. Joint ventures are subject to scrutiny under section 7 of the Clayton Act, since they may eliminate potential competition in a market. They are also scrutinized under section 1 of the Sherman Act.

G. DEPARTMENT OF JUSTICE MERGER GUIDELINES

1. Significance of Guidelines §373
The Guidelines are not binding on the courts or the FTC. However, they are useful in evaluating horizontal, vertical, and conglomerate mergers. Since few *private parties* have standing to enforce section 7, the Guidelines are important aids to the Government's role in preventing anticompetitive mergers.

2. Horizontal Merger Guidelines §375
In addition to focusing on market shares and market concentrations, the Guidelines indicate other factors to be considered in evaluating horizontal mergers: *ease of entry* into the relevant market, *adequacy of irreplaceable raw materials*, *excess capacity of firms* in the market, *increased concentration trends*, and *particular efficiencies* created by the merger. Note the Guidelines' methods for measuring market concentration and defining the relevant market differ from the methods used by the courts.

3. Vertical Merger Guidelines §379
The Guidelines for vertical mergers focus on three dangers resulting from such mergers: *barriers to entry*, *collusion*, and *avoidance of rate regulations*. The Guidelines are more lenient to vertical mergers than case law, but the FTC, which has not adopted the vertical guidelines, occasionally does challenge vertical mergers.

4. Conglomerate Merger Guidelines §384
These Guidelines track the case law by threatening to challenge mergers that eliminate actual or potential market entrants.

H. PRE-MERGER NOTIFICATION §385
The Hart-Scott-Rodino Antitrust Improvements Act requires certain merging firms to notify the DOJ of impending mergers. The Act applies only to mergers in which the acquiring firm would hold an aggregate amount of the acquired firm's assets and voting securities either (i) in excess of $200 million *or* (ii) between $50 and $200 million *if* the acquiring firm has total assets or annual net sales of (a) $100 million, and is acquiring voting shares or assets of a manufacturing firm that has annual net sales or assets of $10 million; (b) $100 million and is acquiring voting securities or assets of a non-manufacturing firm with total assets of $10 million; *or* (c) $10 million and is acquiring voting securities or assets of a firm with annual net sales or total assets of $100 million or more.

VII. PRICE DISCRIMINATION—THE ROBINSON-PATMAN ACT

A. ECONOMIC ANALYSIS OF PRICE DISCRIMINATION §387
Price discrimination occurs when identical or similar products, having the same

marginal production costs, are sold at different prices. Conditions necessary for illegal price discrimination are **market power**, **differences in elasticity of demand** (inelasticity results in little or no bargaining power on the part of buyers), and the ability to easily **identify and separate buyers** (by geography, age, income) based on the elasticity of demand.

1. **Effects of Price Discrimination** §392

   Positive effects include incentives for **increased output**, facilitation of the introduction of **new products**, and possibly **more price competition in oligopolistic markets**. Adverse economic effects include **excessive profits**, **predatory pricing practices** (the injured firm suffers a **primary line injury**), and **injury to competitors** who are forced to pay a higher price (the firm at a competitive disadvantage suffers a **secondary line injury** while its customers may suffer a **tertiary line** injury if they compete with customers of the preferentially treated firm).

2. **Purposes of Robinson-Patman Act** §394

   Clayton Act section 2 originally was aimed at preventing primary line injury caused by geographic price discrimination. The Robinson-Patman amendments ("chain store bill") were enacted to ensure that sellers would not treat small businesses differently than larger businesses at the same competitive level.

B. **ELEMENTS OF A PRIMA FACIE ROBINSON-PATMAN VIOLATION** §395

   Under section 2(a) of the Clayton Act (the Robinson-Patman Act), it is unlawful for any person **engaged in commerce** to **discriminate in price between different purchasers** of commodities of **like grade and quality**, where the **effect** may be **to substantially lessen competition** in any line of commerce (or tend to create a monopoly) or to **injure, destroy, or prevent competition** with any person who either grants **or** knowingly receives the benefits of such discrimination, **or** with customers of either of them. The Act applies to both the **seller** who offers and the **preferred buyer** who knowingly receives the discriminatory price.

1. **"Engaged in Commerce"** §396

   This has been construed as a narrow jurisdictional requirement that necessitates that at least one of the two transactions which, when compared, generates a discrimination across a state line (no "affecting commerce" test).

2. **"Discriminate in Price Between Different Purchasers"** §397

   The Act requires that there be **at least two purchases** and that the sales at different prices be during a **fairly contemporaneous** period. **Indirect price discrimination** (discriminatory non-price terms, e.g., preferential credit terms, or freight charges) is also prohibited. Courts will scrutinize the facts of each situation to determine whether buyers receiving different prices are in fact competitors at the same level, even though they may have different titles or names.

3. **"Commodities of Like Grade and Quantity"** §406

   This means **tangible articles** and excludes services and intangibles. **Mixed sales**, such as construction contracts (services and materials) are also excluded.

a. **Other antitrust laws**
Price discrimination in services and intangibles may violate the **Sherman Act** if there is a **restraint of trade** or an **attempt to monopolize**. Or, it may be **unfair competition** under section 5 of the **FTC Act**.

4. **"Injure Competition with Any Person Who Grants Such Discrimination"**
The Act permits recovery for primary line, secondary line, and tertiary line injury. Primary line injury occurs when there is a **substantial and sustained drop in price** in a local area with the **intent or known effect** of destroying, injuring, or disciplining a smaller-scale rival. Note that **predatory pricing** is **not** illegal if it does **not harm competition**. The requirements for proving a predatory pricing claim in a primary line discrimination case are similar to those under the Sherman Act (*e.g.*, proof of pricing below relevant measure of cost).

5. **"Injure Competition with Any Person Who Knowingly Receives Price Discrimination"**
Secondary line injury describes the injury suffered by the competitor of a buyer who has received a discriminatorily low price from a seller. These cases account for the majority of Robinson-Patman Act prosecutions. Generally, one must prove only a difference in price; competitive injury may be **inferred** from the discrimination itself. No injury occurs if the discrimination is **temporary** (*e.g.,* gas station "wars").

6. **"Injure Competition with Customers of Any Person Who Knowingly Receives Price Discrimination"**
Tertiary line injury refers to the injury suffered by a customer of a buyer who was discriminated against, when that customer must then compete with customers of buyers who received favorable treatment from a seller. The standards are similar to those in secondary line cases.

C. DEFENSES TO A PRIMA FACIE VIOLATION OF ROBINSON-PATMAN ACT

1. **De Minimis Effect**
The defendant may assert affirmative defenses or attempt to prove that any prima facie violation had only a de minimis effect on competition.

2. **Cost Differential**
Proving a cost justification (*e.g.*, production or delivery costs) is an **absolute defense** to a prima facie violation.

3. **Changing Conditions**
In rare cases, and usually confined to **temporary** situations caused by the physical nature of a commodity, a defendant might be able to prove that the price was changed in response to changing market conditions, such as imminent deterioration of perishable goods.

4. **Meeting Competition in Good Faith**
Section 2(b) provides that a seller may rebut a prima facie case by showing that the lower price was made in good faith to meet an equally low price of a competitor. This defense is difficult to prove. Seller must establish a **reasonable** basis for its good faith, and it must **meet**, not beat, the competitive price offered by a competitor.

4. Infringement Actions §484

The patentee is entitled to sue for damages or injunctive relief, or both, anyone who makes, uses, sells, offers for sale, or imports the invention without the patentee's consent (*direct infringement*)—even if it is *unintentional*. *Contributory infringement*, where someone aids another in infringement, requires *scienter*.

5. Defenses to Infringement Actions §486

An alleged infringer can defend on the ground that the patent itself is *invalid* (indeed, a present licensee may challenge the validity of a patent) or that the patentee has *misused or abused* the patent (*e.g.*, by attempting to tie an unpatented commodity to it). *Fraudulent procurement or enforcement* of a patent also constitutes an equitable defense to a patent infringement suit, and may also be the basis for an antitrust suit.

C. COPYRIGHTS

1. The Copyright Act §489

The Copyright Act protects *original works of authorship* and gives the owner the exclusive rights to *copy, adapt, distribute, perform, and display* her works. Copyright subject matter includes literary works, works of art, musical compositions, dramatic works, sound recordings, and computer programs.

a. Requirements §491

To receive copyright protection, works must be "*fixed in a tangible medium of expression*" and must possess at least a modicum of *originality.* Further, protection extends only to the *original expression* in a work; ideas themselves cannot be copyrighted.

2. Procedures §494

Copyright protection is *automatic* once a work meets the above criteria. However, owners must *register* their works with the Copyright Office before bringing an infringement suit.

3. Rights §495

The *copyright owner* has the exclusive right to prevent others from copying, adapting, distributing, publicly performing, and publicly displaying the work, although there are certain *limitations* on those exclusive rights (*e.g.*, library exception).

4. Infringement Actions §497

A plaintiff can sue for damages and injunctive relief. Copyright infringement is a *strict liability offense* although the plaintiff must still show copying. Copying can be indirectly proved by showing the defendant had *access* to the work and the works are *substantially similar*.

5. Defenses §500

Defenses include *fair use* (*e.g.*, uses for the public benefit, use noninjurious to plaintiff's market) and *copyright misuse* (*e.g.*, antitrust violation).

D. RELATIONSHIP OF INTELLECTUAL PROPERTY TO ANTITRUST LAWS

1. **Monopolization**
   Since intellectual property rights are **legal monopolies** granted by statute, the patent or other right may provide a defense to a charge of monopolizing under section 2 of the Sherman Act. However, acquiring a patent is an "acquisition of an asset" within the meaning of the Clayton Act and can be enjoined if the effect substantially lessens competition and tends to create a monopoly. Courts can break up a patent "monopoly" by ordering **compulsory licensing** of all interested parties. **Exclusive licensing** is treated as a sale of the property right and may be subject to the Sherman and Clayton Acts.

   §502

   a. **Refusals to deal**
      Courts differ greatly as to whether an owner's refusal to license her rights or sell patented products so that competition is reduced violates antitrust laws.

      §507

2. **Restraints of Trade Found in Certain Patent Licensing Practices**
   The legal monopoly granted by the patent laws extends only as far as the patentee's own use or reasonable exploitation of the invention. This protection does **not** extend to anticompetitive conduct in the licensing or distribution of the product.

   §508

   a. **Restrictions on licensee**
      Generally, once the patentee has **sold** her product, the purchaser is free to use or resell the product without infringing the patent. However, a patentee can **by agreement** restrict a licensee's resale price, but this right is subject to many restrictions; *e.g.*, the patentee cannot fix the price of unpatented products made by the patented machine. The patentee can also enforce certain **use** and **territorial** restrictions.

      §510

   b. **Illegal agreements**
      Grant-back clauses or patent accumulations are not illegal per se, but may violate antitrust provisions of the Sherman Act. Other provisions found to be unlawful include attempts to extend a patent monopoly, exclusive dealing, tying arrangements, agreements extending beyond the expiration date of the patent, royalties as a percentage of sales, block-booking, and required dealing.

      §515

   c. **Patent pools**
      Such pools, whereby parties disputing certain patents give each other the right to a sublicense (cross license) and set a fixed royalty rate by agreement, have been held to be a legitimate method of settling patent disputes, even though the royalty rates were fixed by agreement. However, pools that lack such a justification may be deemed anticompetitive.

      §525

      (1) **Pharmaceutical settlements**
          Settlements involving **pharmaceutical patents** between the pioneer drug company whose patent has expired and the generic manufacturer have been held per se unlawful, while other courts instead apply a rule of reason analysis.

          §527

3. Enforcing Intellectual Property Rights §528

Obtaining and enforcing intellectual property rights against infringers is frequently alleged to be an effort to monopolize, but such claims rarely succeed. However, patentees could be liable for monopolization in cases involving *fraudulent procurement* of patent or bringing a *sham infringement action* for harassment purposes. Note that in all such cases the other elements of a monopolization claim must also be present.

4. Justice Department Guidelines §531

The DOJ and FTC have issued joint guidelines concerning licensing of intellectual property, which changed enforcement policy: The definition of a *relevant market* may now possibly be a market not for goods or services, but for intellectual property itself (a *technology market*), or for future research and development (an *innovation market*). Also, the *rule of reason* applies to intellectual property transactions. Further, an antitrust *safety zone* has been established under which licensing arrangements will not be challenged unless the parties have a greater than 20% market share.

X. EXEMPTIONS FROM THE ANTITRUST LAWS

A. BACKGROUND

1. Rationale for Exemptions §536

Some businesses or industries have been exempted from the prohibitions of the antitrust laws, generally because those businesses or industries are regulated by other governmental agencies charged with protecting the public's interest *or* because the exempted industries are thought to require the special protection that cartelization may provide (*e.g.,* agricultural organizations).

2. Types of Exemptions §538

Exemptions may be *constitutionally mandated, expressly granted* by Congress, *implied by courts* from regulatory schemes created by Congress or implied to avoid conflicts between federal antitrust laws and state laws or practices. Generally speaking, exemptions are *strictly construed and hesitantly created*.

a. Implied antitrust immunity §540

This applies only on a convincing showing of a *clear repugnancy* between the antitrust laws and the regulatory system at issue.

B. AGRICULTURAL ORGANIZATIONS §541

Agricultural or horticultural stock organizations or cooperatives or fishing cooperatives are *expressly exempted* from the antitrust laws. The exemption is *narrowly construed* and extends only to the conduct of persons *actually engaged* in agricultural production.

C. INTERSTATE WATER, MOTOR, RAIL, AND AIR CARRIERS §549

The Federal Maritime Commission has the power to approve agreements among *water carriers* relating to rates, etc., and the approved agreements are expressly *exempt* from the antitrust laws. However, motor, rail, and air carriers are, for the most part, subject to the full force of the antitrust laws.

1. **Distinguish—Federal Action Does Not Necessarily Create Exemption** §551
   Many kinds of federal agency approvals and regulatory structures do *not* create an exemption from antitrust liability (*e.g.,* the fact that electric companies are regulated by the Federal Power Commission does not bar a government antitrust suit).

D. EXPORT TRADE ASSOCIATIONS §552

The Webb-Pomerene Export Trade Associations Act provides an *express* antitrust *exemption* for agreements or acts done in the course of export trade by an association of producers formed *solely* for the purpose of engaging in export trade following the filing of a statement and subsequent annual reports with the FTC. However, the exemption is inapplicable if the activities have the effect of restraining trade *within* the United States.

1. **Export Trading Company Act** §555
   Because Webb-Pomerene had many limitations, few trade associations used its protections. The Export Trading Company Act was enacted to provide a stronger express antitrust exemption. An exporter must apply for and receive a certificate from the Commerce Department stating that the proposed activities will not have anticompetitive effects in the United States. Companies obtaining such certificates are not liable under the general antitrust laws.

E. BANK MERGERS §558

Special legislation *expressly exempts* bank mergers from private enforcement of antitrust laws. Special procedures are established for challenging bank mergers that have been approved by various governmental authorities regulating banks.

F. INSURANCE §561

The McCarran-Ferguson Act *expressly exempts* the business of insurance from federal antitrust law to the extent that such business is *regulated by state law.* However, state regulation cannot render lawful any act or agreement to boycott, coerce, or intimidate. The "business of insurance" has been *narrowly construed* to *not exempt* activities that merely reduce costs rather than spread risks.

G. STOCK EXCHANGES §567

Although the 1934 Securities Exchange Act contains no express exemption from the antitrust laws, one has been *implied* for stock exchanges registered with the SEC. Thus, such exchanges are permitted to fix minimum brokerage commissions. This implied immunity will probably not be applied where government regulation and the antitrust laws are compatible.

H. LABOR UNIONS §568

Collective bargaining by labor unions and related labor union activities are *generally exempt* from the antitrust laws. However, there are a number of limitations (*e.g.,* the exemption does not extend to labor union activities in aid of nonlabor groups, or to control the marketing of goods and services).

I. PROFESSIONAL BASEBALL §572

Professional baseball has been exempted from the impact of the antitrust laws by *stare decisis*. **Other sports,** however, never received the judicially created exemption extended to baseball.

J. "STATE ACTION" EXEMPTION

1. Deference to State Regulatory Schemes §574

The Supreme Court has created an exemption for governmental action that *articulates clear regulatory schemes* and is *affirmatively designed* to displace competition. However, mere approval by a state commission of conduct by a regulated company does not necessarily exempt the conduct from antitrust laws. The state regulatory scheme must be clearly articulated and the state's participation substantial. Further, the "state action" exemption is applicable only to *governmental functions* performed by the state.

2. Action of Municipality §578

The state action exemption does *not* exempt municipal action, unless a state is directly involved (*e.g.*, there is a *clear delegation of power* from the state to a municipality). Note that the Local Government Antitrust Immunity Act protects municipalities and government officials from damages liability for antitrust violations.

K. CONCERTED ACTION BY COMPETITORS DESIGNED TO INFLUENCE GOVERNMENTAL ACTION

1. *Noerr-Pennington* Doctrine §582

Efforts by individuals or groups to petition the government are protected by the *antitrust immunity (Noerr-Pennington) doctrine*, and are not illegal even if undertaken for *anticompetitive purposes*. The basis for this exemption is the *right to petition* in the Bill of Rights and the First Amendment protection of political activities. The doctrine applies to attempts to influence legislators, administrative agencies, courts, and foreign governments.

2. Limitations §586

The *Noerr-Pennington* doctrine does not apply to attempts to influence governmental action when the conduct is a "mere sham" covering what is actually harassment of a competitor. Sham lawsuits must be *both objectively baseless and improperly motivated*.

L. REJECTION OF "LEARNED PROFESSION" EXEMPTION §587

There is *no* sweeping exemption for learned professions. Thus, minimum fee schedules for attorneys have been held illegal, as have provisions in an engineers' ethical code *prohibiting competitive bidding*. However, application of antitrust laws has been inconsistent. The Court has held some concerted actions to be per se illegal, and has also suggested application of a rule of reason analysis for concerted actions of a learned profession.

1. State Action Exception §590

An exception may exist if a state regulatory scheme or body is clearly exercising state power over a learned profession.

XI. APPENDIX—COMPETITION AS AN ECONOMIC MODEL §591

The primary goal of the antitrust laws is the protection of competition. An understanding of "competition" requires a basic knowledge of how the price system affects the rationing of resources and the distribution of income in a market economy. The Appendix discusses the basic tools of economic analysis (including demand concepts, cost concepts, and revenue concepts), and the traditional classification of market structures (including competition, monopoly, and oligopoly). Finally, the Appendix discusses the impact of market structures upon the price system and its ability to ration resources and distribute income. A study of this material provides the foundation for understanding why competition is an ideal worth striving for. Competition promotes efficiency, innovation, stability, equity, and fairness.

Approach to Exams

A. INTRODUCTION

1. Purposes of Federal Antitrust Laws

The antitrust laws are primarily concerned with controlling private economic power through competition. Competition is considered desirable for a variety of reasons:

a. Efficiency in resource allocation

Competition tends to keep costs and prices lower and to encourage the efficient allocation of economic resources.

b. Consumer choice

A free competitive market is also thought to give producers greater opportunities to succeed and to offer consumers a broader choice.

c. Avoidance of concentrated political power

By preventing any single person or group from acquiring dominant economic power, the antitrust laws help to avoid undue concentration of political power as well.

d. Fairness

Finally, the antitrust laws encourage fairness in economic behavior among competitors. Through competition, resources are allocated through market forces and not on the basis of favoritism or prejudice. Competition may also promote equitable distribution of income.

2. Sources of Antitrust Law

Federal antitrust law is founded on three basic statutes: the Sherman Act, the Clayton Act, and the Robinson-Patman Act, together with various amendments thereto.

a. Imprecise statutory standards

These statutes are extremely broad, general, and vague in their terms (*e.g.*, banning "restraints of trade," "monopolizing," "unfair methods of competition," "conduct which tends substantially to lessen competition or create a monopoly," etc.).

b. Importance of judicial interpretations

As a result of these broad statutory standards, most key principles of antitrust law are found in judicial decisions interpreting and applying the statutes. In effect, a "common law of antitrust" has been created to flesh out the general statutory language, and this case law (rather than statutory standards alone) will generally determine the legality of particular conduct.

3. Impact of Economics

In deciding antitrust issues, the Supreme Court uses basic economic concepts such as demand, cost, and revenue, and market structure. Familiarity with these basic concepts will greatly facilitate an understanding of antitrust law. (*See* the Appendix to this Summary, "Competition as an Economic Model" (§§591 *et seq.*). For those *without a strong economics background*, the Appendix should be reviewed *before* studying the body of this Summary.

B. APPROACH

In analyzing conduct that might violate federal antitrust law, the following factors are usually relevant:

1. Jurisdiction and Standing

Before deciding whether a violation of the antitrust laws can be established, consider:

a. Jurisdiction

Does the court have jurisdiction over the particular violation?

(1) Is the "interstate commerce" or "foreign commerce" requirement met in appropriate cases?

(2) Note that the jurisdiction under the Clayton Act and the Robinson-Patman Act is more limited than under the Sherman Act.

b. Standing

Who has standing to complain (the government, private parties, the states)? Note that only the FTC can enforce the FTC Act.

(1) If the plaintiff is a *private party*, can she show *antitrust injury—i.e.,* injury of the type the antitrust laws were intended to prevent and which flows from that which makes the conduct unlawful?

c. Government action

In the event of a government suit, can private parties sue for the same violation or intervene in the government suit? What is the effect of a decree obtained by the government?

2. Monopoly and Attempts to Monopolize

Does the question involve the behavior or economic power of a single firm?

a. Power

If so, does the firm have economic power sufficient to allow it to raise prices or exclude competition in a relevant market? In answering this question, consider both the relevant *product market* and the *geographic market*.

b.   Behavior

Monopoly power alone is not illegal. Has the firm engaged in *anticompetitive conduct* to acquire or maintain its power?

c.   Attempt to monopolize

Even if the firm lacks monopoly power, consider whether its *behavior* toward competitors can be characterized as an *attempt* to monopolize (*e.g.*, intentional, unfair conduct, etc.).

3.   Horizontal Restraints

Are two or more competitors acting together in restraint of trade?

a.   Agreement

First of all, can some type of *"contract, combination, or conspiracy"* be shown between or among the competitors? If no express agreement exists, can an agreement be *implied* by their conduct? (Consider the impact of "conscious parallelism.")

b.   Anticompetitive purpose or effect—per se violations

Assuming that a sufficient agreement can be shown, what is the *purpose* of the agreement? How have courts *characterized* that particular purpose or conduct? Even if there is no anticompetitive purpose, is there a substantial anticompetitive *effect*?

(1)   Would the court hold the conduct *per se illegal* by characterizing it as *price fixing, division of markets, group boycotts,* or the like?

(2)   Conversely, is the conduct involved *constitutionally protected* as, *e.g.*, freedom of petition or free speech (*Noerr-Pennington* doctrine)?

c.   Rule of reason

Assuming that the agreement is *not* characterized as per se illegal, does it nevertheless have such an adverse effect on competition that it will be held illegal under the rule of reason? Consider:

(1)   Exactly what anticompetitive *effects* flow from the conduct involved? If there are none as yet, is there a risk of future anticompetitive effects, and if so, how great is the risk?

(2)   Can any redeeming competitive *virtues* be claimed for the conduct in question? Does it perfect a market or provide integrative efficiencies? If so, how significant are such virtues?

(3)   Are there *alternative means*, less restrictive of competition, that can achieve the same legitimate ends?

4.   Vertical Restraints

Is the restraint imposed between companies that are not direct competitors, but act at different stages of the production process (*e.g.*, manufacturer-distributor-retailer, etc.)?

a. Relationship
First of all, what legal *relationship* exists between the party imposing the restraint and the party against whom it is imposed? (The name the parties give it is not conclusive.)

b. Anticompetitive purpose or effect
What is the *purpose* and *effect* of the restraint? How have courts *characterized* such purpose or conduct (recognizing that the label the court attaches may well predetermine its legality)?

(1) Is the purpose or activity one that the court will *almost always uphold*, *e.g.*, a "pure" exclusive distributorship?

(2) Is the purpose or activity one that the court may hold *per se illegal*—*e.g.*, by characterizing it as *resale price maintenance*?

(3) If not characterized as per se illegal, does the conduct have an *adverse effect on competition*? Is coercion or market foreclosure present? If so, what is its lawfulness under the rule of reason (applying the same basic tests indicated above)?

(4) Are there any *defenses* available?

5. Mergers
Do the facts show an unlawful "merger" between two or more companies?

a. Definition of merger
Is there an "acquisition" by one company of any part of the stock or assets of another? Even if there is no merger or acquisition in the normal sense, is there a business relationship that may be treated as if it were a merger (*e.g.*, a joint venture; *see Penn-Olin*)?

b. Statutory tests
Does it—

(1) *"Substantially lessen competition"*?

(2) *"In any line of commerce"* (relevant product market)?

(3) *"In any section of the country"* (relevant geographic market)?

c. Substantial lessening of competition
In determining whether there is a "substantial lessening of competition" consider:

(1) Vertical mergers

As to vertical mergers, consider the percentage share of the market foreclosed. If more than de minimis, consider other economic and historical factors, especially any trend toward concentration and the nature and purpose of the merger.

(2) Horizontal mergers

As to horizontal mergers (between competitors), lessening of competition may be *presumed* if the merging parties occupy a sufficiently large share of the market. Parties to the merger must prove that the merger does not produce a firm controlling an "undue" percentage of the relevant market and that results in a significant increase in concentration in the relevant market.

(3) Conglomerate mergers

As to conglomerate mergers, is there (i) any threat to *potential* competition; (ii) a threat of potential reciprocity; or (iii) a showing of "unfair advantage"? Will the merger substantially affect the *character* of competition in either the acquired firm's market or the acquiring firm's market?

(4) Department of Justice Merger Guidelines

6. Price Discrimination

a. Violation

Do the facts show a prima facie violation of the Robinson-Patman Act?

(1) A discrimination in *price* (which includes freight charges or allowances);

(2) Between different *purchasers* (substantially contemporaneous);

(3) Of *commodities* (not services or intangibles) of *like grade and quality;*

(4) Where the *effect* is either—

(a) To *injure, destroy, or prevent competition* with the person who grants or receives the favored price; or

(b) Otherwise to *substantially lessen* competition in any line of commerce or tend to create a monopoly?

b. By whom

If so, is the violation by the seller alone, or also by the buyer (if inducement or knowing receipt can be shown)?

c. Defense

If a prima facie violation is shown, do the facts indicate any available *defense?* Consider:

(1) Cost differentials.

(2) Changed conditions.

(3) Meeting competitive prices in good faith.

7. Remedies

Assuming an antitrust violation is established, consider:

a. Injunctive relief

Is injunctive relief proper, and if so, what kind of remedy should be fashioned (cease and desist order, divestiture, free royalties, etc.)?

b. Damages

Is an award of damages proper, and if so, what is the *measure* thereof? Are there any *defenses* to a damages action (*e.g.*, statute of limitations)?

8. Judicial Administration

When evaluating rules of law or remedies, it is important to remember that the antitrust laws are primarily enforced through courts. Thus, rules of law and remedies must be capable of being understood, susceptible of proof, and easily administered.

Chapter One:
Restraints of Trade—
at Common Law

CONTENTS

Chapter Approach

Chapter Approach

Exam questions on the drawbacks of the common law that prompted the enactment of the antitrust laws are rare. Nevertheless, knowledge of those drawbacks is necessary for a complete understanding of antitrust policy. The English common law metamorphosed over several centuries, changing from a system that forbade nearly all covenants in restraint of trade to a system that permitted nearly all such agreements. Modern American common law is more hostile to restraints of trade and to monopolistic combinations, but all such laws share the same shortcomings: They apply only to limit the rights of the parties to the covenants in question and afford no remedies to third parties harmed by the restraints of trade they create; and they are not uniform, varying widely from state to state within our federal system.

Despite the modern hostility to restraints of trade, note that only ***unreasonable restraints*** of trade are unlawful. This notion, developed at common law and described in the Restatement of Contracts, forms the centerpiece of judicial interpretation of the broad language of section 1 of the Sherman Act (discussed *infra*, in chapter II). By its terms, section 1 condemns "*every* contract, combination . . . or conspiracy in restraint of trade," but the Supreme Court has interpreted this language to prohibit only "unreasonable" restraints.

A. Contracts in Restraint of Trade

1. **Early Common Law [§1]**
   The earliest common law cases held that any contract in which one party covenanted not to engage in some lawful trade or calling was *void per se*. [**Dyer's Case**, Y.B. 2 Hen., f. 5, pl. 26 (1415)]

   a. **Rationale**
   This rule was formulated not so much to protect free competition in the local economy, but to prevent the covenantor (having bound himself not to practice his trade) from becoming a public charge.

2. **Later Common Law [§2]**
   In the 17th and 18th centuries, the English courts began to hold that certain contracts in restraint of trade were valid and enforceable.

   a. **Requirements [§3]**
   For such a contract to be enforced, the cases generally required that the restraint be:

(i) *Ancillary to some otherwise lawful transaction—typically, the sale of a business* in which the seller covenanted not to compete with the buyer. Some (but not all) courts were willing to uphold covenants not to compete in *employment* contracts, as well.

(ii) *Reasonably limited as to time, scope, and locality—i.e.,* a "partial," rather than a "total," restraint on the covenantor.

(iii) *Reasonable as to both the public interest and the interests of the parties—i.e.,* it could not pose any threat of harm to the public, unreasonable lessening of competition, increase in prices, etc.

---

e.g. **Example:** In a leading case, **Mitchel v. Reynolds,** 24 Eng. Rep. 347 (1711), a baker sold his bakery and covenanted to the buyer that he would not compete in the immediate locality for five years. This covenant was held enforceable because it was "ancillary" to the sale of the bakery, "partial" (*i.e.,* limited both in time and geography), and "reasonable" from the standpoint of the parties and the public interest.

---

b. Later developments [§4]

What began as narrow exceptions to the rule that contracts in restraint of trade were unenforceable later became broader than the rule itself. By the 19th century, English courts justified nearly any restraint as "reasonable" and, in fact, often upheld "naked" restraints (including price-fixing agreements) that were *not* "ancillary" to an otherwise lawful agreement.

3. Modern Common Law Rules [§5]

American courts generally have been more hostile to contracts in restraint of trade, and this position has continued to the present time. The basic American common law is found in Restatement of the Law of Contracts ("Restatement"). The Restatement defines "restraint of trade" and the factors for determining whether the restraint is reasonable. [Restatement §§186-188]

a. "Restraint of trade" [§6]

A contract is deemed in "restraint of trade" when "its performance would limit competition in any business, or restrict a promisor in the exercise of gainful occupation."

b. Illegality of restraint of trade [§7]

A contract that restrains trade is *not always illegal.* Rather, it is illegal only if *unreasonable* (*see* chart, *infra*).

(1) Application—enforceable ("reasonable") restraints [§8]

Within the above limits, the following types of restraints have been upheld:

(a) Covenants not to compete by seller of business [§9]

Covenants by the seller of a business (or other property) not to compete with the buyer in such a way as to injure the value of the property or business sold have been upheld. [**Reeves v. Sargent**, 21 S.E.2d 184 (S.C. 1942)]

1) Note

The goodwill of the business need *not* be transferred in order to sustain the covenant. [**Sauser v. Kearney**, 126 N.W. 322 (Iowa 1910)]

2) Distinguish

However, where the goodwill *is* transferred, some courts hold that a covenant not to compete will be *implied*, and the buyer is thereby protected even in the absence of an express promise from the seller. *Rationale:* What value does a sale of goodwill have if the transferor is free to recapture it? [**Tobin v. Cody**, 180 N.E.2d 652 (Mass. 1962)]

a) But note

Other courts disagree on this point. [*See* **Cotrell v. Babcock Printing**, 6 A. 791 (Conn. 1886); **Diller v. Schindler**, 88 Cal. App. 250 (1928)] Still others take a middle position, holding that the seller cannot specifically solicit customers of the transferred business but is otherwise free to engage in the same line of business. [**Von Bremen v. MacMonnies,** 200 N.Y. 41 (1910)]

(b) Covenant by buyer or lessee of property [§10]

A promise by the buyer or lessee of property or a business not to use it in competition with, or to the injury of, the seller or lessor has also been upheld. [**Messett v. Cowell,** 79 P.2d 337 (Wash. 1938)]

(c) Covenant by partner [§11]

Agreements by a person entering into a partnership not to compete with the business of the partnership while it continues or, within reasonable limits, after his withdrawal therefrom are also valid. [*But see* **Lynch v. Bailey,** 275 App. Div. 527 (1949)—invalidating as unreasonable a restraint in partnership agreement among accountants that effectively prohibited a partner who voluntarily withdrew from practicing accountancy at all]

(d) Covenant by employee [§12]

An agreement by an employee not to compete with his employer during the term of employment or thereafter, within such territory and during such time as may be reasonably necessary to protect the employer, but without imposing undue hardship on the employee, has also been upheld.

1) "Reasonableness"

Virtually all states impose an overarching requirement of *reasonableness* on employee noncompetition agreements. Such agreements *must be limited* as to: (i) the type of work prohibited; (ii) the geographic range in which they apply; and (iii) the time they are in force (generally limited to one year or less). [**Comprehensive Technologies v. Software Artisans,** 3 F.3d 730 (4th Cir. 1993)]

2) Requirements for equitable relief

To obtain equitable relief (injunction), the employer must also generally show that the employee's services had some *unique value* (*e.g.*, personal service contract) or that some *confidential* aspect of the employment (*e.g.*, customers' lists, trade secrets) might be jeopardized by the employee working for a competitor. [**Corpin v. Wheatley,** 227 App. Div. 212 (1929); *and see* Remedies Summary]

(2) Application—unenforceable ("unreasonable") restraints

(a) "Naked" restraints [§13]

A "bare" or "naked" covenant is one that is *not incidental* to the sale of a business or other property. Such agreements are not likely to be upheld. *Rationale:* "Naked" restraints are often used as tools of oppression.

> **Example:** Where A pays B to agree not to compete with A (so as to preserve A's virtual monopoly), the covenant is contrary to public policy and void. [**Vancouver Malt v. Vancouver Breweries,** 1934 A.C. 181]

> **Example:** Likewise, if two theater companies already compete and one merely pays the other to stop competing, that promise is void. [**Robey v. Plain City Theatre,** 186 N.E. 1 (Ohio 1933)]

> **Compare:** If one theater had bought out the other's business or property, a promise to stop competing would be valid. [**Robey v. Plain City Theatre,** *supra*]

1) Test [§14]

In determining whether a restraint is "naked" or merely "incidental" to the sale of a business or employment relation, courts look to the substance rather than the form of the transaction. [**Purchasing Associates, Inc. v. Weitz,** 13 N.Y.2d 267 (1963)—transfer of "partnership" assets to company constituted an employment contract (rather than a sale of the business) when the only assets of the partnership were the personal talents of the partners]

a) But note

A covenant incidental to the sale of business goodwill alone will be upheld (*i.e.*, is not "bare")—even though the physical plant is not sold. [**Brett v. Ebel,** 29 App. Div. 256 (1898)] Transfer of the goodwill may *imply* an enforceable restraint (*see supra*, §9).

(b) Exclusive dealing contracts [§15]

Exclusive dealing contracts (*i.e.*, contracts to purchase or sell exclusively to another) are *not* illegal per se [*see* Restatement §516(e)], even at common law; but when such an agreement is used as an attempt to obtain a monopoly, it is illegal (*see infra*, §§33-42).

(3) Time limitations affecting "reasonableness" [§16]

There is no hard and fast rule regarding limitations on the time of the restraint. The question is simply whether the length of the restraint is *fair under all the circumstances*—i.e., how long must it run to give the buyer needed protection without unduly interfering with the seller's right to engage in his own livelihood?

e.g. **Example—sale of business:** According to some courts, a covenant not to compete that is ancillary to the sale of a business and limited to a *reasonable geographic location* may be upheld even though *no* duration is specified; hence, it may run for the life of the covenantor. This is not necessarily unfair if the covenantor has ample opportunity to engage in the same business or profession in another community or in a different local business. [*See* **Reeves v. Sargeant**, 21 S.E.2d 184 (S.C. 1942)] *But note:* Most states limit the length of any covenant not to compete to the length of time the buyer or any transferee carries on a "like" business. [*See* Cal. Bus. & Prof. Code §16601; *and see infra*, §26]

cf. **Compare—employment contract:** If the contract is not for the sale of business, but is between an employer and an employee, virtually all states limit the amount of time the employee can be prevented from competing after employment terminates. (*See supra*, §12.)

(4) Geographic limitations affecting "reasonableness" [§17]
A restraint that is unlimited as to territory is almost always unreasonable. The courts insist that the territory protected be no greater than that in which the business was previously conducted *plus* the area in which it may be conducted in the *reasonably foreseeable* future.

(a) Expanding business [§18]
Of course, where the business sold is expanding nationwide, very broad restraints may be upheld as necessary to protect the buyer's interests.

e.g. **Example:** Although the business sold reached only 10 states, a seller's covenant not to compete anywhere in the United States except two states was held *not* too broad in view of the nature of the business. [**Diamond Match Co. v. Roeber**, 106 N.Y. 473 (1887)]

e.g. **Example:** Similarly, an employee's covenant not to compete "within a 1,500 mile radius of Chicago" was enforced where the employer's business extended throughout the greater portion of that territory and the employee had knowledge of trade secrets, the disclosure of which would have endangered the employer's market. [**Harrison v. Glucose Sugar Refining**, 116 F. 304 (7th Cir. 1902)]

(b) Scattered market [§19]
If, *e.g.*, a company has sales in only 10 states, but those sales are not concentrated in any geographic region, and the company competes with firms across the nation, a nationwide restriction on employment

is reasonable. [**Comprehensive Technologies v. Software Artisans,** *supra*, §12]

EXAMPLES OF COMMON LAW RESTRAINTS OF TRADE **gilbert**	
ENFORCEABLE	**UNENFORCEABLE**
Covenant *incidental to sale* of business or property	*"Bare" or "naked"* covenant (*i.e.*, *not* incidental to sale of business or property)
Covenant by partner not to compete *during partnership* or within *reasonable limits after withdrawal*	Covenant by partner or employee that is *not reasonable* in: • type of work • geographic location • length of time
Covenant by employee not to compete *during term of employment* or within *reasonable limits* thereafter	

c. Enforcement of restraint [§20]

A valid covenant not to compete is enforceable both at law and in equity.

(1) Damages [§21]

The legal remedy of damages is frequently unsatisfactory, however, because the covenantee cannot prove exactly how much business, if any, was lost as a result of the covenantor's breach. Also, the breach may cause an injury (*e.g.*, loss of trade secrets) that is simply not compensable in monetary terms.

(2) Injunction [§22]

Since the legal remedy (*i.e.*, damages) is usually inadequate, most covenantees seek equitable relief (*i.e.*, an injunction) to prevent the covenantor from competing.

(a) But note

Going into equity permits the assertion of various equitable *defenses* (laches, unclean hands, etc.) which may bar relief. (*See* Remedies Summary.)

(3) "Blue pencil rule" [§23]

Where the scope of the restraint is broader than necessary to protect the buyer's interest, many courts will exercise their equitable powers to "blue pencil" the restraint—*i.e.*, *reform* it to whatever *time or geographical area is "reasonable"* under the circumstances—rather than refuse enforcement altogether. [**Stanley v. Lagomarsino,** 53 F.2d 112 (S.D.N.Y. 1931)]

(a) Application

Reformation is predicated on the public policy of enforcing an agreement of the parties to the greatest extent possible. The "blue pencil" rule is most frequently used to whittle down a statewide or nationwide restraint to the area in which the business sold is actually conducted (or property sold is actually located). In the case of employment contracts, reformation may narrow the area to that in which the employer is, or may be, engaged in competition. [**Whiting Milk v. Grondin,** 184 N.E. 379 (Mass. 1933)]

(b) But note

Some courts, however, refuse to rewrite the contract for the parties, holding that if the restraint is too broad, the *contract is invalid.* [**Beit v. Beit,** 63 A.2d 161 (Conn. 1948)] In fact, in jurisdictions following this view, an overly broad covenant not to compete that is an essential provision of the sale, and therefore nondivisible, might result in rescission of the entire sale. (*See* Contracts Summary.)

4. Statutes [§24]

The common law rules above have been changed by statute in many jurisdictions. While these statutes vary considerably from state to state, the general trend is to *limit* enforceable restraints.

Examples: California Business and Professions Code section 16600 goes further than most: "Except as provided in this chapter, every contract by which anyone is restrained from engaging in a lawful profession, trade or business of any kind is to that extent void." And courts in Texas have questioned whether restraints on competition are "ancillary" to an employment contract if the contract is for employment at will. [**Light v. Centel Cellular Co.,** 883 S.W.2d 642 (Tex. 1994)]

---

a. Exceptions to statutory prohibitions [§25]

Despite the general trend, certain restraints are still upheld under most statutes.

(1) Sale of goodwill of business [§26]

Any person selling the goodwill of a business is bound by his promise not to carry on a similar business within the area in which the business sold has been conducted, for so long as the buyer (or any transferee) carries on the business. [Cal. Bus. & Prof. Code §16601]

(a) Note

This exception has been construed rather broadly. For example, while the statute refers only to sale of the goodwill of a "business," it has also been held applicable to the goodwill of a professional practice. [**Crutchett v. Lawton,** 139 Cal. App. 411 (1934)]

(b) And note

The provision that a seller can be enjoined from carrying on a "similar business" is interpreted to mean any related enterprise that is or may be in competition with the business sold. [**Laird v. Steinman**, 97 Cal. App. 2d 781 (1950)—industrial towel business was sold; seller was restrained from laundering work clothes commercially because business sold was expanding into that area]

(2) Sale of corporate shares [§27]

Similarly, a shareholder (controlling or otherwise) who sells *all* of her stock in a corporation may be bound by her promise not to compete in the area in which the corporate business has been carried on. [Cal. Bus. & Prof. Code §16601]

(3) Sale of corporate business [§28]

Also, if the corporation sells one of its divisions or subsidiaries, together with the *goodwill* thereof (or all of the shares of any subsidiary corporation), the shareholders of the parent corporation are bound by a promise not to compete with the buyer. [Cal. Bus. & Prof. Code §16601]

(4) Dissolution of partnership [§29]

Finally, an agreement among partners that, in the event of withdrawal or dissolution, the terminating partner shall not carry on a similar business within the same area as that in which the partnership business is conducted is enforceable. [Cal. Bus. & Prof. Code §16602]

b. Unenforceable restraints [§30]

Certain restraints are entirely invalid under a particular statute. For example, *exclusive dealing contracts* are entirely unenforceable under the strict California statute above. [**Getz Bros. & Co. v. Federal Salt Co.**, 147 Cal. 115 (1905)] Also, covenants not to compete by *agents or employees*, and agreements not to accept employment offered by a competitor of the employer are likewise invalid.

(1) But note

Even though a covenant not to compete is unenforceable per se, an employee's conduct that amounts to an independent tort (*e.g.*, disclosure of trade secrets, customers' lists, etc.) *may* be enjoined. (*See* Remedies Summary.)

B. Common Law Monopolies and Combinations in Restraint of Trade

1. **Definitions**

   a. **Monopoly [§31]**
   Originally, a monopoly was a license or privilege *granted by the King* that gave an individual *exclusive power* to buy, sell, trade, or deal in any particular commodity (all others being restrained from dealing in that commodity).

      (1) **Modern application**
      Under more modern usage, a monopoly consists of the ownership of so large a part of the market supply or output of a commodity as to *stifle competition* and thereby give the monopolist effective control over prices, distribution, and other aspects of commerce in that commodity. [*See* **State v. Atlantic Ice & Coal Co.**, 188 S.E. 412 (N.C. 1936)]

   b. **Combination in restraint of trade [§32]**
   Concerted action among competitors that tends to *create a monopoly* or otherwise endanger competition is termed a *combination* in restraint of trade. Examples include agreements limiting output or fixing price in any business or profession.

      (1) **Note**
      If there was an intent to restrain trade or monopolize, the agreement could be punishable as a criminal *conspiracy* (*see* below).

2. **Early Common Law**

   a. **"Middleman offenses" [§33]**
   Even where there was no combination or concerted action, early statutes (1266 A.D.) made it a crime for any person to attempt to corner the market for any goods or wares so as to interfere with normal supply and demand.

      Example: These statutory offenses included "forestalling" (buying goods before they came on the market); "engrossing" (buying crops while still in the fields or being harvested); and "regrating" (buying in large quantities and reselling smaller quantities).

      (1) **Note**
      Such "middleman offenses" were gradually abandoned as the English economy emerged from a feudal state into a national economy, and there are no such offenses under modern law.

   b. **Local guild restrictions [§34]**
   Along similar lines, many English towns (in order to preserve their home market for local craftsmen) adopted laws restricting the rights of outsiders to trade in particular commodities. English courts occasionally struck down such restrictions on the ground that the towns were not authorized by the Crown to create or grant local monopolies.

c. **Judicial interpretation of monopolies [§35]**
Darcy v. Allen, 77 Eng. Rep. 1260 (1603), is the first reported case dealing squarely with the issue of the legality of a monopoly. The court held that Queen Elizabeth's grant to the plaintiff of the sole right to import playing cards was a monopoly and "utterly void," because it was "contrary to the common law."

d. **Statute of Monopolies [§36]**
To combat further royal grants to preferred businessmen, Parliament enacted the Statute of Monopolies in 1623. This statute voided "all" monopolies, although broad exceptions were retained for local guilds, and the statute permitted Parliament itself to create monopolies by appropriate grants.

e. **Private monopolies [§37]**
The early English cases dealt almost entirely with monopolies created by public grant, rather than by private agreement or combinations among competitors. However, there are dicta in some cases to the effect that any agreement between individuals for the purpose of fixing prices or restraining trade was illegal per se.

(1) **Criminal conspiracy [§38]**
If the subject of the agreement to restrain trade was a "necessity of life" (*e.g.,* food, clothing, shelter), the early rule held that the agreement was punishable as a criminal conspiracy. [**King v. Norris,** 96 Eng. Rep. 1189 (1758)—price fixing by salt merchants] At common law, it was a criminal conspiracy for two or more persons to combine for an objective contrary to the public interest, *even where such acts would not necessarily be unlawful if done individually* (*see* Criminal Law Summary).

3. **Later Common Law—"Rule of Reason" Approach [§39]**
Under the later common law cases, combinations and agreements to regulate prices or competition in business were *not* unlawful per se. They were valid if "*reasonable*," and *if they did not create a monopoly* (*i.e.,* did not include all members of a certain trade or producers of a certain commodity, or otherwise materially affect the freedom of commerce). [**Herriman v. Menzies,** 115 Cal. 16 (1896)]

a. **Determinative factors [§40]**
The "reasonableness" of the combination represented the court's conclusion as to whether the restriction went beyond fair protection to the parties to endanger the public interest. The following factors were generally significant:

(1) *The parties' comparative position* with respect to each other before and after the combination;

(2) *The object of the combination*—to fix prices and eliminate competition, or merely to regulate trade practices, etc.;

(3) *The form of the combination*—loose-knit trade association, or corporate integration (vertical or horizontal); and

(4) *Problems of proof*—formal agreement between the parties, as opposed to conduct of the parties, custom in the trade, etc.

b. Limitation against monopolistic combinations [§41]
If the combination posed any threat of monopolizing an industry, this ordinarily was enough to render the combination *unreasonable* and illegal. [**Craft v. McConoughy,** 79 Ill. 346 (1875)—partnership among grain dealers to fix local prices]

(1) Exception for "distress industries" [§42]
However, in a *few* cases, a combination among all producers or sellers in a distress industry was upheld as "reasonable" where it appeared that cutthroat competition was driving the whole industry to financial ruin. In such cases, the courts concluded that the combination—albeit monopolistic—was serving public policy by keeping the industry intact. [**Skrainka v. Scharringhausen,** 8 Mo. App. 522 (1880)—stone quarry operators' agreement to restrain production and market through one sales agent to eliminate previous cutthroat competition upheld; prices set were reasonable and newcomers were not excluded from the industry]

(a) But note
Other courts *refused* to recognize any such exception. [*See* **Cummings v. Union Blue Stone Co.,** 164 N.Y. 401 (1900)—contra to the Skrainka case, above, on very similar facts] These courts emphasized that the power to fix prices tends to create a monopoly, is illegal per se regardless of the "reasonableness" of the prices set, and could *not* be justified by "distress" conditions in the industry. [*See* **Endicott v. Rosenthal,** 216 Cal. 721 (1932)]

Chapter Two:
The Federal Antitrust Laws—In General

CONTENTS

Chapter Approach

This chapter first discusses the statutes that regulate competitive behavior and then presents the general considerations that may apply in any antitrust situation. These considerations are also important in analyzing any exam question.

1. **Antitrust Jurisdiction**
   Be sure to determine whether:

   a. The *interstate commerce requirement* is satisfied—*i.e.*, the activity at least *affects interstate commerce*.

   b. If *foreign commerce* is at issue, that the *intent* of the parties is to *affect commerce* in the United States *and* the conduct *actually does have effects* in the United States.

2. **Antitrust Remedies**
   Recall that both criminal and civil penalties may be appropriate.

   a. Only certain antitrust laws provide for *criminal penalties*. Keep in mind that criminal convictions require proof of intent and impose a higher standard of proof.

   b. *Equitable remedies* are available to either the government or private parties in appropriate situations.

   c. *Damages* are available to private parties, state attorneys general acting as parens patriae, and even foreign governments *if*:

      (1) The damage or injury is *to a business* in which plaintiff is engaged or prepared to become engaged, or to plaintiff's *property*;

      (2) Plaintiff's injury is the *direct result of defendant's conduct*;

      (3) The *injury results from the anticompetitive effects* of the conduct; and

      (4) The plaintiff is a *direct purchaser* from defendant and the injury is *not too remote*.

   d. *Attorneys' fees* are also available to private antitrust plaintiffs.

   e. Successful private parties may recover *treble damages*. The federal government may recover *single damages*.

3. **Antitrust Defenses**
   Defenses include the statute of limitations, state action immunity, and *Noerr-Pennington*

immunity (*see infra*, §§582-584). In an answer to an exam question, you may want to discuss defenses that are not available (*e.g.*, "unclean hands") and the reasons why the Supreme Court has rejected or limited the application of those defenses.

A. Background

1. Economic Factors [§43]

In the last half of the 19th century, the American economy rapidly changed from a primarily rural, agriculturally based economy to an urbanized, industrial economy. With that change came some developments that spurred federal antitrust legislation.

a. Agrarian discontent [§44]

As the role of agriculture began to diminish, farmers found themselves facing lower prices for their crops and higher costs for manufactured goods and railroad services. Farmers then began to organize and voice demands against the "industrial giants" who ran the railroads and manufacturing industries.

b. Predatory practices [§45]

Public opinion also became increasingly aroused by the methods used by many large industrial concerns to force their smaller competitors out of business (*e.g.*, predatory price cuts and secret rebates). Moreover, national and international *cartels* were sometimes formed to restrict output and drive up prices.

2. Shortcomings of Common Law [§46]

The common law (*see* chapter I) was largely ineffective in dealing with these abuses.

a. No positive prohibition [§47]

At most, the common law rules on combinations in restraint of trade merely made certain combinations or agreements **unenforceable**. No absolute prohibitions existed which could be enforced by the government or by private parties.

b. Lack of uniformity [§48]

Also, there was no uniform common law approach to these problems. Some states took a relatively stringent view of combinations in restraint of trade, while others did not. More importantly, state law proved impotent to deal with the anticompetitive abuses of growing multistate corporations.

3. Relationship of Sherman Act to Common Law [§49]

The Sherman Act of 1890 was passed by Congress as a federal response to these problems. Although the Act used certain common law terminology (*e.g.*, "restraint of trade," "conspiracy"), it was **not** meant simply to incorporate the existing common law into federal law.

a. **Uniform, national law [§50]**

The Act gave *federal* courts the jurisdiction to develop a "new common law" of competitive behavior by elaborating and refining the meaning of "old common law" terms. This "new common law" became a uniform, national law, superseding the numerous state rules then in effect.

b. **Scope of Act exceeded common law [§51]**

As will be seen, the Sherman Act went far beyond the common law by (i) establishing **absolute prohibitions** on certain conduct (punishable as crimes), (ii) invoking the equity power of federal courts to **restrain** violations, and (iii) providing for effective **private damages** actions.

c. **Economic rationale [§52]**

The economic rationale for the federal law is discussed in "Competition as an Economic Model," *infra*, §§591 *et seq.*

B. Summary of Principal Statutes Regulating Competitive Behavior

1. **Federal Statutes of General Application [§53]**

The following are the most important provisions of the basic federal enactments:

a. **Sherman Act [§54]**

The Sherman Act [15 U.S.C. §§1-7] was enacted in 1890.

(i) *Section 1* makes unlawful (and criminal) "every contract, combination . . . or conspiracy in restraint of trade" in interstate or foreign commerce. Supreme Court decisions have limited this language, interpreting it to prohibit only "**unreasonable**" restraints of trade.

(ii) *Section 2* prohibits monopolizing, attempts to monopolize, and combinations or conspiracies to monopolize any part of interstate or foreign commerce.

Section 2 is typically used to attack the activity of a single firm with monopoly power. Combinations and conspiracies to monopolize are normally prosecuted as violations of section 1.

b. **Clayton Act [§55]**

The Clayton Act [15 U.S.C. §§12-27, 44] was enacted in 1914 in response to perceived deficiencies or loopholes in the Sherman Act.

(1) *Section 3* prohibits sales on the condition that the buyer not deal with competitors of the seller ("tie-in" sales, exclusive dealing arrangements,

and requirements contracts) where the effect "may be to substantially lessen competition or tend to create a monopoly in any line of commerce." However, this limitation applies only to the sale of *goods*, not to services.

(2) *Section 4* allows private parties injured by violations of the Sherman and Clayton Acts to sue for *treble damages*.

(3) *Section 6* basically exempts labor unions and agricultural organizations from the Sherman and Clayton Acts.

(4) *Section 7* prohibits acquisitions or mergers where the effect "may be substantially to lessen competition, or tend to create a monopoly" in "any line of commerce in any section of the country."

(5) *Section 8* prohibits any person from being a director of two or more competing corporations, any one of which has capital in excess of $10 million. (This section has been largely unenforced; *see infra*, §266.)

c. Federal Trade Commission Act [§56]

The Federal Trade Commission Act [15 U.S.C. §§41-57a] was also enacted in 1914. The Act creates the Federal Trade Commission ("FTC"), an administrative agency, and gives it broad powers to enforce the antitrust laws.

(1) Provisions of Act [§57]

Section 5(a)(1) prohibits "unfair methods of competition in or affecting commerce, and unfair or deceptive acts or practices in or affecting commerce."

(a) Exclusive enforcement of FTC Act [§58]

The FTC has *exclusive* authority to enforce section 5 of the FTC Act (*see* above); *i.e.*, *private individuals have no standing* to sue to enjoin violations of the FTC Act or to seek damages for such violations. [**Holloway v. Bristol-Myers Corp.**, 485 F.2d 986 (D.C. Cir. 1973)]

(b) Enforcement of other antitrust laws

1) Clayton Act [§59]

The FTC is also given authority, *concurrent with the federal courts*, to enforce the Clayton Act (*see infra*, §136).

2) Sherman Act [§60]

While the FTC is not specifically charged with enforcing the Sherman Act, section 5 of the FTC Act is "all encompassing" and has been broadly read to authorize the FTC to issue cease and desist orders against violations of the Sherman Act (*see infra*, §452). However, only the Department of Justice can enforce the Sherman Act through criminal actions. The FTC is limited to pursuing civil actions to enforce the Sherman Act.

(c) Regulation of conduct not otherwise violative of antitrust laws [§61]
Moreover, the language of section 5 is so broad that it has been held to give the FTC quasi-legislative authority to determine what "methods" of competition are undesirable, and thus to reach even conduct that *does not in itself* violate the antitrust laws (*see infra*, §§456-458).

d. Amendments to the antitrust laws [§62]
The three basic statutes above have been amended since their enactment. The most important of these amendments still in force are:

(1) Robinson-Patman Act of 1936 [§63]
The Robinson-Patman Act substantially rewrote and amended section 2 of the Clayton Act, dealing with price discrimination (*see infra*, §§395 *et seq.*). [15 U.S.C. §13]

(2) Celler-Kefauver Act of 1950 [§64]
The Celler-Kefauver Act amended section 7 of the Clayton Act to close loopholes relating to asset acquisitions, and generally to tighten its anti-merger provisions (*see infra*, §323). [15 U.S.C. §§18, 21]

(3) Hart-Scott-Rodino Antitrust Improvements Act of 1976 [§65]
The Hart-Scott-Rodino Act made several important changes. It expands the power of the Department of Justice to investigate antitrust violations by permitting broad use of Civil Investigatory Demands; requires *pre-merger notification* and a waiting period by parties to mergers of certain sizes; and authorizes and establishes procedures for state attorneys general to sue, as *parens patriae*, for antitrust violations causing injury to state citizens. [15 U.S.C. §§1311-1314; 18 U.S.C. §1505]

2. Federal Statutes Covering Specific Industries [§66]
In addition to the basic antitrust statutes above, many federal statutes impact competition in specific industries. Such statutes may or may not involve regulation by an administrative agency, and some contain *exemptions* from the general antitrust laws (*see infra*, §§536 *et seq.*). The following are brief examples of such acts:

a. *Federal Aviation Act* (under which the Federal Aviation Administration is authorized to control competition for air routes);

b. *Federal Communications Act* (regulating competition for radio and television outlets, etc.);

c. *Federal Food, Drug, and Cosmetics Act;*

    d.   *Federal Power Act;*

    e.   *Federal Reserve Act;*

    f.   *Webb-Pomerene Export Trade Associations Act;* and

    g.   *Wilson Tariff Act* (covering restraints in the import trade).

C. Antitrust Jurisdiction

1. "Interstate Commerce" Requirement

a. Sherman Act [§67]

Sections 1 and 2 cover restraints of *"commerce among the several States* or with foreign nations"; and monopolizing "any part of . . . commerce among the several States, or with foreign nations."

(1) Historical view [§68]

In its first Sherman Act decision, the Supreme Court read this interstate commerce requirement very stringently, holding that the mere manufacture or production of goods was not "commerce" even though the goods might be destined for shipment to another state. [**United States v. E.C. Knight Co.,** 156 U.S. 1 (1896)—sugar monopoly not subject to Sherman Act]

(2) Present view [§69]

The Court subsequently abandoned this restrictive interpretation. Today, the commerce requirement is satisfied simply by showing that the business or activity—even where purely *intrastate*—has a *substantial economic effect* on interstate commerce. [**Mandeville Island Farms, Inc. v. American Crystal Sugar Co.,** 334 U.S. 219 (1948)—price fixing by sugar refiners a violation of the Sherman Act] Thus, the activity need only "affect" interstate commerce. [**Mandeville Island Farms, Inc. v. American Crystal Sugar Co.,** *supra*]

(a) Statute extends to limits of congressional power [§70]

The Supreme Court has ruled that Congress intended in the Sherman Act to use its full constitutional powers under the Commerce Clause to reach restraints on trade. [**United States v. South-Eastern Underwriters Association,** 322 U.S. 533 (1944)] Thus, "[if] it is interstate commerce that feels the pinch, it does not matter how local the operation which applies the squeeze." [**United States v. Women's Sportswear Association,** 336 U.S. 460 (1949)]

> **Example:** Wholesale liquor dealers in Oklahoma agreed to divide the state market among them. This "intrastate" agreement meant standardized prices, less sales competition, and fewer purchases from out-of-state distillers. Hence, the agreement "inevitably affected *interstate* commerce" and fell under the Act. [**Burke v. Ford,** 389 U.S. 320 (1968)]

(3) Problem areas

(a) Restraint itself does not affect commerce [§71]

To support a cause of action under the Sherman Act, the restraint itself need not affect interstate commerce; it is enough that the business or activity affects interstate commerce.

> **Example:** A complaint alleging a conspiracy by real estate firms to set minimum brokerage rates alleges an effect sufficiently substantial to state a cause of action under the Sherman Act. Proving a substantial effect on interstate commerce by the *general activities* of the brokers is sufficient; there is no need to make the more particularized showing of an effect on interstate commerce caused by the alleged rate fixing conspiracy or by the other allegedly illegal activities. [**McLain v. Real Estate Board of New Orleans,** 444 U.S. 232 (1980)]

EXAM TIP   **gilbert**

This is an important point that bears repeating: On an exam, you are not concerned about whether the restraint has an effect on interstate commerce. Rather, you must look at the *business or activity* to see if *it* affects interstate commerce.

(b) "De minimis" exception [§72]

Even where there is an effect on interstate commerce, some courts have held that there is no jurisdiction under the Sherman Act if the effect is *de minimis or insubstantial*. This is obviously a matter of degree and turns on the facts in each case. *But note:* Most courts, however, find the commerce requirement satisfied despite the de minimis exception.

> **Example:** Certain local hospitals allegedly conspired to block expansion of another local hospital. Despite a lower court finding that hospital services were an intrastate activity and that effects on interstate commerce were insubstantial, the Supreme Court held that the commerce requirement *had* been satisfied. [**Hospital Building Co. v. Trustees of Rex Hospital,** 425 U.S. 738 (1976)] The Court

based its finding of a substantial interstate effect on the following factors: (i) a substantial portion of the hospital's supplies (exceeding $100,000 per year) came from out-of-state sellers; (ii) the hospital derived significant revenue from out-of-state insurance companies and the federal government; (iii) it paid management fees to an out-of-state corporation; and (iv) a large proportion of financing for expansion would come from out-of-state lenders.

1) Note—effect need not be direct

The Court indicated that the illegal conduct need not be directed at interstate commerce, nor affect interstate market prices, in order to be "substantial" under the commerce requirement.

Example: An alleged conspiracy to drive a Los Angeles ophthalmologist out of the market satisfied the interstate commerce requirement because the ophthalmologist's services were performed for out-of-state patients and generated revenues from out-of-state sources, and if the alleged conspiracy was successful, there would be a reduction of ophthalmological services in the Los Angeles market. [**Summit Health, Ltd. v. Pinhas,** 500 U.S. 322 (1991)]

2) But note

At least one court has held that none of the factors relied upon in *Trustees of Rex Hospital* (*supra*) was sufficient by itself to satisfy the "interstate commerce" jurisdictional requirement, and that mere purchase of supplies from out of state did not substantially affect interstate commerce. [*See* **Musick v. Burke,** 913 F.2d 1390 (9th Cir. 1990)]

3) Distinguish—criminal standard [§73]

There is a higher standard in criminal prosecutions. Thus, in a criminal prosecution under section 1 for conspiring to divide the market for waste disposal on a Hawaiian island, the court concluded that allegations of effect on interstate commerce were "utterly conclusory." The government was required to allege a *demonstrable nexus* between the defendants' activity and interstate commerce. [**United States v. ORS, Inc.,** 997 F.2d 628 (9th Cir. 1993)]

(c) Nonprofit activities [§74]

A charitable activity may have an effect on commerce sufficient to support a cause of action.

> **Example:** In a civil action charging that Ivy League colleges set uniform standards for financial aid, the court rejected the argument that the agreement did not implicate interstate commerce because it was charitable in nature. The effect of the agreement was commercial because it had a financial effect on both the students and the colleges. [*See* **United States v. Brown University**, 5 F.3d 658 (3d Cir. 1993)]

b. **Clayton Act [§75]**

Originally, the Clayton Act applied only to corporations engaged in interstate commerce, which the Supreme Court defined as "directly engaged in the production, distribution, or acquisition of goods or services in interstate commerce." [**United States v. American Building Maintenance Industries**, 422 U.S. 271 (1975)] Thus, the jurisdictional standard was narrower than the "affecting commerce" standard applicable to the Sherman Act and the Federal Trade Commission Act. However, Congress remedied this situation in the Antitrust Procedural Improvements Act of 1980, which provides that the Clayton Act applies to *persons* engaged in commerce or in any activity *affecting* commerce.

c. **Robinson-Patman Act [§76]**

The Robinson-Patman Act (dealing with price discrimination and discussed *infra*, §§395 *et seq*.) has more stringent requirements than either the Sherman or Clayton Act: The discriminating seller must be engaged in interstate commerce *and* at least one of the two sales upon which the claim of discrimination is based must be *across state lines*.

d. **"Instrumentalities" of interstate commerce not enough [§77]**

Under the Robinson-Patman Act and under the Clayton Act as it existed prior to 1980, the Supreme Court *rejected* the argument that conduct involving a product used to construct an instrumentality of interstate commerce is thereby "in interstate commerce."

> **Example:** Asphaltic concrete, produced and sold solely within the state of California, was used to pave interstate highways in the state. The Supreme Court found no jurisdiction under the Clayton or Robinson-Patman Act for claims involving such concrete, because (i) one of the two defendants did not engage in interstate commercial activities at all; (ii) the other defendant's alleged "exclusive dealing" arrangement did not arise in the course of interstate activities; and (iii) no discriminatory sale was made in interstate commerce. [**Gulf Oil Corp. v. Copp Paving Co.**, 419 U.S. 186 (1974)]

e. **Burden of proof [§78]**

Regardless of whether an "engaged in commerce" or "affecting commerce" standard applies, the *plaintiff has the burden* of alleging and proving the jurisdictional commerce requirement. [**Gulf Oil Corp. v. Copp Paving Co.**, *supra*]

2. "Foreign Commerce"

a. Statutory coverage [§79]

International law recognizes that conduct beyond the territorial borders of a country can still be subject to the laws of that country where the conduct has effects within the country. The Sherman Act has been interpreted as covering activities outside the United States where the *intent* of the parties is *to affect commerce* with the United States *and where the conduct actually does cause effects* in the United States. [**United States v. Aluminum Co. of America**, 148 F.2d 416 (2d Cir. 1945)—the "Alcoa Case"]

(1) Note

Once the plaintiff proves such intent, *the burden shifts to the defendant* to prove that the conduct in fact had no effect in the United States. [**Alcoa Case**, *supra*]

EXAM TIP	gilbert

Be sure to remember that there are *two* threshold inquiries if foreign commerce is at issue: (i) whether the *intent* of the parties is to affect commerce in the United States, *and* (ii) whether the commerce *actually does* have such effects.

---

b. Conflicts with foreign law [§80]

The application of American antitrust law to firms in international trade can, and frequently does, involve policy conflicts with foreign governments—especially when the rights of persons in foreign countries (who are not before the American courts) are affected. [*See* **United States v. Imperial Chemical Industries**, 100 F. Supp. 504 (S.D.N.Y. 1951); **British Nylon Spinners v. Imperial Chemical Industries**, 1 Ch. 37 (1955)—clash of American and British court rulings]

(1) Limitations [§81]

Accordingly, some limitations on the application of American antitrust law are recognized. If the defendant's foreign activities are *required by foreign law*, for example, that activity cannot be condemned by the American antitrust laws. Similarly, the Act of State Doctrine prohibits American courts from passing on the validity of the acts of foreign governments. However, this does not mean that an American court will refuse to hear a case simply because to do so might embarrass a foreign government. [**W.S. Kirkpatrick & Co. v. Environmental Tectonics Corp. International**, 493 U.S. 400 (1990)] And absent a clear congressional statement to the contrary, the antitrust laws will *not* be applied where they conflict with principles of international law. [**Pacific Seafarers, Inc. v. Pacific Far East Lines, Inc.**, 404 F.2d 804 (D.C. Cir.), *cert. denied*, 393 U.S. 1093 (1969)]

(a) But note

Despite the limitations, American courts have applied the antitrust laws to foreign commerce in a wide variety of situations. [*See, e.g.,* **Pacific Seafarers Inc. v. Pacific Far East Lines, Inc.,** *supra*—Sherman Act was applicable to an alleged conspiracy among American shippers to destroy plaintiff's business of shipping U.S. financed cargoes between Taiwan and South Vietnam; **Laker Airways v. Sabena Belgian World Airlines,** 731 F.2d 909 (D.C. Cir. 1984)—court upheld the district court's injunction restraining defendants from taking part in a British case designed to prevent the district court from hearing the American antitrust claims; **Hartford Fire Insurance Co. v. California,** 509 U.S. 764 (1993)—international comity does not bar conspiracy claims under the Sherman Act against domestic and foreign insurers]

3. United States Territories [§82]

Section 3 of the Sherman Act covers combinations in restraint of trade or monopolies in "trade or commerce in any territory of the United States," or between such a territory and a state or foreign nation. [*See* **United States v. Standard Oil,** 404 U.S. 558 (1972)—Samoa is a "territory" of the United States for purposes of Sherman Act §3]

D. Antitrust Remedies

1. Criminal Sanctions

a. Statutory violations as crimes [§83]

Only some of the antitrust laws contain penal provisions.

(1) Sherman Act sections 1 and 2 [§84]

Violations of sections 1 and 2 of the Sherman Act are criminal felonies. Individuals can be punished by a fine up to $350,000, three years in prison, or both. Corporations can be fined up to $10 million. Alternatively, federal law permits the government to recover twice the pecuniary gain received by a convicted defendant or twice the loss imposed on its victims. [18 U.S.C. §3571(d); **United States v. Andreas,** 1999 WL 116218 (N.D. Ill. 1999)]

(a) Must prove intent [§85]

"Criminal intent" is a necessary element. While a *civil violation* can be established by proof of either an unlawful purpose *or* an anticompetitive effect [**United States v. Container Corp.,** 393 U.S. 333 (1969)], a *criminal conviction* requires proof of criminal intent *and* an anticompetitive effect. The level of criminal intent required is "*knowledge* of [the act's] probable consequences." [**United States v. United States Gypsum Co.,** 438 U.S. 422 (1978)] However, "specific intent" is not required.

EXAM TIP gilbert

Be sure to keep in mind that although both civil and criminal penalties may be appropriate, a *higher standard of proof is required for a criminal conviction* than for civil liability. For civil liability it's an "either-or"—an unlawful purpose *or* an anticompetitive effect, but for criminal liability, there must be *both* criminal intent *and* an anticompetitive effect.

---

(2) FTC Act or Clayton Act [§86]

There are *no* criminal sanctions for violations of the FTC Act or the Clayton Act (including those portions of the Robinson-Patman price discrimination law codified in section 2 of the Clayton Act).

(a) But note—Robinson-Patman Act section 3 [§87]

Certain instances of intentional price discrimination (*e.g.*, in rebates, discounts, or advertising service charges) *are* criminal by virtue of section 3 of the Robinson-Patman Act. [15 U.S.C. §13a]

(3) Corporate violation of penal provisions [§88]

If a corporation violates any of the penal provisions of the antitrust laws, the *individual* directors, officers, and agents who either authorized or committed the criminal acts may be guilty of misdemeanors, punishable by a $5,000 fine, one year in jail, or both. [Clayton Act §14; 15 U.S.C. §24]

b. Enforcement [§89]

The Antitrust Division of the Justice Department, or the local United States Attorney (subject to the control of the Attorney General), is responsible for criminal antitrust prosecutions.

(1) Discovery [§90]

The Antitrust Civil Process Act [15 U.S.C. §§1311-1314] authorizes the Justice Department to issue a "civil investigative demand" to any person who possesses documentary material relevant to an antitrust investigation, prior to the institution of any civil or criminal proceedings.

(2) Indictment vs. information [§91]

When the Justice Department decides to seek a criminal prosecution, it usually convenes a grand jury and seeks an indictment (rather than merely filing an information). This procedure allows the department to use the grand jury's broad powers to compel the production of evidence and testimony. (*See* Criminal Procedure Summary.)

(a) Note

Transcripts of grand jury proceedings are generally secret and are not made available to private antitrust plaintiffs unless plaintiffs are able to show special circumstances; *i.e.*, the material sought is needed to avoid a possible injustice, the need for disclosure is greater than the need for continued secrecy, *and* the request is structured to cover only the material so needed. [**Douglas Oil Co. v. Petrol Stops Northwest,** 441 U.S. 211 (1979)]

(3) Criminal vs. civil suits [§92]

In practice, however, the Justice Department uses criminal proceedings under the antitrust laws less frequently than it seeks equitable relief, and usually only for conduct constituting a per se violation of the antitrust laws or egregious predatory conduct.

2. Equitable Relief [§93]

Both the government and private parties can obtain injunctive relief to "prevent and restrain" antitrust violations. [Sherman Act §4; Clayton Act §§15, 16] Note that a private plaintiff seeking injunctive relief does not have to prove that it has suffered actual injury, but only needs to show a "threatened loss or damage." [**Cargill, Inc. v. Monfort of Colorado, Inc.,** 479 U.S. 104 (1986); 15 U.S.C. §26]

a. Scope—suits by government [§94]

The equitable power of the federal courts to remedy antitrust violations in government cases is extremely broad. Federal courts can:

(1) *Restrain* particular acts or conduct;

(2) *Compel divestiture* of subsidiaries;

(3) *Divide a company's assets* to create a competing entity;

(4) *Compel a company to license* its patents on a reasonable royalty basis [*see* **United States v. Glaxo Group, Ltd.,** 410 U.S. 52 (1973)];

(5) *Cancel contracts* [*see* **Utah Public Service Commission v. El Paso Natural Gas Co.,** 376 U.S. 651 (1964)]; and

(6) *Compel dealings* with third parties [*see* **Paschall v. Kansas City Star,** 695 F.2d 322 (8th Cir. 1982)].

b. Scope—private suits [§95]

The court's equitable powers in private lawsuits are apparently as broad as in government actions. Resolving a dispute between the circuits, the Supreme Court has held that divestiture is available to private parties. [**California v. American Stores Co.,** 495 U.S. 271 (1990)—although complainant was the state of California, the court's language makes clear that divestiture should be available to all plaintiffs]

c. Private decree does not bar government suit [§96]

The fact that a private party has already obtained relief does not preclude the government from obtaining an injunction against future illegal activities. The private and public remedies in the antitrust laws are *cumulative* and can be pursued simultaneously. [**United States v. Borden Co.,** 347 U.S. 514 (1954)—government's duty to protect the public interest exists without regard to any private suit or decree]

d. Preliminary injunctions available to prevent irreparable injury [§97]

Both the government and private plaintiffs can obtain preliminary injunctive relief against conduct that would *irreparably injure* the plaintiff, including mergers or the termination of distributors. To obtain such relief, the plaintiff must also show likelihood of success on the merits and a public interest in the injunction. [**Roland Machinery v. Dresser Industries,** 749 F.2d 380 (7th Cir. 1984)]

3. Actions for Damages [§98]

Section 4 of the Clayton Act [15 U.S.C. §15] allows "any person . . . *injured in his business or property* by reason of anything forbidden in the antitrust laws" (*i.e.,* for a violation of either the Sherman or Clayton Act) to "recover *threefold* the *damages* by him sustained, and the *cost of suit,* including a *reasonable attorneys' fee.*" This provision for treble damages plus costs and attorneys' fees constitutes not only an effective remedy wherever actual damages can be shown, but also a powerful incentive for *private* enforcement of the antitrust laws.

a. Who may sue for damages [§99]

Several cases and further statutory development have clarified the language of section 4 of the Clayton Act.

(1) "Person" [§100]

In addition to providing standing for injured individuals and corporations, the term "person" includes:

(a) Foreign governments [§101]

The term "person" within section 4 also permits suits brought by foreign governments. Though Congress had never explicitly considered the question at the time the Sherman and Clayton Acts were enacted, the Court reasoned that the congressional goals of deterrence and compensation were served by extending the protection of the antitrust laws to foreign governments. [**Pfizer, Inc. v. Government of India,** 434 U.S. 308 (1978)]

1) But note

In 1982, Congress enacted legislation amending section 4 to limit a foreign state seeking recovery for violations of the antitrust laws to *actual* (as opposed to treble) damages, plus costs and attorneys' fees, except in certain specified cases. [15 U.S.C. §15(b)]

(b) State attorneys general [§102]

The Hart-Scott-Rodino Antitrust Act of 1976 amended section 4 of the Clayton Act by permitting state attorneys general to sue for damages as *parens patriae* for injured state citizens (typically consumer actions) and by specifying procedures for protecting defendants against double recovery, measuring damages by statistical methods, and distributing any monetary award to the injured state citizens. [15 U.S.C. §§15c-15h]

(2) "Business or property" [§103]

Injury to "business or property" includes:

(a) Plaintiff in business [§104]

Injury to "business" requires that the plaintiff actually be in business, or prepared to go into business; a mere intent to compete in the future is not enough. [**Martin v. Phillips Petroleum Co.**, 365 F.2d 629 (5th Cir.), *cert. denied*, 385 U.S. 991 (1966)] However, the plaintiff need not be an entrepreneur himself; *e.g.*, an employee who lost his job due to a conspiracy among employers can recover. [**Nichols v. Spenser International Press**, 371 F.2d 332 (7th Cir. 1967)]

1) But note

Employees who lost their jobs when their employer went bankrupt lacked standing to complain about the acts of a competitor which allegedly drove their employer out of business. Their injury was only an "indirect consequence" of the real injury to the bankrupt employer. [**Sharp v. United Airlines**, 967 F.2d 404 (10th Cir. 1992)]

(b) Consumers [§105]

Injury to "property" *includes* the monetary loss suffered by *consumers* who are the victims of price fixing or other anticompetitive activities. Thus, consumers so injured may sue for treble damages under section 4, provided all other requirements for suit are met. [**Reiter v. Sonotone Corp.**, 442 U.S. 330 (1979)]

(c) Unions [§106]

The question of whether a union may recover under section 4 requires an evaluation of the union's harm, the alleged wrongdoing by the defendants, and the relationship between them. Thus, a union's allegations that a multi-employer association conspired to boycott subcontractors that had signed collective bargaining contracts with the union were held insufficient as a matter of law because: (i) the union was neither a consumer nor a competitor in the market; (ii) the asserted injury was indirect and speculative; (iii) the potential existed for duplicative recovery or complex apportionment of damages; and

(iv) more direct victims existed. [**Associated General Contractors v. Carpenters**, 459 U.S. 519 (1983)]

(3) Plaintiff must be injured by defendant [§107]

"Proximate cause" is necessary for recovery. The injury to the plaintiff must be the *direct result* of the defendant's action. [**Melrose Realty v. Loew's**, 234 F.2d 518 (3d Cir. 1956)—lessor with percentage lease cannot sue for injury due to reduction in lessee's business; *but compare* **Hoopes v. Union Oil**, 374 F.2d 480 (9th Cir. 1967)—lessor who was unable to find lessee because of defendant's conduct can recover damages]

(a) "Target area" theory [§108]

However, some decisions avoid the difficult "direct-indirect" determination by adopting a "target area" theory: If plaintiff was *among the competitors* against whom defendant's alleged violation was directed, the plaintiff may recover. [**SCM Corp. v. Radio Corp. of America**, 407 F.2d 166 (2d Cir.), *cert. denied*, 395 U.S. 943 (1969)]

(b) Market affected [§109]

Alternatively, courts have asked whether plaintiff was a member of the relevant market affected by defendant's violation. [**Hiland Dairy, Inc. v. Kroger Co.**, 402 F.2d 968 (8th Cir. 1968), *cert. denied*, 395 U.S. 961 (1969)]

(4) Injury suffered must be "antitrust injury" [§110]

To recover damages, plaintiff must be able to prove "antitrust injury," defined as an injury of the type the antitrust laws were intended to prevent and which flows from that which makes the defendant's conduct unlawful. For example, plaintiff cannot recover for an alleged injury due to the fact that a competitor remained in business because of an allegedly illegal merger (thereby denying plaintiff an anticipated increase in its market share). [**Brunswick Corp. v. Pueblo Bowl-O-Mat, Inc.**, 429 U.S. 477 (1977)] Nor could another plaintiff recover damages for sales lost to a competitor charging "nonpredatory" prices under a vertical maximum price fixing scheme. [**Atlantic Richfield Co. v. USA Petroleum Co.**, 495 U.S. 328 (1990)]

(a) Rationale

The basic purpose of the antitrust laws is to protect *competition*, not competitors. In *Brunswick*, the Court rejected the plaintiff's antitrust claim because its alleged injury was caused by an *increase* in competition, not a reduction in competition. Although the incumbent firm would suffer injury in the form of lost sales to the new competitor, this injury is not "antitrust injury."

(b) No claim where plaintiff benefits [§111]

Where the antitrust plaintiff actually stands to *benefit* from the anticompetitive acts, it cannot claim antitrust injury. Thus, a claim that competitors agreed to raise prices cannot be brought by a seller in the market, because the seller would gain from any such conspiracy. [**Matsushita Electric Industrial Co. v. Zenith Radio Corp.**, 475 U.S. 574 (1986)]

(c) Equitable remedies [§112]

The Supreme Court has extended the *Brunswick* doctrine to apply to actions in which the plaintiff seeks equitable relief, as opposed to damages. [**Cargill, Inc. v. Monfort of Colorado, Inc.**, *supra*, §93—injury due to threat of increased competition resulting from horizontal merger to two of plaintiff's competitors was not an antitrust injury and, consequently, the merger would not be enjoined]

(5) Additional standing requirements [§113]

Even if a plaintiff has suffered antitrust injury caused by the defendant's antitrust violation, a court may still deny standing to sue for jurisprudential reasons. [**Cargill, Inc. v. Monfort of Colorado, Inc.**, *supra*] Thus, an antitrust plaintiff will be denied standing if it is not a direct purchaser from the defendant or the injury is otherwise deemed too remote.

(a) Direct purchasers [§114]

Only *direct purchasers* can sue for damages under section 4. [**Illinois Brick Co. v. Illinois**, 431 U.S. 720 (1977)—*rejecting* plaintiff's claim that *indirect purchasers* down the distributional chain from the alleged price fixing are "injured" under section 4]

1) "Direct" vs. "indirect" [§115]

In a price fixing case, the *direct purchaser* is one who purchases price-fixed goods directly from the alleged price fixer. The direct purchaser may later resell the goods to others in a chain of distribution, who are thus *indirect* purchasers. For example, manufacturers of auto parts may sell the parts to distributors (direct purchasers), with the distributors selling to auto parts stores, who in turn resell the parts to consumers. The auto parts stores and consumers are both indirect purchasers (with respect to the manufacturer) of the parts.

2) Rationale for the *Illinois Brick* decision [§116]

In **Hanover Shoe, Inc. v. United Shoe Machinery Corp.**, 392 U.S. 481 (1968), the Supreme Court held that a defendant could not defend a price fixing claim by alleging that the plaintiff (who was a direct purchaser) had *"passed on"* any overcharges to its customers (indirect purchasers) and, therefore, was not injured within the meaning of section 4. *Defensive use* of "passing on" was *not permitted*. In *Illinois Brick*, indirect purchasers claimed that overcharges occurring upstream in the distributional chain had been "passed on" to them. The plaintiffs thus attempted to use "passing on" offensively to show they were injured. The Court felt bound by *Hanover Shoe* **to reject offensive use** of "passing on" as well.

3) Further justifications [§117]

The Court in *Illinois Brick* noted that in cases involving a multi-stage chain of distribution, it becomes very difficult to analyze the economic effects of an overcharge on price and output at each purchasing level. In the interests of simplifying litigation, the Court deemed it preferable to limit damage claims to the first purchaser in line, absent very limited exceptions (*i.e.*, pre-existing cost-plus contract between plaintiff and direct purchaser, or plaintiff who owns or controls direct purchaser). Moreover, the Court noted that permitting indirect purchasers to recover damages might subject defendants to multiple liability, if all purchasers were not joined in the same action. It was likewise felt that concentrating recovery in direct purchasers would have a stronger deterrent effect, on the assumption that such purchasers would have larger claims than indirect purchasers and hence be more willing to sue.

4) Contrary state rules [§118]

In **California v. ARC America Corp.**, 490 U.S. 93 (1989), the Supreme Court chipped away slightly at *Illinois Brick*, holding that the federal rule barring recovery by indirect purchasers did not preempt *state* antitrust statutes allowing recovery by indirect purchasers.

(b) Standing issues related to remoteness [§119]

Even if a plaintiff has suffered antitrust injury and there is no *Illinois Brick* issue, courts may still deny standing if they conclude that the injury is too remote. To determine this, courts look to a variety of factors, including whether the plaintiff is "a consumer or competitor in the market in which trade was restrained," "the directness or indirectness of asserted injury," whether the damages are speculative, "the nature of the [plaintiff's] injury, the tenuous and speculative character of the relationship between the alleged antitrust violation and the [plaintiff's] alleged injury, the potential for duplicative recovery or complex apportionment of damages, and the existence of more direct victims of the alleged conspiracy." [**Associated General Contractors of California v. California State Council of Carpenters**, 459 U.S. 519 (1983)]

b. Types of damages recoverable [§120]

Plaintiffs can recover for (i) *lost profits* that could have been earned in a freely competitive market; (ii) *increased costs* of business actually transacted or purchases made; *and/or* (iii) the *decrease in value* of an investment in tangible or intangible property. Private parties may recover treble these damages (*see supra,* §98).

c. Amount of damages [§121]

Although damages—especially lost profits—are difficult to prove in antitrust cases, verdicts are upheld if a "just and reasonable estimate of the damage based on relevant data is made." The wrongdoer bears the risk of uncertainty. [**Bigelow v. RKO Radio,** 327 U.S. 251 (1946)]

(1) Note

Even so, plaintiff must prove the *fact* of injury before the jury will be allowed to estimate the *amount* of damages. [**Flintkote Co. v. Lysfjord,** 246 F.2d 368 (9th Cir. 1957)]

(2) And note

While proof of damages is relaxed in antitrust cases, some evidence allowing a reasonable estimation of damages is required. [**J. Truett Payne v. Chrysler Motor Corp.,** 451 U.S. 557 (1980)] Thus, where the plaintiff did not distinguish between injury resulting from anticompetitive acts and injury resulting from lawful competition, the court reversed an award of damages. [**MCI Communications v. AT&T,** 708 F.2d 1081 (7th Cir. 1983)]

d. Costs [§122]

Section 4 provides that the injured party is also entitled to recover the "cost of suit, including a reasonable attorney's fee." The purpose is to give the private plaintiff some protection against having a damage recovery diluted by the cost of litigating.

(1) Note

A successful claimant is entitled to court costs and reasonable attorneys' fees in the trial court, *and in appellate* proceedings if successful on appeal. [**Perkins v. Standard Oil**, 399 U.S. 222 (1970)]

SUMMARY OF ANTITRUST REMEDIES			gilbert
	CLAYTON ACT	**SHERMAN ACT**	**ROBINSON-PATMAN ACT**
CIVIL SANCTIONS: PRIVATE PARTIES	*Treble* damages and cost of suit, including attorneys' fees; equitable relief	*Treble* damages and cost of suit, including attorneys' fees; equitable relief	Not applicable
CIVIL SANCTIONS: FOREIGN GOVERNMENTS	*Actual* damages plus costs and attorneys' fees	*Actual* damages plus costs and attorneys' fees	Not applicable
CRIMINAL SANCTIONS	No criminal sanctions	Felony conviction punishable by fine up to $350,000*, three years in prison,* or both for individuals. Corporations may be fined up to $10 million.*	Misdemeanor conviction punishable by a $5,000 fine, one year in jail, or both
	*These sanctions are applicable as of the date of publication. However, the government is increasing the individual punishment to a potential maximum fine of $1 million and 10 years in prison. For corporations, the fine will be a maximum of $100 million.		

e. Defenses

(1) "Passing on" rejected [§123]

As discussed above (*see supra*, §116), the *Hanover Shoe* case generally prevents a defendant from claiming that a plaintiff was not injured because the plaintiff "passed on" any overcharges to other purchasers, although certain minor exceptions were noted where the defense might still be viable (*e.g.*, in cases where the plaintiff and subsequent purchasers have cost-plus contracts, which make it considerably easier to trace and prove the amount of an overcharge passed on).

(2) "Unclean hands" (*in pari delicto* defense) rejected [§124]

Earlier decisions allowed as a defense to antitrust actions proof that the plaintiff was a party or accomplice to the illegal combination or conspiracy, or had otherwise violated the antitrust laws. This is *not* true today.

(a) Rationale

Supreme Court decisions now hold that the antitrust laws are best served if there is "an ever-present threat" to violators, including the threat of a private damages action by one's own accomplices in an anticompetitive scheme. [**Perma Life Mufflers, Inc. v. International Parts Corp.,** 392 U.S. 134 (1968)]

Example: The Court has allowed a price-fixing wholesaler to recover from a price-fixing supplier. [**Kiefer-Stewart Co. v. Joseph E. Seagram & Sons,** 340 U.S. 211 (1951)]

Compare: However, in a breach of contract action, the Supreme Court held that the defendant could assert as a defense that the contract violated federal antitrust laws. [**Kaiser Steel v. Mullins,** 455 U.S. 72 (1982)]

(3) Statute of limitations [§125]

There is a four-year statute of limitations on private damage actions. [Clayton Act §4B]

(a) When statute commences [§126]

Normally, the limitations period runs from the date the *damage is suffered*, rather than from the date the anticompetitive conduct took place. Thus, if the damages were sustained within four years of filing the complaint, the action is timely—even if the unlawful conduct occurred earlier. [**Zenith Radio Corp. v. Hazeltine Research, Inc.,** 401 U.S. 321 (1971)]

(b) Exception—fraudulent concealment [§127]

Courts have also adopted a "fraudulent concealment" exception—*i.e.*, where the defendant has fraudulently concealed the facts constituting the violation, the statutory period commences only *when plaintiff discovers* (or in the exercise of reasonable diligence should have discovered) that her rights have been invaded. [**Kansas City v. Federal Pacific Electric Co.,** 310 F.2d 271 (8th Cir. 1962)]

(c) Statute tolled by proceedings instituted by government [§128]

The institution of a suit by the government or FTC proceedings *tolls* the normal four-year statute of limitations on private actions as to any matter complained of in those proceedings. If the four-year statute of limitations has run, the private action must be brought *within one year after* conclusion of the government proceedings. [15 U.S.C. §16(i); Clayton Act §5(b); **Minnesota Mining & Manufacturing v. New Jersey Wood Finishing,** 381 U.S. 311 (1965)]

f. Effect of government judgment [§129]

A final judgment in a suit *by the government* that a person has violated the antitrust laws is *prima facie evidence* against the defendant in a subsequent private damage action. [Clayton Act §5(a)]

(1) Limitation [§130]

This rule does *not* apply to consent decrees or pleas of nolo contendere. For this reason, consent decrees and pleas of nolo contendere are accepted only in the discretion of the court. [**United States v. Standard Ultramarine and Color,** 137 F. Supp. 167 (S.D.N.Y. 1955)]

g. No right to contribution [§131]

Antitrust defendants are *not* entitled to contribution from co-conspirators. Nothing in the Sherman or Clayton Act indicates that contribution is permitted, and federal courts are not empowered to fashion a federal common law right of contribution because "uniquely federal rights" are not involved. [**Texas Industries, Inc. v. Radcliff Materials Inc.,** 451 U.S. 630 (1982)]

4. Consent Decrees [§132]

Often the government and the defendant agree to settle a government antitrust action by a consent decree, which is a stipulation by both parties as to what remedy or relief the court should order (without an acknowledgment of guilt by the defendant).

a. Limitation [§133]

However, the ultimate responsibility in fashioning an antitrust decree lies with the court, to determine what is or is not in the "public interest." The court is not relieved thereof simply because all parties to the proceeding—including the government—have agreed upon or requested a particular form of relief. [Tunney Act, 15 U.S.C. §16(e)]

(1) But note

The court has only limited discretion to reject a proposed consent decree. The court is not entitled to look beyond the parameters of the complaint to consider anticompetitive acts not alleged by the government. [**United States v. Microsoft Corp.,** 56 F.3d 1448 (D.C. Cir. 1995)]

5. Intervention [§134]

Private parties (often customers or competitors of the defendant) may attempt to intervene in government antitrust suits—often for the purpose of objecting to a proposed settlement or consent decree. Typically, the courts have *denied* nonparties any right to intervene in government antitrust suits. *Rationale:* Such suits are brought to protect public, rather than private, interests, and this obligation of the Attorney General should not be subject to interference by private parties.

a. Limited exception [§135]

In exceptional circumstances, the Court has held that nonparties may be entitled to intervene.

e.g. **Example:** In **Cascade Natural Gas Corp. v. El Paso Natural Gas Co.**, 386 U.S. 129 (1967), where the government suit charged that defendant's acquisition of a pipeline company was an attempt to strangle competition in the sale of natural gas in California, the state of California and Southern California Edison Co. (the state's largest industrial user) were held entitled to intervene as a matter of right.

6. Federal Trade Commission Remedies for Antitrust Violations

a. FTC authority [§136]

As described in more detail *infra* (§§448 *et seq.*), the FTC has *exclusive authority* to enforce section 5 of the Federal Trade Commission Act prohibiting "unfair methods of competition in or affecting commerce," and *concurrent authority* (with court and other agencies) to enforce sections 2, 3, 7, and 8 of the Clayton Act.

b. Cease and desist order [§137]

If, after a hearing on an administrative complaint, the FTC finds a violation of section 5 or the antitrust laws, the FTC may issue an order requiring the respondent to cease and desist from violating the laws. [15 U.S.C. §45(b)]

c. Civil action for penalties [§138]

The FTC may bring a civil action seeking penalties of up to $10,000 per day for violation of a final cease and desist order or FTC rule. [15 U.S.C. §45(m)]

d. Preliminary injunctions [§139]

The FTC may also seek preliminary injunctions. [15 U.S.C. §45]

(1) Acquisitions [§140]

To obtain a preliminary injunction on the grounds that an acquisition violates section 7 of the Clayton Act, the FTC must prove: (i) a likelihood of success on the merits, and (ii) that the equities favor granting the injunction. In weighing the equities, the court considers both "the public interest in effective antitrust enforcement" and the "private equities," such as the interests of the shareholders of the acquired company and the interest in decreasing unemployment where the acquired company is located. [**FTC v. Weyerhaeuser**, 655 F.2d 1072 (D.C. Cir. 1981)]

e. Restitution [§141]

In 1974, the Ninth Circuit held that the FTC did not have authority under the Act to order restitution. [**Heater v. FTC**, 503 F.2d 321 (9th Cir. 1974)] However, in 1975, Congress amended the Act specifically to provide that the FTC may institute actions on behalf of consumers or other persons injured by violations of cease and desist orders or rules, and that, with respect to such action, the court has jurisdiction "to grant such relief as the court finds necessary . . . includ[ing] . . . the refund of money or return of property [or] the payment of damages." [15 U.S.C. §57b]

Chapter Three: Monopolization

CONTENTS

Chapter Approach

Unilateral actions by a firm to acquire or to maintain monopoly power are addressed in section 2 of the Sherman Act. It is important to remember that section 2 does not forbid mere possession of monopoly power nor does it proscribe monopolies resulting from a superior product, business acumen, or historical accident. For a firm to violate section 2's prohibition on monopolization, it must:

(i) *Possess monopoly power* (the ability to raise price and/or exclude competition) *in a relevant market* (for a particular product in a particular geographic area); *and*

(ii) *Take some purposeful and intentional action* (such as predatory pricing) to *acquire or maintain* that power.

Section 2 also proscribes attempts to monopolize. To be liable for attempted monopolization, a firm must engage in *anticompetitive conduct* with a *specific intent to monopolize*, and a *dangerous probability must exist* that the firm *could monopolize a relevant market*.

Finally, note that the offense of *conspiracy to monopolize*, which is contemplated by section 2, is nearly always prosecuted under section 1's broader prohibition of conspiracies in restraint of trade.

A. Monopolization by a Single Firm

1. In General [§142]
Firms with monopoly power are able to reduce output and thereby raise prices for goods or services. This results in higher ("monopoly") profits than would be earned in a competitive market structure. (*See* the Appendix, *infra*, §§591 *et seq.*) Monopoly profits will result even if the firm's monopoly power is *innocently acquired* or maintained. However, the Sherman Act does *not* condemn the mere status of monopoly—more is required.

2. Definition of "Monopolizing" [§143]
Section 2 of the Sherman Act does not specifically outlaw monopolies as such, but rather, it forbids the *act of monopolizing*. ("Every person who shall monopolize, or attempt to monopolize . . . .") This has been interpreted to require proof of two basic elements:

(i) *The possession of monopoly power* in a *relevant market*; and

Plaintiff must first define:

- The **relevant product market**
  (what products are reasonably interchangeable?)

- The **relevant geographic market**
  (where can purchasers practically turn to for the product?)

Plaintiff then asks:

Does defendant have **monopoly power** (*i.e.,* the power to control prices or exclude competition) in that relevant market? (Look for **high market share**.)

NO →

YES ↓

Are there **barriers to entry** into that market?

NO →

YES ↓

Plaintiff **cannot prove a prima facie case;** defendant wins.

Has defendant **acquired or maintained** its monopoly power **through anticompetitive conduct**?

NO →

YES ↓

Plaintiff **can establish a prima facie case** for monopolization.

(ii) ***The willful acquisition or maintenance of that power,*** as distinguished from growth or development as a consequence of a superior product, business acumen, or historic accident. This is known as the "purposeful act" requirement. [**United States v. Grinnell Corp.,** 384 U.S. 563 (1966); **United States v. Aluminum Co. of America (Alcoa),** *supra,* §79]

3. Monopoly Power in a Relevant Market [§144]

To determine whether a defendant has monopoly power, the plaintiff must first define the relevant market. Market definition will often determine the outcome of a monopolization case. The plaintiff will argue for a narrow market definition, which will make the defendant appear to be the dominant player in the market. Naturally, the defendant in a section 2 case will argue for an expansive market definition, which will make her market share very small and lead the court to conclude that the defendant is not a monopolist. The definition is obviously critical and should correspond to commercial realities. The relevant market is composed of two parts: the relevant ***product market*** and the relevant ***geographic market.*** Thus, to establish the first element, an antitrust plaintiff must: (i) define the relevant product market, (ii) define the relevant geographic market, and (iii) prove that the defendant has monopoly power in the relevant market that it has defined.

EXAM TIP   **gilbert**

Keep in mind that order is important here. The relevant product market and the relevant geographic market must be determined by the plaintiff ***before*** attempting to establish that the defendant has monopoly power in the relevant market it defined. On an exam, your analysis of the issues should likewise follow that order.

---

a. Relevant product market [§145]

The relevant product market is largely determined by consumer preferences, and the extent to which physically dissimilar products can fulfill the same consumer need; *i.e.,* what products are viewed as being reasonably interchangeable?

(1) The Cellophane Case [§146]

The principal Supreme Court opinion outlining the criteria for determining the relevant product market is the **"Cellophane Case"—United States v. E. I. duPont,** 351 U.S. 377 (1956). The general rule announced in that case was that *"commodities reasonably interchangeable by consumers* for the same purposes make up the 'part of the trade or commerce,' monopolization of which may be illegal."

(a) Application

In the **Cellophane Case,** the government brought an action alleging that duPont was monopolizing the cellophane market with 75% under its control. However, duPont argued that the relevant product market was flexible wrapping materials and that it controlled only 20% of that market. The Supreme Court agreed that the relevant market was flexible wrapping materials, not merely cellophane. The Court stressed the *cross-elasticity of demand* (*see infra,* §601), *competition with other products,* and *the functional interchangeability of those products.*

(b) Cellophane Case criticized

Commentators have criticized the economic analysis employed by the Court, noting that high cross-elasticities of demand between products (which the Court used to justify a broad market definition of flexible wrapping material) may very well indicate that a monopolist is *already* extracting the full amount of monopoly profits possible and it is only for that reason that consumers find other products to be substitutes. This is known as the "*Cellophane* trap."

(2) Narrower definition of relevant product market [§147]

Although the Supreme Court has continued to cite the **Cellophane Case** with approval, many modern cases seem to have defined the relevant product market more *narrowly* than required by the **Cellophane Case**.

Example: The Supreme Court held that professional *championship* boxing matches constitute a market distinct from professional boxing matches generally. *Rationale:* Such matches are the "cream" of the boxing business and hence are a separate market. [**International Boxing Club v. United States**, 358 U.S. 242 (1959)]

Example: Similarly, "gospel music" was held to be a market distinct from music generally. [**Affiliated Music Enterprises v. Sesac**, 268 F.2d 13 (2d Cir.), *cert. denied*, 361 U.S. 831 (1959)]

Example: In a section 1 case, college football broadcasts were held to constitute a separate market because "intercollegiate football telecasts generate an audience uniquely attractive to advertisers and . . . competitors are unable to offer programming that can attract a similar audience." [**NCAA v. Board of Regents**, 468 U.S. 85 (1984)]

Compare: In a case involving IBM, however, the court of appeals *reversed* a narrow definition of product market by the trial court. The trial court had found the market to be only peripheral computer equipment that was "plug compatible" with IBM units, but the court of appeals held that the relevant market included *all* peripheral equipment (whether or not "plug compatible" with IBM units). *Rationale:* All such equipment would be *reasonably interchangeable* with IBM units if interfaces were used, and the IBM units *competed with* other central processing units as to which all peripheral equipment would be plug-compatible. [**Telex Corp. v. IBM**, 510 F.2d 894 (10th Cir.), *cert. denied*, 423 U.S. 802 (1975)]

(3) Single-brand markets [§148]

The Supreme Court has held as a matter of law that a single brand of product or service can be a relevant market under the Sherman Act.

[**Eastman Kodak Co. v. Image Technical Services, Inc.,** 504 U.S. 451 (1992)] *But note:* Application of the single-brand theory remains controversial.

(a) *Kodak* **case**

Kodak sold high-end copiers to businesses. It also sold replacement parts, and serviced Kodak copiers for a fee. To eliminate competition from independent service organizations, Kodak refused to make parts available to customers unless they agreed to purchase service from Kodak as well. The court concluded that the relevant markets for antitrust analysis were the markets for service and parts for Kodak machines. *Rationale:* Despite the fact that Kodak competed vigorously with others in the market for machines, those who had already bought Kodak copiers were "locked in" to the "aftermarkets" for parts and service specific to those copiers. Parts and service for other copiers were *not reasonably interchangeable*. The aftermarket therefore was a single-brand market.

(b) **Reaction**

A number of commentators have been critical of the *Kodak* decision. Courts since *Kodak* have tried to limit the scope of the Court's holding, refusing to read it as a general affirmation of the idea of single-brand markets. [*See, e.g.,* **TV Communications Network v. Turner Network Television,** 964 F.2d 1022 (10th Cir. 1992)—access to TNT television channel is not a relevant product market] It is also important to note that the *Kodak* rationale does not apply where there is no "lock in" effect from a prior purchase. [*See* **Collins v. Associated Pathologists,** 844 F.2d 473 (7th Cir. 1988)]

EXAM TIP **gilbert**

Relevant market definition is one of the most hotly contested issues in antitrust litigation. Because of the numerous factors involved in defining a relevant market, there is often room for considerable disagreement, and thus, on an exam, you must make a *fact-based determination* using the above cases as guidelines. Ask yourself, for example, what products do consumers *actually find interchangeable*? *Under what conditions*? *How far* are consumers *willing to travel for a substitute*? Not surprisingly, cases can be found to support narrow definitions or broad definitions. The outcome of a particular case will often turn on the facts and the skillfulness of their evidentiary presentation.

---

b. **Relevant geographic market [§149]**

The geographic market is generally defined by the area in which the defendant and competing sellers sell the product. Depending on the case, the relevant market may be local, regional, or national. The question is to what geographic area can purchasers *practically* turn for a product or service?

(1) Submarkets [§150]

There may be submarkets where a number of local sellers compete with nationwide sellers (*e.g.*, the market for beer). In this case, a court may deem the submarket a relevant market. [**Rothery Storage & Van Co. v. Atlas Van Lines**, 792 F.2d 210 (D.C. Cir. 1986)]

(2) Factors in determining relevant geographic market [§151]

In addition to considering price data, the court considers such factors as transportation costs, delivery limitations, customer convenience and preference, and the location and facilities of other producers and distributors. "A geographic market is only relevant for monopoly purposes where these factors show that consumers within the geographic area cannot realistically turn to outside sellers should prices rise within the defined area." [**T. Harris Young & Associates, Inc. v. Marquette Electronics, Inc.**, 931 F.2d 816 (11th Cir.), *cert. denied*, 502 U.S. 1013 (1991)]

(3) Single-customer markets [§152]

In one case, the plaintiffs attempted to define a "geographic" market as limited to sales to a single customer (the federal government). The court held that such a market could *not* exist absent *unique characteristics* that distinguished this customer from others. [**International Logistics Group v. Chrysler Corp.**, 884 F.2d 904 (6th Cir. 1989)]

c. Proving monopoly power [§153]

"Monopoly power" is the power to *control prices* or *exclude competition* in the relevant market. [**Cellophane Case**, *supra*, §146]

(1) Economic definition of "market power" [§154]

"Market power," in the economic sense, is principally a function of the elasticity of the demand curve facing the firm. The more elastic the demand, the less market power the firm has. (For an explanation and discussion of "elasticity" and "demand" concepts, *see infra*, §§592-600.)

(a) Market power in competitive market [§155]

The demand curve facing a truly competitive firm is infinitely elastic; *i.e.*, such a firm has no market power at all. The prices at which it sells its products are dictated by market conditions that are entirely beyond its control. If a firm attempted to raise its price, it would lose all of its sales to competitors charging the competitive price.

(b) Market power in imperfect market [§156]

The monopolist, oligopolist, and monopolistic competitor (*see* discussion of these terms, *infra*, §§614, 616-617) are said to possess some market power, since the elasticities of their demand are not infinite; *i.e.*, they can raise their prices without losing all their customers.

1) Note

For the monopolist, the power to raise prices is limited only by the present and potential availability of other products that consumers find acceptable ("substitutes"). For the oligopolist and the monopolistic competitor, competition from other sellers or from potential entrants to the market are additional limitations on market power.

(c) Lower costs give seller market power [§157]

Any seller may have significant market power if she has *lower costs*, which permit her to sell profitably at a lower price than her competitors. If such a seller does lower her price and capture the entire market, this is not in itself a violation of section 2—since the monopoly would be due to efficiency, a type of superior "business acumen" (within the meaning of **United States v. Grinnell Corp.**, *supra*, §143). This holds unless the price charged is predatory (*see infra*, §413).

(2) Measuring "market power" [§158]

At some inexact point, "market power" *becomes* "monopoly power" within the Supreme Court definition (*i.e.*, the power to control prices or to exclude competitors). [**Cellophane Case**, *supra*] Such power is marked by high (monopoly) profits over an extended period of time and the failure of other goods or services to respond as substitutes.

(a) Market share as prime measure [§159]

Courts take the share of the market that an alleged monopolist has *presently* captured as the principal sign of "monopoly power."

1) Market share sufficient [§160]

A market share *in excess of 70%* is strongly suggestive of monopoly power and thus is generally held to be sufficient. [**United States v. Aluminum Co. of America (Alcoa)**, *supra*, §143—90% sufficient; **United States v. Grinnell Corp.**, *supra*—85% sufficient; **United States v. United Shoe Machinery Corp.**, 110 F. Supp. 295 (D. Mass. 1953)—75% sufficient; **Heatransfer Corp. v. Volkswagenwerk, A.G.**, 553 F.2d 964 (5th Cir. 1977), *cert. denied*, 434 U.S. 1087 (1978)—71-76% sufficient]

a) But note—market share not sole determinant [§161]

Market share alone is not determinative. A 100% market share has been found *not* to constitute monopoly power where there were no barriers to entry by potentially competing firms. [**Los Angeles Land Co. v. Brunswick Corp.**, 6 F.3d 1422 (9th Cir. 1993)] *Rationale:* If entry is easy, the defendant cannot raise prices or rival firms will enter the market to compete.

2) **Market share doubtful [§162]**
There is more uncertainty whether market shares *between 40% and 70%* connote monopoly power.

a) **Sufficient**
Courts have found the following market shares to be sufficient: 58% [**Arthur S. Langendurfter, Inc. v. S.E. Johnson Co.,** 917 F.2d 1413 (6th Cir. 1990)], and less than 50% [**Hayden Publishing Co. v. Cox Broadcasting Corp.,** 730 F.2d 64 (2d Cir. 1984); **Yoder Bros. v. California Florida Plant Corp.,** 537 F.2d 1347 (5th Cir. 1976), *cert. denied,* 429 U.S. 1094 (1977)].

b) **Insufficient**
However, other courts have disagreed. [**United States v. Aluminum Co. of America (Alcoa),** *supra*—"doubtful" whether 60% share sufficient; **Fineman v. Armstrong World Industries, Inc.,** 980 F.2d 171 (3d Cir. 1992), *cert. denied,* 507 U.S. 921 (1993)—55% insufficient; **Twin City Sportservice, Inc. v. Charles O. Finley & Co.,** 512 F.2d 1264 (9th Cir. 1975), *cert. denied,* 459 U.S. 1009 (1982)—50% insufficient]

3) **Market share insufficient [§163]**
A market share *below 40%* generally is not enough to prove monopoly power. [**Cellophane Case,** *supra*—20% insufficient; **United Airlines v. Austin Travel Corp.,** 867 F.2d 737 (2d Cir. 1989)]

MARKET SHARE AS MEASURE OF MARKET POWER	gilbert
IN EXCESS OF 70%	*Strongly suggestive* of monopoly power
70 - 40%	*Uncertain* as to whether percentage of market share will prove monopoly power
UNDER 40%	Market share is *probably insufficient* to connote monopoly power

(b) **Other factors [§164]**
As stated above, market share is not the sole determinant of monopoly power. Other factors must also be considered.

1) **No or low barriers to entry [§165]**
As discussed above, companies with a high market share do not

possess monopoly power if other companies can easily enter the market to compete with them. (*See supra,* §161.) Examples of barriers to entry include government regulation, intellectual property rights, and lack of access to necessary inputs.

2) Future market potential [§166]

Similarly, a company that has nearly depleted its reserves and thus **will not continue to dominate** the market may not possess monopoly power. For example, a coal producer with a major percentage of past sales of coal did not have market power where its coal reserves were all but depleted, precluding it from dominating the market in the future. [**United States v. General Dynamics Corp.**, 415 U.S. 486 (1974)—Clayton Act §7 case]

(c) Distinguish—mergers, tie-ins [§167]

The market share required for a section 2 violation is generally much greater than required for antitrust violations such as mergers or tie-ins (*see infra,* §§304-309, 320 *et seq.*). *Rationale:* Section 7 of the Clayton Act, unlike section 2, is designed to address threats to competition "in their incipiency."

4. "Purposeful Act" Requirement—Prohibited Market Behavior [§168]

As already indicated, monopoly power alone is not unlawful under section 2 of the Sherman Act; some additional act or conduct is required. The "act" or "conduct" referred to is that by which the alleged monopolist *obtained and/or maintains a monopolistic position*. This second element is also referred to as "monopoly conduct," "anticompetitive conduct," "exclusionary conduct," and/or "predatory conduct." The terms can be used more or less interchangeably.

a. Acts that violate the antitrust laws [§169]

If, in order to obtain or maintain monopoly power, the monopolist engaged in predatory or other coercive conduct that *itself* violated the antitrust laws—*e.g.,* acts constituting a restraint of trade under section 1 (*infra,* §202), or a merger in violation of the Clayton Act, section 7 (*infra,* §323)—this is clearly sufficient to establish a violation of the Sherman Act, section 2. [*See* **Standard Oil v. United States**, 221 U.S. 1 (1911)]

b. "Deliberate or purposeful" acts [§170]

In addition, Judge Learned Hand in the landmark *Alcoa* decision (*supra,* §162) indicated that acts and conduct, otherwise lawful, might also violate section 2 where monopoly power was involved; *i.e.,* it is sufficient to establish a violation of section 2 that the company having monopoly power *purposefully and intentionally acquired, maintained, or exercised* that power—*unless* it is shown that the monopoly power was either (i) *attained by "superior skill, foresight, or industry"*; or (ii) *"thrust upon"* the defendant because of a thin market or economies of scale (*e.g.*, *natural monopolies*). [*See* **American Tobacco Co. v. United States**, 328 U.S. 781 (1946); **United States v. Grinnell**, *supra*, §143—expressly endorsing the Hand opinion]

(1) Note—specific intent not required [§171]

As the *Alcoa* decision makes clear, there is no violation of section 2 unless it is shown that the monopolist *deliberately and purposefully* exercised his monopoly power to acquire or maintain the market (as distinguished from inadvertent or accidental conduct). But a *specific intent* to monopolize is *not required*.

c. Determining whether conduct is "anticompetitive" [§172]

There is no clear test for determining what conduct satisfies the second element of the monopolization test. However, the Supreme Court has stated that "'exclusionary' comprehends, at the most, behavior that not only (1) tends to *impair the opportunities* of rivals, but also (2) either *does not further competition* on the merits or does so in an unnecessarily restrictive way." [**Aspen Skiing Co. v. Aspen Highlands Skiing Co.**, 472 U.S. 585 (1985)(emphasis added)—*quoting* 3 P. Areeda & D. Turner, *Antitrust Law* 78 (1978)]

(1) Note

The primary way for a plaintiff to satisfy the monopoly conduct is by pointing to cases that have found conduct to be exclusionary and arguing that the defendant's conduct in the case at hand is similar to the defendants' conduct in those cases.

d. Examples of anticompetitive conduct

(1) Exclusionary conduct impairing competition [§173]

A violation may be found for exclusionary conduct that unnecessarily impairs or restricts the ability of competitors to compete. In *Alcoa*, the court thought it sufficient that the firm kept increasing its production capacity to supply all demand, before a competitor could enter the field. [**United States v. Aluminum Co. of America**, *supra*, §162] Similarly, in *United Shoe*, the defendant's "lease only" policy and the extended terms of its leases (10-year minimum) were viewed as exclusionary. [**United States v. United Shoe Machinery Corp.**, *supra*, §160]

(a) But note

Expanding into new markets is not anticompetitive. [**Pacific Express, Inc. v. United Airlines**, 959 F.2d 814 (9th Cir. 1992)]

(2) Predatory pricing [§174]

A violation may be found for predatory pricing, often defined as *pricing below average or marginal cost*, although there is debate as to the requirements for a prima facie case. However, it is often difficult to prove predatory conduct or distinguish it clearly from honestly industrial, competitive behavior. And the Supreme Court has made it clear that charges of predatory pricing must make economic sense (*i.e.*, the plaintiff must present evidence that a predatory pricing scheme carries a reasonable chance of success at a reasonable cost to the defendant) for such charges to survive a defense motion for summary judgment. [**Matsushita Electric Industrial Co. v. Zenith Radio Corp.**, *supra*, §111]

(a) Supreme Court test [§175]

The Supreme Court in dicta has articulated a two-pronged test for predatory pricing under section 2: (i) plaintiff must prove *below-cost pricing* by defendant; and (ii) defendant must have a *dangerous probability of recouping* the money it lost on below-cost pricing. Recoupment is essential to a finding of illegal predatory pricing, because without recoupment, defendant's below-cost pricing actually enhances consumer welfare by lowering aggregate prices in the market. In other words, if competition in the relevant market is such that one party's predatory pricing, even if it harms a particular rival, can never put the defendant in a position to recover the profits lost in the predatory pricing scheme, then no violation of the antitrust laws has occurred. Those laws protect competition, not individual competitors. [**Brooke Group Ltd. v. Brown & Williamson Tobacco Corp.**, 509 U.S. 209 (1993)]

(b) Definition of below-cost pricing [§176]

Areeda and Turner define predatory pricing as pricing below short-run marginal cost. They argue that if a monopolist prices above marginal cost, only less efficient firms will be harmed, thereby maximizing social welfare by avoiding the wasteful idling of productive resources. They also suggest that average variable cost can be substituted for marginal cost because of the difficulty in ascertaining marginal cost. A number of courts have held that pricing below average variable cost is *presumptively predatory*. [*See, e.g.*, **California Computer Products v. IBM Corp.**, 613 F.2d 727 (9th Cir. 1979)]

1) Distinguish

In **Inglis & Sons Baking, Inc. v. ITT Continental Baking Co.**, 668 F.2d 1014 (9th Cir. 1981), *cert. denied*, 459 U.S. 955 (1982), the Ninth Circuit apparently backed off from a strict following of the Areeda and Turner cost-based rule. "Predation exists where the justification for (lowered) prices is based not on their effectiveness but on their *tendency to eliminate rivals* and create a market enabling the *seller to recoup his losses*. This is the ultimate standard and not rigid adherence to a particular cost-based formula." [Emphasis added]

2) Note

Inglis laid down a cost-based test for allocating the burden of proof on the predation issue, under which the defendant must prove a lack of predation if prices are below average variable cost, and the plaintiff must prove predation if prices are above average variable cost and below average total cost. [*See* **Transamerica Computer Co. v. IBM Corp.**, 698 F.2d 1377 (9th Cir.), *cert. denied*, 464 U.S. 955 (1983)—where prices exceed average total cost, plaintiff has the burden of proving predation by clear and convincing evidence]

3) But note

At least one court has specifically refused to adopt the Ninth Circuit's approach to predatory pricing. [*See* **Barry Wright Corp. v. ITT Grinnell Corp.**, 724 F.2d 227 (1st Cir. 1983)—endorsing the Areeda-Turner approach that pricing above both incremental cost and average cost is lawful]

(3) Refusals to deal [§177]

There is no general requirement that a company deal with its competitors, or with particular downstream purchasers. There are, however, narrow exceptions to this rule:

(a) Essential facilities [§178]

If a company possesses exclusive access to a facility that is "essential" to competition and that it could feasibly share, the company may be required to provide access to that facility on a reasonable, nondiscriminatory basis—even to its competitors. The four elements necessary to establish liability under the essential facilities doctrine are: (i) control of the essential facility by a monopolist; (ii) a competitor's inability practically or reasonably to duplicate the essential facility; (iii) the denial of the use of the facility to a competitor; and (iv) the feasibility of providing the facility. [**MCI v. AT&T**, 708 F.2d 1081 (7th Cir. 1983)]

Example: The Terminal Railroad Association controlled access to the only rail yard in the major hub city of St. Louis. Thus, members of the Association could not deny access to the rail yard to competing railroads who were willing to pay market rates for access. [**United States v. Terminal Railroad Association**, 224 U.S. 383 (1912)]

1) But note

It is extremely rare for courts to find a competitor's facility to be "essential." Only if the control of the facility carries with it the power to *eliminate* competition will it be considered essential.

[*See, e.g.,* **Alaska Airlines v. United Airlines,** 948 F.2d 536 (9th Cir. 1991)—access to airline computer reservation system not essential; **City of Anaheim v. Southern California Edison Co.,** 955 F.2d 1373 (9th Cir. 1992)—electric power transmission lines not essential]

2) Caveat

The Supreme Court asserted in **Verizon Communications, Inc. v. Trinko,** 124 S. Ct. 872 (2004), that it has never recognized the essential facilities doctrine, though it declined "to recognize it or to repudiate it" in that case.

(b) Canceling existing deals [§179]

Although the refusal to deal with competitors is *not* generally proscribed, the Supreme Court has held that a firm with monopoly power in the Aspen, Colorado mountain ski facilities market violated section 2 when it attempted to force its sole rival to accept deep concessions in the distribution of proceeds of "all-Aspen tickets" or it would not participate in the program. The tickets entitled their bearers to use each of the four major mountain ski facilities in Aspen. The tickets had been issued for many years, and revenues from their sales had been distributed to the competitors on the basis of surveys designed to determine the number of skiers who used each facility. The accused monopolist, which initially owned only one such facility, later acquired a second and eventually opened a third (the area's fourth). It then demanded that its competitor accept a fixed share of revenues from sales of the all-Aspen tickets, which share was significantly below the competitor's historical average based on usage. [**Aspen Skiing Co. v. Aspen Highlands Skiing Corp.,** 472 U.S. 585 (1985)]

1) Limiting *Aspen Skiing*

Finding that its decision in *"Aspen Skiing* is at or near the outer boundary of section 2 liability," the Supreme Court in *Trinko* suggested that the presence of a regulatory scheme, such as the Telecommunications Act of 1996, may allow a refusal to deal to escape antitrust liability. [**Verizon Communications, Inc. v. Trinko,** *supra*]

(4) Monopoly leveraging [§180]

Courts differ on whether using monopoly power in one market to "leverage" power in another market violates section 2 of the Sherman Act.

(a) Tying [§181]

Special rules govern the use of "tying arrangements," *i.e.,* where a monopolist conditions the sale of one good on sales of other goods. (*See infra,* §§290 *et seq.*)

(b) No duty to disclose to competitors [§182]

Even in circuits where leveraging is illegal, there is no affirmative duty to protect competitors in "leveraged" markets.

(e.g.) Example: In **Berkey Photo, Inc. v. Eastman Kodak Co.,** 603 F.2d 263 (2d Cir. 1979), *cert. denied,* 444 U.S. 1093 (1980), Kodak clearly had monopoly power in the film market and was accused of introducing a new film and camera package in an attempt to leverage its monopoly in the film market into the camera and photofinishing markets. The plaintiff alleged that, among other things, the defendant, as a monopolist, had a duty to predisclose new innovations to competitors, but the court rejected this and found no section 2 violation. A monopolist is encouraged by section 2 to compete aggressively on the merits, and none of Kodak's acts were unreasonably restrictive of competition. They were simply the products of "invention and innovation" and merely "reflected Kodak's superior product, business acumen, skill and foresight and did not constitute willful maintenance of monopoly power." Although the court found no liability on the facts before it, it nevertheless opined that "a firm violates section 2 by using its monopoly power in one market to gain a competitive advantage in another."

(c) Ninth Circuit—leveraging not illegal [§183]

The Ninth Circuit has held that leveraging a monopoly is not an independent offense under section 2; it is illegal only if the leveraged market is itself monopolized, or some other antitrust law is violated. [**Alaska Airlines v. United Airlines,** *supra,* §178] The court acknowledged that its decision conflicted with cases in the Second and Sixth Circuits. The Third Circuit has followed the Ninth Circuit. [**Fineman v. Armstrong World Industries, Inc.,** *supra,* §162]

(d) Supreme Court resolution [§184]

The Supreme Court in **Verizon Communications, Inc. v. Trinko,** *supra,* §178, seemed to resolve the debate in favor of the Ninth Circuit position, reasoning that monopoly leveraging cannot be a section 2 violation unless there is a dangerous probability of success that the defendant will monopolize the second market.

(5) Accumulation of patents [§185]

Although "the mere accumulation of patents, no matter how many, is not in itself illegal" [**Automatic Radio Manufacturing Co. v. Hazeltine Research,** 339 U.S. 827 (1950)], the acquisition of additional patents to perpetuate control over an industry may be prohibited if it would tend to dissuade market participants from conducting research and development [*see* **United States v. General Electric**, 82 F. Supp. 753 (D.N.J. 1949); *see infra*, §504].

(6) Foreclosing distribution chains and other dirty tricks [§186]

Microsoft Corp. was found to have illegally monopolized the market for Intel-based PC operating systems by *thwarting the development and evolution of two technologies*—Netscape's browser and Sun Microsystem's Java—which Microsoft saw as long-term competitive threats. Microsoft illegally prevented Netscape from getting its browser to market by convincing original equipment manufacturers, internet access providers, internet content providers, independent software vendors, and other distribution channels to discriminate against Netscape. Microsoft also integrated its own competing browser code, Internet Explorer ("IE"), into its operating system code in such a manner that its customers could not remove IE without disabling their computer. Finally, Microsoft illegally interfered with Sun's Java Virtual Machine—a programming language that allowed software developers to write applications that could run on any operating system, which would make consumers and software application developers less dependent on Microsoft's operating system—by creating and distributing its own "polluted" version of Java, while falsely informing software developers that programs written on Microsoft's version of Java would run on other operating systems, just like programs written in regular Java. [**United States v. Microsoft Corp.**, 253 F.3d 34 (D.C. Cir. 2001)]

(7) Bundled rebates [§187]

The Third Circuit (en banc) held that 3M illegally monopolized the market for transparent tape by offering bundled rebates that essentially required its customers to buy all of their tape from 3M (and none from competitors) in order to receive significant rebates on other 3M products. [**LePage's, Inc. v. 3M**, 324 F.3d 141 (3d Cir. 2003)]

5. "Monopsony" Power [§188]

The Court has also held that section 2 applies to monopoly *buying* power ("monopsony" power), as well as monopoly selling power. Thus, a buyer (*e.g.*, a film exhibitor) cannot use his monopsony power in one geographic area to extract preferences (*e.g.*, from a film distributor) over competitors of the buyer in other areas where the buyer does not possess such power. Such use of monopsony power constitutes an act of "monopolizing" within the meaning of section 2. [**United States v. Griffith**, 334 U.S. 100 (1948)]

6. Defense—"Innocently Acquired" or "Natural" Monopolies [§189]

Where the monopoly power was acquired "innocently" (*e.g.*, as the result of "superior skill") or thrust upon the defendant (*e.g.*, as a "natural" monopoly), section 2 is not violated. Such monopolies are the result of a superior product, business acumen, historical accident, or natural advantage.

e.g. **Examples:** The following are examples of such lawful monopolies:

(i) *A small town newspaper*, where the town market can support only one paper [**Union Leader Corp. v. Newspapers of New England**, 284 F.2d 582 (1st Cir. 1960), *cert. denied*, 365 U.S. 833 (1961)];

(ii) *A professional football team* in a city where there are not enough sports fans to support more than one team [**American Football League v. National Football League**, 323 F.2d 124 (4th Cir. 1963)]; and

(iii) *A manufacturer who has the only facilities* required to supply the market [**Ovitron Corp. v. General Motors**, 295 F. Supp. 373 (S.D.N.Y. 1969)—Delco was the only manufacturer able to supply squad radios in quantities required by Army].

a. Limitation [§190]

Even though monopoly power has been innocently acquired, if it is thereafter *exercised in a "ruthless, predatory, or exclusionary" manner*, it will constitute a violation of section 2. [**Ovitron Corp. v. General Motors**, *supra*—Delco allegedly bid below cost to keep all competitors out of market in which it had natural monopoly]

e.g. **Example:** Power Company had obtained exclusive franchises (lawful monopoly) from various small towns to sell electric power. As these franchises expired, Power Company attempted to prevent the towns from setting up their own power facilities by refusing to sell wholesale power to them or allow any transfer of power across its lines. *Held:* This action violated section 2. [**Otter Tail Power Co. v. United States**, 410 U.S. 366 (1973)]

7. AT&T Case [§191]

The Justice Department and AT&T agreed in January 1982 to settle the largest antitrust case in history under terms that required AT&T to divest all 22 of its local operating companies, which comprised approximately two-thirds of AT&T's total assets. AT&T continues to own its long distance intercity lines, Bell Telephone Labs, and Western Electric. [**United States v. AT&T**, 552 F. Supp. 131 (D.D.C. 1982), *aff'd sub nom.* **Maryland v. United States**, 460 U.S. 1001 (1983)] The divestiture decree opened the long-distance and telephone product markets to competition.

B. Attempts to Monopolize

1. In General [§192]

As noted (*supra*, §143), section 2 also outlaws "*attempts* to monopolize." This provision permits some degree of control over predatory or exclusionary single-firm

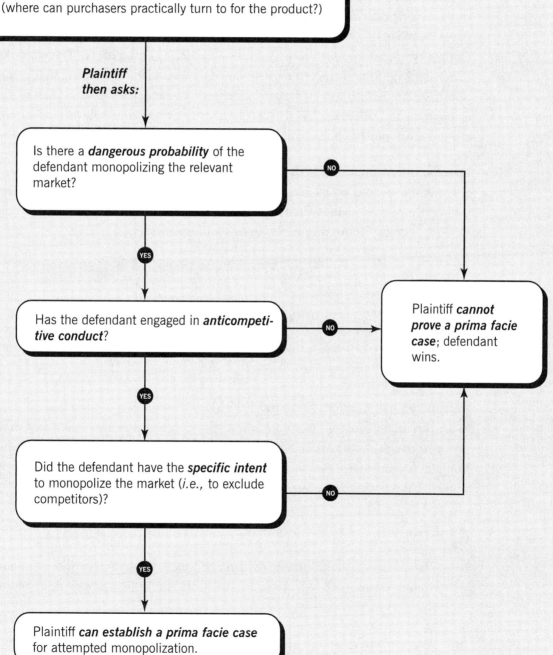

Plaintiff must first define:

- The **relevant product market**
  (what products are reasonably interchangeable?)

- The **relevant geographic market**
  (where can purchasers practically turn to for the product?)

Plaintiff then asks:

Is there a **dangerous probability** of the defendant monopolizing the relevant market?

NO →

YES ↓

Has the defendant engaged in **anticompetitive conduct**?

NO →

YES ↓

Did the defendant have the **specific intent** to monopolize the market (*i.e.*, to exclude competitors)?

NO →

Plaintiff **cannot prove a prima facie case**; defendant wins.

YES ↓

Plaintiff **can establish a prima facie case** for attempted monopolization.

conduct in cases where the offending firm does not possess clear monopoly power. The Supreme Court has explained that "it is generally required that to demonstrate attempted monopolization a plaintiff must prove (i) that the defendant has engaged in *predatory or anticompetitive conduct* with (ii) *a specific intent* to monopolize and (iii) *a dangerous probability of achieving monopoly power.*" [**Spectrum Sports, Inc. v. McQuillan,** 506 U.S. 447 (1993)]

2. Dangerous Probability of Success Required [§193]

An attempt to monopolize is "the employment of methods, means and practices which would, if successful, accomplish monopolization, and which, though falling short, nevertheless approaches so close as to create a *dangerous probability* of it. . . ." [**Spectrum Sports, Inc. v. McQuillan,** 506 U.S. 447 (1993)] In *Spectrum Sports*, the Court reversed a line of Ninth Circuit cases [*see, e.g.,* **Lessig v. Tidewater Oil Co.,** 327 F.2d 459 (9th Cir.), *cert. denied*, 377 U.S. 993 (1964)] holding that evidence of unfair or predatory conduct might satisfy the "dangerous probability of success" element of the offense even in the absence of proof of a relevant market or the alleged monopolist's power therein.

3. Specific Intent Required [§194]

An attempt to monopolize requires a *specific intent to exclude competitors* and gain monopoly power. [**Times-Picayune Publishing Co. v. United States,** 345 U.S. 594 (1952)] Specific intent may be *inferred from conduct.*

EXAM TIP   **gilbert**

Be sure to note the difference in the types of intent required for monopolization versus attempted monopolization. To prove *monopolization*, all a plaintiff must show is a *deliberate and purposeful act*—i.e., not accidental (see *supra*, §§170-171). However, for *attempted monopolization*, the plaintiff's proof must be more substantial; the plaintiff must prove the defendant's *specific intent to exclude competitors*.

---

4. Anticompetitive Conduct Required [§195]

Since the intent must be to monopolize, the defendant must be seeking monopoly power through means *other than* "business acumen"; *i.e.*, defendant must be using "unfair means." The conduct discussed in the prior section regarding monopolization is also relevant here. (*See supra*, §§173 *et seq.*)

 Examples: The following are examples of unfair means:

(i) *The inducement of others to boycott one's competitors* [**Lorain Journal v. United States,** 342 U.S. 143 (1951); **Klors Inc. v. Broadway-Hale Stores,** 359 U.S. 207 (1959)];

(ii) *Discriminatory pricing* [**Union Leader Corp. v. Newspapers of New England,** *supra*, §189]; or

(iii) *Refusal by a manufacturer with a dominant market position to deal with an independent dealer*, after the dealer refused to sell out to the manufacturer. [**Eastman Kodak Co. v. Southern Photo Materials**, 273 U.S. 359 (1927); *but see* **FTC v. Raymond Bros.-Clark Co.**, 263 U.S. 565 (1924)—similar refusal to deal deemed permissible where defendant lacked "dominant control" of the relevant market]

a. Aggressive competition allowed [§196]

In attempted monopolization cases, courts emphasize that aggressive efforts to compete are not illegal; indeed, they are to be encouraged. [*See* **Pacific Express, Inc. v. United Airlines**, *supra*, §173; **Midwest Radio Co. v. Forum Publishing Co.**, 1991-2 Trade Cas. ¶69,547 (8th Cir. 1991)—hiring competitor's employees to improve performance not anticompetitive]

C. Conspiracy to Monopolize

1. In General [§197]

Section 2 likewise makes it illegal for any person "to conspire with any other person or persons to monopolize. . . ." However, this part of section 2 entirely overlaps with section 1, which prohibits "conspiracies in restraint of trade" (*see infra*, §251). Since monopolizing is an extreme form of a restraint of trade, any conspiracy to monopolize would necessarily be a conspiracy in restraint of trade. The converse is not true, however; indeed, the Supreme Court has ruled that a conspiracy in restraint of trade can fall short of a conspiracy to monopolize. [*See* **American Tobacco Co. v. United States**, *supra*, §170]

EXAM TIP	gilbert

If an exam question indicates a conspiracy to monopolize under section 2, remember that *section 1 is more frequently used to prosecute such offenses*, and tailor your discussion accordingly.

2. Conscious Commitment Requirement [§198]

A section 2 conspiracy claim requires proof that the parties to the conspiracy were "consciously committed" to the anticompetitive scheme. [**Morgan, Strand, Wheeler & Biggs v. Radiology, Ltd.**, 924 F.2d 1484 (9th Cir. 1991)]

Chapter Four: Collaboration Among Competitors— Horizontal Restraints

CONTENTS

Chapter Approach

Section 1 of the Sherman Act has been applied by the Supreme Court to prohibit agreements that unreasonably restrain trade. This chapter focuses on the courts' treatment of agreements and collaborations between market *competitors*, so-called horizontal restraints.

These restraints take several forms. Price fixing agreements, market allocations, and group boycotts are the most obvious and the most odious, and these arrangements are frequently declared *per se unlawful*. Remember that under the per se approach, the courts limit their inquiry into such factors as the subjective intent of the parties, relevant markets, and market power, on the theory that certain agreements are so objectionable and so lacking in competitive justification that they must be eliminated.

Still other horizontal restraints, such as joint ventures and trade associations, have more ambiguous effects on the marketplace. Thus, these restraints are evaluated on the totality of their circumstances under what courts call the *rule of reason* analysis.

Finally, this chapter considers *what constitutes an "agreement"* that violates section 1. Although there may be direct evidence of such an agreement, be sure to consider facts amounting to circumstantial evidence of an agreement. Look especially for "conscious parallelism" in price or other terms.

A. Introduction

1. Horizontal Restraints [§199]

A primary concern of the antitrust laws has been to preserve and encourage competition among firms in the same industry. The antitrust laws—primarily through *section 1 of the Sherman Act*—place limits on collaboration among competing firms, so-called horizontal restraints.

a. Necessity of agreement [§200]

Unilateral action does not violate section 1; there must be some kind of agreement between competitors. However, whether an action is unilateral or not may be difficult to determine. (*See infra*, §§249 *et seq.*)

b. Basic elements of a section 1 claim [§201]

In order to establish liability under section 1 of the Sherman Act, the plaintiff must prove: (i) an *agreement or concerted action*; (ii) that *unreasonably restrains trade*; and (iii) that has an *effect on interstate commerce*. To show that a particular restraint of trade is unreasonable, courts generally apply one of two tests: the per se rule and the rule of reason.

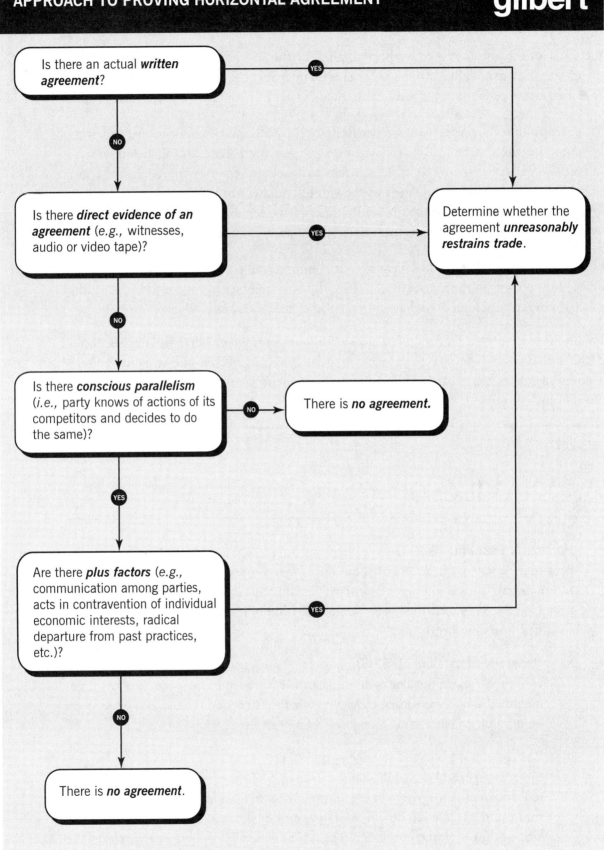

Is there an actual **written agreement**?

— YES →

Is there **direct evidence of an agreement** (*e.g.*, witnesses, audio or video tape)?

— YES →

Determine whether the agreement **unreasonably restrains trade**.

Is there **conscious parallelism** (*i.e.*, party knows of actions of its competitors and decides to do the same)?

— NO → There is **no agreement.**

Are there **plus factors** (*e.g.*, communication among parties, acts in contravention of individual economic interests, radical departure from past practices, etc.)?

— YES →

— NO →

There is **no agreement**.

2. Rule of Reason vs. Per Se Violations

a. Rule of reason test [§202]

The language of Sherman Act section 1 condemns "*every* contract, combination . . . or conspiracy in restraint of trade." Although one early case appears to have taken this language literally [**United States v. Trans-Missouri Freight Association,** 166 U.S. 290 (1897)], the Supreme Court soon adopted the "rule of reason" and declared that *only agreements that unreasonably restrain* trade are unlawful. [**Standard Oil Co. v. United States,** *supra,* §169]

(1) Rationale

An all-inclusive condemnation of every restraint, if applied literally, would make section 1 unworkable since it would condemn much business behavior that is economically and socially beneficial. After all, every contract between two firms for the sale of goods is to some extent a "restraint" in that it requires those particular goods to be purchased from the seller and not one of the seller's competitors.

(2) Effect

The *Standard Oil* rule of reason test focuses on market structure and behavior, and acknowledges that there is a range of economic effects that may result from different kinds of restraints in different market structures; *i.e.,* the rule requires a *case-by-case determination* of the "reasonableness" of any particular combination or agreement among competitors.

(3) Inquiry limited [§203]

The rule of reason, however, does not permit a broad inquiry that would balance anticompetitive effects of an agreement against its alleged social or political benefits. Rather, the inquiry is more narrow: Is the challenged agreement one that *promotes competition or suppresses competition*? "The statutory policy [of the Sherman Act] precludes inquiry into the question whether competition is good or bad." [**National Society of Professional Engineers v. United States,** 435 U.S. 679 (1978)]

> **Example:** In **National Society of Professional Engineers v. United States,** *supra,* the defendants argued that their otherwise anticompetitive bidding rules should be saved from the force of the Sherman Act because they were designed to ensure public safety (through better engineering designs and specifications) that allegedly would result from removing engineers from the pressures associated with competitive bidding. The court rejected that argument. Once an agreement has been found to have substantial anticompetitive effects, the defendants cannot defend by acknowledging the restraint on competition and then arguing that public safety or some other social benefit is served by the agreement. Such arguments should be addressed to Congress as the basis for an exemption from the antitrust laws.

(4) Factors considered in rule of reason analysis [§204]

To measure and evaluate a challenged restraint's impact on competition, courts will consider: the structure of the industry, facts peculiar to the firm's operation in that industry (including the firm's power and position), the history and duration of the restraint, the reasons why the restraint was adopted, and the effects on the competitive market, including price and output. [**Chicago Board of Trade v. United States**, 246 U.S. 231 (1918); **National Society of Professional Engineers v. United States**, *supra*]

(a) But note

Many rule of reason cases do not seem to analyze a firm's market power carefully or expressly. When such analysis is made, it often tends to be curtailed and far less rigorous than the analysis typically associated with monopolization or merger cases.

b. Per se violations [§205]

Following the *Standard Oil* decision, the Court held that certain types of business agreements among competitors would be held *unreasonable as a matter of law—i.e., illegal per se.*

(1) Rationale

Certain agreements almost always result in substantial restraint of trade, without any redeeming procompetitive benefits. A case-by-case inquiry into reasonableness is therefore unwarranted.

(2) Effect

Trials are simplified and shortened because the issues are limited and not as far-ranging as permitted under a rule of reason analysis. Moreover, some commentators have noted that per se rules provide predictive advantages by giving businesses bright-line standards and at the same time lightening the administrative burden that would be felt by courts if they continually had to monitor conduct to determine its reasonableness.

(3) Application

The Supreme Court has said that "[i]t is only after considerable experience with certain business relationships that courts classify them as per se violations of the Sherman Act." [**United States v. Topco Associates, Inc.**, 405 U.S. 596 (1972)] The prime examples of per se violations are horizontal price fixing and horizontal market division. Other areas where per se rules are employed include certain types of tie-ins and boycotts. Minimum resale price maintenance (so-called vertical price fixing) is also per se illegal. (These areas are discussed *infra*.)

c. Problem of characterization [§206]

Characterizing conduct or the likely effects of an agreement is a critical step in determining whether the rule of reason or the per se rule analysis applies.

(1) Per se category [§207]

The initial inquiry should be to determine whether the conduct or effect *fits within a recognized per se category.* If so, then the analysis need not go further. Thus, for example, one might ask whether the *likely purpose or effect* of an agreement is *to raise prices.* If the answer is yes (and provided the effect is not de minimis), the agreement should be condemned as a per se violation.

Example: Two competitors agreed to allocate the Georgia bar review course market exclusively to one of them. The Court held that this was illegal per se; the anticompetitive effect of the arrangement was clear from the fact that the price for the review course jumped from $150 to $400 immediately after the agreement was instituted. **[Palmer v. BRG of Georgia,** 498 U.S. 46 (1990)]

(a) But note

In addressing a plan by NCAA member schools to limit the number of televised intercollegiate football games, the Supreme Court observed that the plan constituted horizontal price fixing and output limitation, which would ordinarily be illegal per se. However, the Court reasoned that horizontal restraints were necessary to even have the "product" of college football, and the Court applied the rule of reason analysis and determined that the plan violated section 1. [**National Collegiate Athletic Association v. Board of Regents,** *supra,* §147]

(2) Rule of reason [§208]

However, if the *purpose or effect is unclear,* or the defendant is able to make a plausible argument that the agreement or conduct (i) enhances the market by making it *more competitive,* or (ii) *increases efficiency* through integration, then a rule of reason analysis should be conducted, balancing the anticompetitive harms and the procompetitive benefits. [**Broadcast Music, Inc. v. Columbia Broadcasting System,** 441 U.S. 1 (1979)]

Example: *Broadcast Music, Inc.* ("BMI") provides an example of the process. ASCAP is composed of composer members and acts as a clearinghouse for copyright owners and users. The court of appeals had found a per se price fixing violation in ASCAP's "blanket licensing" requirements, which forced a user of ASCAP's copyrighted music to purchase a blanket license for use of all ASCAP's music, even though the user desired only some of the copyrighted music. The Supreme Court reversed, holding that the practice could not be clearly characterized as price fixing and that, because courts had little previous experience with this type of marketing, and the ASCAP blanket license scheme arguably created efficiencies through integration, the rule of reason analysis should be applied. [**Broadcast Music, Inc. v. Columbia Broadcasting System**, *supra*; *and see* **National Collegiate Athletic Association v. Board of Regents**, *supra*—Supreme Court held it inappropriate to apply per se rule to a situation in which horizontal restraints were necessary to make product available in the first place]

d. "Quick look" rule of reason [§209]

On occasion, courts will employ an intermediate measure between the per se rule and the rule of reason, *i.e.*, a *"quick look"* analysis. This intermediate standard applies in cases where per se condemnation is inappropriate, but where no elaborate industry analysis is required to demonstrate the anticompetitive character of an *inherently suspect restraint*. [**FTC v. Indiana Federation of Dentists**, 476 U.S. 447 (1986); **United States v. Brown University**, *supra*, §75]

(1) But note

Courts will not employ "quick look" analysis if it appears that the defendants have a plausible procompetitive justification for their concerted action. Thus, *e.g.*, the Supreme Court held that a dental association's rule requiring several disclosures if a dentist wanted to advertise a price discount should not be condemned under the abbreviated rule of reason because, although the rule could possibly have anticompetitive effects, it could also enhance competition by eliminating deceptive advertising. [**California Dental Association v. FTC**, 526 U.S. 756 (1999)]

e. Practical effect of characterization [§210]

Because the court must decide in each case whether to apply the per se rule or the rule of reason, defendants will almost always have some opportunity to argue that the challenged restraint is actually procompetitive.

MODES OF ANALYSIS FOR HORIZONTAL RESTRAINTS	**gilbert**
ANALYSIS	**RESTRAINTS**
PER SE VIOLATION	- Price fixing - Output restriction - Market division - Some group boycotts
"QUICK LOOK" TEST	- Agreements that facially restrain competition - Some group boycotts
RULE OF REASON TEST	- All horizontal agreements that do not fall in any of the above categories

B. Price Fixing Among Competitors

1. Per Se Violation [§211]

The Supreme Court has stated that: "Any combination or agreement between competitors, formed for the purpose and with the effect of raising, depressing, fixing, pegging, or stabilizing the price of a commodity in interstate or foreign commerce is *illegal per se*." [**United States v. Socony-Vacuum Oil Co.**, 310 U.S. 150 (1940)—to avoid temporary depressions in gasoline prices caused by oversupply, major oil companies agreed to purchase surplus gasoline from independent refiners who lacked storage facilities; such agreement was illegal per se as a price fixing conspiracy]

2. No Justification Permitted [§212]

The general rule is that no defense or justification of any kind is recognized where horizontal price fixing is shown. "Whatever economic justification particular price fixing agreements may be thought to have, the law does not permit inquiry into their reasonableness. They are all banned because of their *actual or potential* threat to the central nervous system of the economy." [**United States v. Socony-Vacuum Oil Co.**, *supra*] This rule has consistently been applied to reject *noneconomic* justifications for price fixing.

Example: It is not a defense that the price fixed was actually a "reasonable" price. [**United States v. Addyston Pipe & Steel Co.**, 85 F. 271 (6th Cir. 1898), *modified*, 175 U.S. 211 (1899); **United States v. Trenton Potteries Co.**, 273 U.S. 392 (1927)]

Example: It is not a justification that the purpose of the price fixing was to end "ruinous competition" in the marketplace, or to eliminate an instability of prices which plagued both producers and consumers. [*See* **United States v. Socony-Vacuum Oil Co.**, *supra*]

Example: Even the First Amendment cannot protect participants in a price fixing boycott. Where District of Columbia attorneys who had regularly accepted court appointments to represent indigent defendants attempted to extract an increase in the fees for that representation by agreeing among themselves not to accept any new appointments, such conduct violated section 1. The First Amendment offered no protection because the purpose of the boycott was to gain an economic advantage for the participants. [**FTC v. Superior Court Trial Lawyers Association**, 493 U.S. 411 (1990)]

a. And note

Also, it is immaterial that adherence to the fixed price schedule was not mandatory and that no penalties were imposed for deviation therefrom. [**United States v. National Association of Real Estate Boards**, 339 U.S. 385 (1950)—adoption by real estate associations of standard commission rates held illegal per se, even though only "ethical" or "moral" sanctions imposed against those who deviated]

3. Exception—Making a Market More Competitive [§213]

If a credible argument can be made that an agreement has the purpose and effect of making a market function more competitively or of creating integrative efficiencies, the effect on prices may be viewed as an ancillary restraint and subject to a rule of reason analysis. Some commentators have rationalized **Chicago Board of Trade v. United States,** *supra*, §204, and **United States v. Appalachian Coals, Inc.,** 228 U.S. 344 (1933), in this manner.

---

e.g. Example: The *BMI* and *National Collegiate Athletic Association* cases (*supra*, §208) cast doubt upon the breadth of the *Socony-Vacuum Oil* test quoted above (*supra*, §211). The restraints in *BMI* and *NCAA* were both formed for the purpose and with the effect of raising or stabilizing prices. Yet the Supreme Court applied the rule of reason analysis to both cases, striking down the *NCAA* arrangement while leaving the *BMI* system intact. In **United States v. Brown University,** *supra*, §209, the court of appeals reversed a lower court's application of a "quick look" rule of reason test to an agreement among colleges to make uniform determinations as to the amount of financial aid and scholarships to be available to particular students (a per se restraint). Citing the public interest in the furtherance of higher education and several "procompetitive" justifications for the practice offered by the defendants, the court held that the case required *full rule of reason* scrutiny.

EXAM TIP	gilbert

Note that if the facts of a case or exam question trigger this exception, it doesn't mean that the defendant has beat the antitrust rap. It merely means that, rather than finding a per se violation, the court will instead **analyze the facts under the rule of reason**, and, depending on the results of that analysis, the agreement may be allowed or struck down.

4. Exception for Regulated Industries [§214]

Businesses that have government-regulated prices (*e.g.*, railroads, shipping, etc.) may be allowed to fix prices or rates without violating the antitrust laws—if the appropriate governmental agency (the Interstate Commerce Commission, etc.) has determined that the rates set are in the "public interest." (*See infra*, §§536-537.)

5. Evidence of Unlawful Purpose or Anticompetitive Effect Sufficient [§215]

As a general rule, a violation "can be established by proof of *either an unlawful purpose or an anticompetitive effect*." [**United States v. United States Gypsum Co.,** *supra*, §85] Thus, if the purpose of an agreement is unlawful (*i.e.*, to restrain competition by affecting price), it is not necessary to establish market power to set or influence prices. [*See* **United States v. Socony-Vacuum Oil Co.,** *supra*]

6. What Constitutes "Price Fixing" [§216]

As noted above, the courts in each case must determine whether the particular conduct involved actually constitutes "price fixing." For the most part, an *expansive* interpretation of "price fixing" has been followed.

a. Minimum prices [§217]

Clearly, any agreement among competitors fixing *minimum* prices constitutes illegal price fixing. [**Goldfarb v. Virginia State Bar**, 421 U.S. 773 (1975)—minimum fee schedule adopted by bar association violates section 1; *see* discussion *infra*, §588]

b. Maximum prices [§218]

An agreement among competitors fixing *maximum* resale prices for a commodity is *just as illegal* as an agreement fixing minimum prices. Even though the competitors are free to sell at less than the maximum, the presence of the maximum price tends to stabilize prices and distort resource allocation. [**Arizona v. Maricopa County Medical Society**, 457 U.S. 332 (1982)—agreement between doctors and insurers fixing maximum prices for the doctors' services held per se illegal]

c. Negotiable "list prices" [§219]

Similarly, an agreement among auto dealers to use common "list prices" has been proscribed, even though the list price was merely the starting point for customer bargaining. [**Plymouth Dealers Association v. United States**, 279 F.2d 128 (9th Cir. 1960)]

d. Production limits [§220]

An agreement between competitors on *how much they will sell or produce* is likewise an illegal price fixing scheme, even though no specific fixed price is agreed upon. [**National Collegiate Athletic Association v. Board of Regents**, *supra*, §213; **Hartford-Empire Co. v. United States**, 323 U.S. 386 (1945)]

e. Purchase price limits [§221]

An agreement *among buyers* on the *price* they will *offer* is illegal per se as a price fixing scheme [**Mandeville Island Farms, Inc. v. American Crystal Sugar Co.**, *supra*, §69], as is an agreement among buyers to *limit purchases* (so as to depress the market price) [**National Macaroni Manufacturers v. FTC**, 345 F.2d 421 (7th Cir. 1975)].

f. Elimination of competitive bidding [§222]

Although an agreement (including an agreed-upon ethical canon) does not expressly fix prices or even a specific method of calculating fees, it will nevertheless constitute price fixing and a *per se violation* of the Sherman Act if it *prohibits competitive bidding*. [**National Society of Professional Engineers v. United States**, *supra*, §203]

g. Elimination of short-term credit [§223]

Concluding that credit terms are an "inseparable part of the price" of a product, the Supreme Court held that an agreement among beer distributors to eliminate free short-term credit on sales to retailers was "tantamount to an agreement to eliminate discounts, and thus falls squarely within the traditional per se rule against price fixing." [**Catalano, Inc. v. Target Sales, Inc.,** 446 U.S. 643 (1980)]

SUMMARY OF ACTIONS THAT CONSTITUTE HORIZONTAL PRICE FIXING — **gilbert**

THE FOLLOWING HAVE BEEN HELD TO CONSTITUTE HORIZONTAL PRICE FIXING:

☑ Fixing *minimum* prices;

☑ Fixing *maximum* prices;

☑ *Negotiable list prices;*

☑ *Production limits;*

☑ *Purchase price limits;*

☑ *Eliminating competitive bidding;* and

☑ *Eliminating short-term credit.*

---

7. **Importance of Initial Characterization [§224]**

Because of the strict rules governing price fixing, antitrust defendants frequently try to characterize their agreement as something other than a *"naked* agreement to fix prices" so that they can avoid the per se rule.

C. Division of Markets

1. **Per Se Violation [§225]**

Any agreement (explicit or tacit) among businesses performing similar services or dealing in similar products whereby the available market is divided up and each is given a share is *illegal per se.* [**Addyston Pipe & Steel Co. v. United States,** 175 U.S. 211 (1899); **United States v. Topco Associates, Inc.,** *supra,* §205; **Palmer v. BRG of Georgia,** *supra,* §207]

   a. **Rationale**

   An agreement among competitors to divide the market for a particular product gives each an effective monopoly in his share of the market. Even though other competitive products may be available, each firm has the power to fix prices, etc., as to *a particular product.* [**Timken Roller Bearing Co. v. United States,** 341 U.S. 593 (1951)]

2. **No Justification Permitted [§226]**

As in the case of price fixing, *no* justifications or defenses are recognized. [**United States v. Topco Associates, Inc.,** *supra*—immaterial that purpose of the territorial market division was to enable small grocers to compete with supermarket chains]

a. **But note**

Topco has been criticized because the Court failed to balance the loss of *intrabrand* competition (among the member stores who sold Topco brand products) against the gains of increased *interbrand* competition (because smaller stores selling Topco brand products could better compete against larger grocery store chains). Others have argued *Topco* should have been analyzed under the rule of reason because it was in reality a joint venture with integrative efficiencies. (*See infra*, §§240, 287.)

b. **"Free rider" arguments [§227]**

Circuit courts have periodically suggested that horizontal market divisions may be justified by the need to prevent "free riding" among distributors (*i.e.*, the practice of dealers who do not spend their own money on promotions but exploit the market created by those dealers who did, by underselling the dealers who financed the promotions). The "free riders" thus take advantage of product advertising and service provided by other nearby distributors. [*See* **General Leaseways v. National Truck Leasing**, 744 F.2d 588 (7th Cir. 1984)] In the face of Supreme Court precedent, however, these courts have generally refrained from establishing a legal justification for horizontal market divisions.

3. **Direct or Indirect Divisions [§228]**

The rule applies to both *direct and indirect* agreements among competitors to divide the market.

> **Example:** An example of indirect divisions appeared in **United States v. Sealy, Inc.**, 388 U.S. 350 (1967). There, Sealy mattresses were sold only through franchised dealers. However, the franchises owned and controlled the franchisor, and so they *controlled the franchisor's marketing operations* and were able to divide up the national market for Sealy mattresses as they saw fit. The Supreme Court held that this arrangement was illegal.

4. **Type of Market Divisions [§229]**

Agreements to divide markets are illegal if they divide *territories, customers*, and/or *products*.

a. **But note**

"Areas of primary responsibility" have been permitted. [*See, e.g.,* **Snap-On Tools Corp.**, FTC Docket No. 7116, 3 CCH Trade Reg. Rep. 15,546]

D. Group Boycotts and Concerted Refusals to Deal

1. **In General [§230]**

An *individual* is free to choose those with whom she wishes to deal, except when such a refusal amounts to monopolization or an attempt to monopolize. (*See supra*, §§143, 192—Sherman Act section 2 liability.) However, when a *group of competitors* (two or more) agrees not to deal with a person or firm outside the group, deal only on certain terms, or coerce suppliers or customers not to deal with the boycotted competitor, there is a combination in restraint of trade violating section 1. [**Klors Inc. v. Broadway-Hale Stores**, *supra*, §195]

2. Per Se vs. Rule of Reason [§231]

A great deal of confusion surrounds the proper treatment of group boycotts under section 1. The Supreme Court has issued a number of conflicting pronouncements on this subject.

a. Per se rule [§232]

A number of early cases seemed to establish the rule that horizontal group boycotts were illegal per se. [*See, e.g.*, **United States v. General Motors Corp.**, 384 U.S. 127 (1966); **Klors Inc. v. Broadway-Hale Stores**, *supra*] The Supreme Court's most recent pronouncement on the subject reaffirms the per se rule. In **FTC v. Superior Court Trial Lawyers Association**, *supra*, §212, the Court invalidated a horizontal agreement by attorneys not to work for wages they considered too low, without any demonstration that the attorneys had market power.

(1) Note

Courts may hesitate to find a "boycott" precisely because it is illegal per se. For example, the BankAmericard corporation had a bylaw prohibiting member banks from joining any other national bank credit card system. The trial court held the bylaw a per se violation of section 1, but the court of appeals reversed, because the bank credit card industry was relatively new and important, and because it was reluctant to find a per se violation on the record presented to it for summary judgment. [**Worthen Bank v. National BankAmericard, Inc.**, 485 F.2d 119 (8th Cir. 1973), *cert. denied*, 415 U.S. 918 (1974)]

(2) And note

It is not a per se illegal boycott for a single buyer to purchase from one supplier instead of the preferred supplier's competitor. [**NYNEX Corp. v. Discon, Inc.**, 525 U.S. 128 (1998)]

b. Rule of reason [§233]

Even some early cases rejected the application of the per se rule to group boycotts. [*See* **Apex Hosiery Co. v. Leader**, 310 U.S. 469 (1940)] In **Northwest Wholesale Stationers v. Pacific Stationery & Printing**, 472 U.S. 284 (1985), the Court refused to apply the per se rule to a boycott of a competitor by a wholesale purchasing cooperative. *Rationale:* Unless the plaintiff could show the probability of an anticompetitive effect, the challenged practice could not be classified as per se illegal. In that case, there could be no anticompetitive effect unless the cooperative had market power.

(1) Comment

Some courts suggest that the per se rule against group boycotts applies when "(1) the boycotting firm has cut off access to a supply, facility, or market necessary for the boycotted firm . . . to compete; (2) the boycotting firm possesses a 'dominant' position in the market (where 'dominant' is an undefined term, but plainly chosen to stand for something different from antitrust's term of art 'monopoly'); and (3) the boycott . . . cannot be justified by plausible arguments that it was designed to enhance overall efficiency." [**Toys "R" Us, Inc. v. FTC**, 221 F.3d 928 (7th Cir. 2000)] This seems inconsistent with the purpose of the per se rule, which is to relieve courts of the burden of determining whether the defendants have market power and whether their agreement has demonstrable anticompetitive effects. Ultimately, it is sometimes difficult to predict whether courts will apply per se or rule of reason analysis to a group boycott.

c. Quick look analysis [§234]

One case applied a "quick look" rule of reason analysis to an agreement by dentists to refuse to submit X-rays to dental insurers reviewing their bills. While the Court did not apply the per se rule, it did condemn the dentists' agreement because it lacked any procompetitive justification. [**FTC v. Indiana Federation of Dentists**, *supra*, §209]

3. Self-Regulation by Industries [§235]

Wherever industry-wide self-regulation operates as a boycott or unreasonable restraint, it is unlawful.

 Example: The activities of a trade association of clothing and garment manufacturers in boycotting retailers who sell cloth or garments involving piracy of design or style were held contrary to the policy of the Sherman Act. [**Fashion Originators' Guild v. FTC**, 312 U.S. 457 (1941)—review of FTC order] The trade association was attempting to exercise "law enforcement" powers against retailers who sold pirated designs. However, such designs were not protected by copyright laws and what the association was doing, in reality, was eliminating competition. The Court deemed it immaterial that the copying might be tortious under state law. Regardless of their purpose, competitors cannot by group boycott inflict their wishes on others.

Example: Similarly, the American Medical Association "rules of ethics" against salaried practice and prepaid medical care was held to violate section 1. [**United States v. American Medical Association**, 130 F.2d 233 (D.C. Cir.), *aff'd*, 317 U.S. 519 (1942)] *Rationale:* The AMA is not a "law enforcement agency" and cannot "destroy competing professional or business groups" in the name of self-discipline and control.

Example: Allegations of a conspiracy between domestic insurers, domestic and foreign reinsurers, insurance brokers, and insurance associations to restrict liability coverage available to commercial firms in the United States by threats of boycotts in the North American market were held sufficient to sustain the complaint against defendants' motion to dismiss. [**Hartford Fire Insurance Co. v. California**, *supra*, §81]

4. Heavily Regulated Industries [§236]

Where the government extensively regulates an industry, courts are more likely to uphold rules imposed by industry groups or trade associations.

Example: The Court refused to invalidate on antitrust grounds the New York Stock Exchange rules limiting membership on the Exchange. The Court concluded that the per se rule did not apply to heavily regulated industries such as stock exchanges. [**Silver v. New York Stock Exchange**, 373 U.S. 341 (1963)]

Example: The suspension of a player by the National Basketball Association for violating an anti-gambling rule was *upheld* as "reasonable" disciplinary action to protect organized sports. [**Molinas v. National Basketball Association**, 190 F. Supp. 241 (S.D.N.Y. 1961)]

5. Political Boycotts [§237]

Boycotts motivated by political rather than commercial purposes are generally beyond the reach of the Sherman Act. [**National Organization for Women v. Scheidler**, 968 F.2d 612 (7th Cir. 1992); **Missouri v. National Organization for Women**, 620 F.2d 1301 (8th Cir. 1980)] Political boycotts may also be protected speech under the *Noerr* doctrine. (*See infra*, §582.)

E. Joint Ventures by Competitors

1. Definition [§238]

A joint venture is an undertaking by two or more business entities for some limited purpose—something short of a complete merger or combination—*e.g.*, joint sales agency or joint research.

2. Unlawful Purpose—Illegal Per Se [§239]

If the *purpose* of the combination is *illegal per se*, the joint venture is likewise illegal per se.

Example: Two daily newspapers in a city formed a jointly managed subsidiary that ran all departments of their businesses except news and editorials. The subsidiary also *set advertising and subscription rates* for both papers. Because price fixing is illegal per se, so was the joint venture. [**Citizen Publishing Co. v. United States**, 394 U.S. 131 (1969)]

3. Rule of Reason Applied [§240]

However, if the purpose and effect of the combination produces plausible integrative efficiencies, the joint undertaking is judged by the section 1 "rule of reason," as well as by the criteria under section 7 of the Clayton Act (*see infra*, §§320 *et seq.*). [*See* **United States v. Penn-Olin Chemical**, 378 U.S. 158 (1964)]

EXAM TIP | **gilbert**

Note that in real life most joint ventures are *evaluated under the rule of reason*. And, because analysis under the rule of reason would require more discussion than a per se violation, the same will most likely be true on an exam question as well.

---

a. Test [§241]

Under the rule of reason, the question is whether the restraint on competition created by the combination is really necessary to achieve the lawful purpose, or whether there are other means to achieve the purpose which are less restrictive of competition. This requires the court in each case to *balance the anticompetitive effects* of the combination *against any legitimate interest* to be served thereby. (For a more detailed description of the test, *see supra*, §§202-204.)

b. Applications

(1) Joint research projects [§242]

Joint research facilities and activities are generally analyzed under the rule of reason, because, even though they pose a risk of anticompetitive behavior, they also promise the possibility of integrative efficiency and added innovation. [**SCM Corp. v. Xerox Corp.**, 645 F.2d 1195 (2d Cir. 1981); *and see infra*, §247]

---

e.g. **Example—new product:** A joint research and development venture between two competitors in the defense industry resulted in the production of a new airplane that neither venturer could have produced alone. The joint venture survived scrutiny under the rule of reason. [**Northrop Corp. v. McDonnell Douglas Corp.**, 705 F.2d 1030 (9th Cir. 1983)]

---

(2) *Morgan* case [§243]

Major investment banking firms were charged with a section 2 conspiracy to monopolize and a section 1 conspiracy to restrain trade. The firms formed syndicates to underwrite corporate securities offerings, and the syndicates included resale price maintenance agreements and provisions for stabilizing the prices of the securities during the period of the offering. The court held the restraints *reasonable*, emphasizing their *limited duration* and the *necessity* of pooling the capital of several firms to undertake the risk of large underwritings. [**United States v. Morgan**, 118 F. Supp. 621 (S.D.N.Y. 1953)]

(3) Distinguish—*Associated Press* case [§244]

The Court *invalidated* a "veto clause" in the membership provisions of a cooperative news service organized by 1,200 newspaper members. While membership in the Associated Press ("AP") was ostensibly open to all newspapers, this provision in the bylaws allowed any member to block the membership of a competing newspaper. The Court found that the exclusionary clause was a substantial barrier to the entry of new firms into the newspaper business, and rejected the argument that owners of property are free to choose their associates. [**United States v. Associated Press,** 326 U.S. 1 (1945)]

(a) Comment

The membership clause had a clearly anticompetitive thrust and was not intended to protect the newspapers' investment in the AP. A concurring opinion suggested that the AP might be able to "freeze" its membership without violating section 1 (although there might be a section 2 violation if the combination was a monopoly).

(4) *Paramount Pictures* case [§245]

The Court also *condemned* the joint ownership of movie theaters by production companies, because each producer gave the other a preference in the exhibition of movies. [**United States v. Paramount Pictures,** 334 U.S. 131 (1948)]

c. Industry structure important [§246]

Joint activities may have different effects, depending on the structure of a particular market and its general performance. Thus, for example, joint activities by large firms in an oligopolistic market might be viewed as an unreasonable restraint of trade because they aggregate significant market power and raise barriers to entry. A different conclusion might be reached if the industry were more competitive generally and the joint venturers comprised only a small share of the overall market. [*But see* **In re General Motors Corp.,** 103 F.T.C. 374 (1984)—FTC opted not to initiate formal proceedings to block proposed joint venture between GM and Toyota because the parties agreed to order limiting scope and duration of the venture and prohibiting exchange of nonpublic information]

d. National Cooperative Research Act [§247]

In 1984, Congress enacted the National Cooperative Research Act ("NCRA") to provide some protection to research and development joint ventures. Qualifying joint ventures are subject only to rule of reason scrutiny, are liable only for single (not treble) damages, and benefit from a "safe harbor" for ventures below a 20% market share. In 1993, Congress extended the NCRA to protect joint *production* ventures as well, rechristening it the National Cooperative Research and Production Act ("NCRPA"). [15 U.S.C. §4301]

F. Disseminating Information Among Competitors

1. In General [§248]

The legality of competitors exchanging information on prices, costs, production inventories, etc.—generally through a trade association—has been the subject of much litigation under Sherman Act section 1. Because data dissemination takes place through trade associations, "agreement" is generally clear. The central question is whether the exchange constitutes an unreasonable restraint of trade. When analyzing the exchange of information, it is important to be sensitive to whether the exchange helps *perfect the market* or *creates efficiencies*, or whether it *facilitates cartelization* and *lessens competition*.

2. Exchange of Information on Prices [§249]

The exchange of price information is *very suspect* and likely to be held a violation of section 1. Factors that especially indicate unlawful activity are: (i) exchange of information about *current or future prices* (as opposed to past prices); (ii) *identification of parties*, as well as price, in sales transactions; and (iii) a *highly concentrated or oligopolistic market* structure with relatively few sellers. The following cases are illustrative:

Example: In **American Column & Lumber Co.,** the Court held unlawful an "open competition plan" of 365 hardwood manufacturers (who controlled one-third of the market), under which members reported the details of individual sales (including identity of the buyer) and of production, inventories, and current price lists—all of which were regularly disseminated. Monthly meetings were held at which estimated future production and price trends were discussed. At these meetings an expert frequently analyzed the data and warned against "overproduction." After the plan was instituted, prices increased substantially. [**American Column & Lumber Co. v. United States**, 257 U.S. 377 (1921)]

Compare: The Court upheld as *reasonable* (and therefore lawful) the activities of a trade association engaged in cooperative advertising and standardization of products. The association disseminated information on average costs, freight rates, and the terms of past transactions *without identifying individual sellers or buyers*. Meetings were held but future prices were never discussed. [**Maple Flooring Manufacturers Association v. United States**, 268 U.S. 563 (1925)]

a. Analysis

The type of information circulated in *American Column* and *Maple Flooring* was important. Much of the information exchanged in the *American Column* case could only have had an anticompetitive purpose, while the activities of the *Maple Flooring* trade association were evidently supervised by an astute antitrust lawyer. However, the information on average cost and freight rate in *Maple Flooring* arguably was aimed at fixing a uniform marked-up price (as the government unsuccessfully asserted).

e.g. **Example:** In **United States v. Container Corp.**, *supra*, §85, paper box manufacturers who controlled 90% of the market voluntarily exchanged information on the most recent price charged or quoted to a particular (identified) customer. This exchange had the effect of *stabilizing prices*, because competitors normally would quote that customer the same price or one slightly lower. Though stopping short of finding this a per se violation, the Court held that the agreement violated section 1 because "the inferences are irresistible" that the exchange of information had an anticompetitive effect—price being "too critical, too sensitive a control. . . ." The Court viewed the oligopolistic market structure as an important factor.

b. Comment

In view of the sensitivity of this area, many antitrust lawyers advise their business clients not to exchange or explain price information with competitors.

EXAM TIP	gilbert

Note that when competitors exchange *future price information* on an exam, it should be a red flag that section 1 has been violated. However, if the competitors are exchanging information regarding *past transactions or shipping costs*, the activity may well be lawful.

3. Exchange of Information Other than Price [§250]

Where information *other than* price is exchanged by competitors, the courts may be more lenient. Such practices are usually held to violate section 1 only where aimed at *lessening competition*, policing a cartel, or *facilitating interdependent pricing*.

e.g. **Example:** In **Cement Manufacturers Protective Association v. United States**, 268 U.S. 588 (1925), the Court *upheld* a trade association's dissemination of information concerning contractors who abused the free delivery options traditionally given by cement manufacturers to contractors bidding on construction contracts. The Court noted that such information was not designed to lessen competition but to prevent fraud upon members (*i.e.*, by protecting members from delivering more cement than needed on a specific job, and thus receiving a lower price).

a. But note

Where the exchange of information *is aimed at suppressing competition*, the result will be contra. Thus, in **Eastern States Retail Lumber Dealers Association v. United States**, 234 U.S. 600 (1914), the Court held unlawful the circulation by an association of retail lumber dealers of the names of wholesalers who also sold directly to consumers. The court reasoned that a conspiracy not to deal with such wholesalers could be *inferred* from the exchange.

G. What Constitutes an "Agreement," "Combination," or "Conspiracy" Among Competitors

1. In General [§251]

The above practices—price fixing, market division, and group boycotts, etc.—are examples of "contracts, combinations . . . or conspiracies" (*i.e.*, agreements among competitors that violate Sherman Act section 1). The concept of "agreement" is critical in section 1 cases. Sometimes a conspiracy or agreement can be proved by direct evidence. Direct evidence includes copies of the actual written contracts at issue, videotapes and audiotapes of the conspirators agreeing, or testimony of witnesses who observed the agreements being entered into. Often, however, the evidence is only circumstantial and must be inferred. It is important, therefore, to clarify what is meant by "agreement." This is especially true in cases of price leadership or "conscious parallelism" in price (*see* below) or other terms of sale by firms in an oligopolistic market structure. (*See* the discussion of oligopoly, *infra*, §§616, 638-641.)

a. Conscious parallelism defined [§252]

Conscious parallelism is the process "not in itself unlawful, by which firms in a concentrated market might in effect share monopoly power, setting their prices at a profit-maximizing, supracompetitive level by recognizing their shared economic interests." [**Brooke Group Ltd. v. Brown & Williamson Tobacco Corp.**, 509 U.S. 209 (1993)] Conscious parallelism, accompanied by "plus factors" (*see infra*, §256), may provide a way to show an agreement through circumstantial evidence.

2. Interdependent Conscious Parallelism Among Competitors [§253]

The leading case on conscious parallelism is **Interstate Circuit, Inc. v. United States**, 306 U.S. 208 (1939). There, a large theater chain simultaneously announced to a group of film distributors that it would not deal with any distributor unless the distributor agreed not to distribute prime films to "second-run" theaters competing with the exhibitor, except on specified conditions. Each distributor, knowing that a similar proposition had been made to his competitors, accepted the exhibitor's terms. The Supreme Court affirmed a trial court finding that there was an *unlawful agreement among the distributors*.

a. Circumstantial evidence of agreement [§254]

A major issue in *Interstate Circuit* concerned the type of evidence sufficient to support an inference of "agreement" or "conspiracy"—*i.e.*, a "meeting of the minds." In inferring agreement, the Court stressed the *knowledge* of the distributors and the *motive* for concerted action (namely, that each defendant would benefit by the action only if all the other defendants participated), the *substantial unanimity* of the distributors in reaching virtually identical and complex arrangements with the exhibitor, and the failure of the distributors to testify concerning the presence or absence of any agreement. The Court held that: "It was enough that, *knowing that concerted action was contemplated and invited* (by the exhibitor), *the distributors gave their adherence* to the scheme and *participated in it.*" Thus, consciously parallel action that is *interdependent* may provide the basis for inferring agreement.

(1) Note

The parallel actions in *Interstate Circuit* were truly *interdependent* because the benefits of the action accrued only if *all* the defendants participated. That is, there was no explanation for a firm taking such actions independently.

b. Mere conscious parallelism not sufficient [§255]

The Supreme Court in a subsequent case held: "The crucial question is whether respondents' conduct . . . stemmed from independent decision *or from an agreement, tacit or express.* To be sure, business behavior is admissible circumstantial evidence from which the fact finder may infer agreement. But *this Court has never held that proof of parallel business behavior conclusively establishes agreement* or, phrased differently, that such behavior itself constitutes a Sherman Act offense." [**Theatre Enterprises v. Paramount Film Distributor Corp.**, 346 U.S. 537 (1954)]

(1) Note

The *Theatre Enterprises* case (*supra*) involved a situation in which the behavior of each defendant could be explained on the basis of *independent business judgment—i.e.*, each decision was *not* interdependent on the same decision's being made by all competitors, as in *Interstate Circuit*.

c. Plus factors [§256]

In addition to conscious parallelism, an antitrust plaintiff attempting to prove an agreement must also establish the presence of "plus factors." The "plus factors" provide the basis for inferring that the parallel business conduct was the result of an *agreement*. Common plus factors include communication among the defendants, an economic motive for concerted action, defendants' acting in contravention of their individual economic interest, simultaneous action, and radical departure from previous business practices.

EXAM TIP   **gilbert**

When analyzing an exam question on horizontal restraints, remember that your starting point should be to determine *whether there was an agreement*. Resist the temptation to jump into a discussion of conscious parallelism until you check whether there is *direct evidence* of an agreement (e.g., a written contract or some other direct way to prove agreement). If so, you can state that there is an agreement and move on to the issue of whether it unreasonably restrains trade. But in the more likely event that there is no direct evidence, then you should state that fact and next consider whether there is *circumstantial evidence* from which the court can infer an agreement—i.e., conscious parallelism and the plus factors.

d. Conscious parallelism under the FTC Act [§257]

And even though certain parallel business behavior is not illegal under the Sherman Act, it may still constitute an *"unfair method of competition"* under section 5 of the Federal Trade Commission Act (*infra*, §§451 *et seq.*). Section 5 does *not* require any "contract, combination . . . or conspiracy."

> **Example:** The FTC has declared illegal the use of a *basing point price system* adopted by certain cement manufacturers. Under a basing point system, sellers will only quote a *delivered* price (*i.e.*, one including freight); and prices can be kept uniform by establishing one or more basing points (usually centers where a large number of sellers or a dominant firm are located). The price to any buyer includes freight from the nearest base point, regardless of where the goods are actually shipped from, and whether or not the buyer is located at the base point. Thus, a buyer located close to the seller is charged for "phantom" freight. The Supreme Court affirmed the FTC ruling, holding that the basing point system was conducive to price parallelism because a buyer is generally quoted about the same price from all sellers wherever located—*i.e.*, the mill net currently charged at the nearest base point plus the freight from that point. [**FTC v. Cement Institute**, 333 U.S. 683 (1948)]

e. Economic rationality of the conspiracy theory [§258]

Proving conspiracies with indirect or circumstantial evidence was probably made more difficult by the Supreme Court's decision in **Matsushita Electric Industrial Co. v. Zenith Radio Corp.**, *supra*, §174. The Court held that, for conspiracy charges to survive motions for summary judgment, alleged conspiracies must make economic sense and evidence must establish that defendants were not acting independently. [*See also* **E. I. duPont de Nemours & Co. v. FTC**, 729 F.2d 128 (2d Cir. 1984)—even under section 5 of the FTC Act, the FTC must establish anticompetitive intent or purpose and lack of competitive justification for offending conduct]

3. Expanding Concept of "Combination" [§259]

In addition to "contracts" and "conspiracies," *combinations* in restraint of trade violate section 1 of the Sherman Act. For many years it was assumed that "combinations" added nothing to the scope of section 1, but some cases imply an independent meaning for the term. For example, the Supreme Court has suggested that *acquiescence* by a group of retailers to minimum resale prices, where such acquiescence was secured by the manufacturer's threats of termination, constituted a "combination" in violation of section 1. [**United States v. Parke, Davis & Co.**, 362 U.S. 29 (1960); *and see* **Albrecht v. The Herald Co.**, 390 U.S. 145 (1968)]

4. Intra-Corporate Conspiracy [§260]

Generally speaking, the conspiracies condemned by the antitrust laws are conspiracies between or among separate economic entities. Thus, a corporation cannot conspire with itself or with its employees, nor can employees of a corporation "conspire with each other" without the presence of independent parties. [**Copperweld Corp. v. Independence Tube Corp.**, 467 U.S. 752 (1984)]

a. But note
Anticompetitive activities within an entity (or by a single individual), though they fall short of a conspiracy, may still be an illegal "attempt to monopolize" under section 2 (*supra*, §§192-196).

5. Inter-Corporate Conspiracies [§261]
A conspiracy *cannot* exist between a corporation and its *wholly owned* subsidiary under section 1 of the Sherman Act. A parent and its wholly owned subsidiary have a complete unity of interest, and so there is no justification for section 1 scrutiny. [**Copperweld Corp. v. Independence Tube Corp.**, *supra*]

a. Partially-owned subsidiary [§262]
Outstanding post-*Copperweld* issues include whether a corporation can conspire with its partially-owned subsidiary [**Computer Identics Corp. v. Southern Pacific Co.**, 756 F.2d 200 (1st Cir. 1985)] and whether sister corporations— corporations that are owned by the same parent—can conspire in violation of antitrust laws [**Advanced Health-Care Services v. Radford Community Hospital**, 910 F.2d 139 (4th Cir. 1990)—two subsidiaries wholly owned by the same parent cannot conspire].

b. Effect of interlocking directorates (Clayton Act section 8) [§263]
The mere fact that the same persons sit on the boards of several competing corporations may not be enough in itself to establish a "conspiracy" under section 1, but it may violate *section 8 of the Clayton Act* [15 U.S.C. §19].

(1) Terms of section 8 [§264]
Section 8 of the Clayton Act provides that no person shall at the same time be a director in two or more corporations "engaged in whole or part in commerce" if such corporations are "by virtue of their business and location of operation, *competitors*, so that the elimination of competition by agreement between them would constitute a violation of any of the provisions of any of the antitrust laws." Section 8 applies only to interlocks in which each of the corporations has *capital aggregating more than $10 million*, which figure is adjusted annually by "an amount equal to the percentage increase (or decrease) in the gross national product."

(2) Purpose [§265]
Section 8 is directed toward an *obvious competitive danger:* If competitors are controlled by the same individuals, rules against "agreements" by competitors to fix prices, divide markets, or boycott would be useless because behavior could be coordinated without agreement or true conspiracy.

(3) Enforcement [§266]

Nevertheless, the enforcement of section 8 has generally been lax or was abandoned when one of the directorships was resigned. Many interlocking directorates have simply gone unchallenged.

(a) Note

The FTC has generally challenged only directors serving two companies that are substantial and *direct* competitors. Furthermore, when particular directors have been challenged, they have generally been allowed simply to resign one of the directorates (though resignation does not render a case moot once begun [*see* **United States v. W. T. Grant,** 345 U.S. 629 (1953)]).

(b) Bank exemption

Section 8 contains an exemption for banks, which the Supreme Court has interpreted to apply to an interlock between any two firms as long as *either* of the two is a bank (*e.g.,* a bank and an insurance company). [**Bankamerica Corp. v. United States,** 462 U.S. 122 (1983)]

Chapter Five:
Vertical Restraints

CONTENTS

Chapter Approach

In contrast to horizontal restraints, which are combinations or agreements between competitors, vertical restraints involve firms at different levels of the production/distribution chain, such as an agreement between a manufacturer and its distributors. Sections 1 and 2 of the Sherman Act and section 3 of the Clayton Act all apply to various vertical restraints, depending upon circumstances.

When presented with a fact situation showing vertical restraints, keep in mind that some vertical restraints are illegal per se, while others are evaluated under the rule of reason:

1. *Agreements and restraints designed to set minimum resale prices* are generally *illegal per se*, but there are a few exceptions, such as consignment arrangements.

2. *Most other vertical restraints* are judged under the *rule of reason*. These restraints include exclusive distributorship arrangements, customer and territorial restrictions, tying arrangements, and exclusive dealing agreements. Of those, only tie-ins may be illegal per se, and then only in circumstances in which the offending company has sufficient market power.

A. Introduction

1. Definition of "Vertical" Restraints [§267]

There are frequently various stages in the production of a particular item. For example, before a refrigerator is sold to a consumer, several steps must occur: coke and iron ore must be mined and refined into steel ingots; the ingots must be processed into useable sheets of steel; the steel, together with other materials, must be made into a refrigerator; the refrigerator must then be distributed through wholesalers and jobbers until it reaches the retailer; and the retailer must then sell the product to the consumer. This process involves *various levels of production and distribution*, and the relationships between the various levels can be described as *"vertical"* dealings. (*Compare:* Relationships between firms at the same level—*i.e.*, between competitors—are described as *"horizontal"*; *see* chapter IV.)

EXAM TIP   **gilbert**

To determine what relationship exists between the parties in the exam question, look at the levels involved. If the parties are competitors, or firms at the *same level*, it is a *horizontal* restraint. If the facts discuss *multiple levels in the production or distribution chain*, it is a *vertical* restraint.

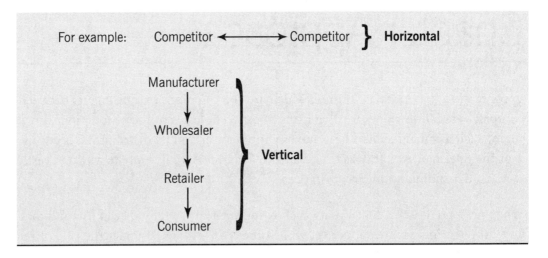

2. Relevant Statutory Provisions [§268]

Contractual and other vertical relationships between different firms may be a restraint of trade in violation of *section 1 of the Sherman Act* and *section 3 of the Clayton Act*, and, if employed in monopolization, can violate *section 2 of the Sherman Act*.

3. Rule of Reason or Per Se Analysis? [§269]

Certain vertical restraints are per se illegal while others are afforded closer, rule of reason scrutiny. The general policy reasons for assigning a restraint to rule of reason or per se analysis are discussed *supra*, §§202 *et seq.*

MODES OF ANALYSIS FOR VERTICAL RESTRAINTS	**gilbert**
PER SE	• Minimum price fixing • Tying arrangements (nominally)
RULE OF REASON	• Maximum price fixing • Nonprice restraints • Exclusive dealing arrangements

B. Resale Price Maintenance by Sellers

1. Minimum Resale Price Maintenance ("RPM") [§270]

It is a *per se violation* of section 1 for a seller (*e.g.*, a manufacturer) contractually to set the minimum price at which the buyer (*e.g.*, a retailer) can resell the product. [**Monsanto Co. v. Spray-Rite Service Corp.**, 465 U.S. 752 (1984)]

a. Economic analysis—maintenance of minimum prices [§271]

A manufacturer normally has no interest in protecting high profits for the retailer by fixing a minimum price for the product, since normally the manufacturer stands to benefit by price competition in the product at the retail level: If retailers compete among themselves, driving down the price and the retailers' profit margins, total sales of the manufacturer's product will increase and so will profits. However, under some circumstances, a manufacturer will be interested in protecting a retailer's profits:

(1) Retailer recommendations

When the retailers also carry competitive products, and customers may tend to rely on a retailer's recommendations, the manufacturer may want to assure profits to the dealer as an incentive for dealer recommendation of the product. Also, the manufacturer may wish to have the retailers provide advertising or a substantial amount of service and advice, and without retail price maintenance, it is arguable that consumers are apt to take the advice from a dealer (take a "free ride") but buy at a lower price at a discount house that did not advertise or where service and advice is not supplied— again reducing the dealer's incentive to "push" the product.

(2) Anticompetitive risk

Resale price maintenance may have been instigated at the request of retailers to help establish or police a cartel whose interest is in selling a product at higher than competitive prices.

2. Maximum RPM [§272]

Although agreements to set a maximum resale price used to be per se illegal [*see* **Albrecht v. Herald Co.,** 390 U.S. 145 (1968)], such agreements are now evaluated under the *rule of reason* [**State Oil Co. v. Khan,** 522 U.S. 3 (1997)]. The Court subjected maximum price setting to the rule of reason because it believed that manufacturers would not set a price that was "too low" and that courts could distinguish maximum price setting from minimum price setting. [**State Oil Co. v. Khan,** *supra*]

a. Standing rules

Even before the Supreme Court removed maximum vertical price fixing from the per se category, the Court announced standing rules that made it difficult for competitors to bring suit. For example, where a retailer challenged a scheme among its competitors to set maximum prices, the Court concluded that the retailer lacked standing to bring the action. [**Atlantic Richfield Co. v. USA Petroleum Co.,** *supra,* §110] *Rationale:* The effect of the price setting scheme was that the plaintiff's competitors lowered their prices. Unless the price charged was predatory (*see supra,* §174), the competitor's "injury" from being unable to raise prices does not reflect anticompetitive harm.

b. Economic analysis—maintenance of maximum prices [§273]

The manufacturer has a clear interest in setting a maximum resale price, because if the retailer has market power and will charge a higher price and sell less than would be sold under conditions of perfect competition, this in turn reduces the sales and profits of the manufacturer.

(1) Manufacturer's options

The manufacturer can either attempt to break the retailer's market position (*e.g.*, by entering retailing himself), or use whatever bargaining power he has to force the retailer not to sell above a set maximum price.

(2) Anticompetitive effect

Although setting a maximum resale price—to the extent that it limits a retailer's market power—can be desirable, there are anticompetitive dangers. The so-called maximum price may be tacitly treated by the manufacturer and retailers as an agreed minimum. Also, a maximum price has the effect of distorting resource allocation and reducing the likelihood of new entry into the market.

3. Exceptions to Per Se Rule Against Minimum Resale Price Maintenance

a. Consignment arrangements [§274]

A consignment arrangement exists when the owner of a product entrusts someone else ("the consignee") to sell her goods for her, but the consignee never takes ownership of the product and can return the product to its owner. Valid consignment plans that are not disguised price maintenance schemes are permitted. However, sham arrangements will be invalidated.

Example: In **United States v. General Electric**, 272 U.S. 476 (1926), the Supreme Court upheld an arrangement under which GE placed patented light bulbs with retailers on "consignment" at a fixed retail price, paying the retailers a "commission" on each sale. The Court held that a *genuine agency* relation existed because the risk of loss or price decline was on GE, and hence no illegal resale price maintenance was involved. (But note that after the GE patents expired, at least one district court ruled that the GE consignment system was a *per se* violation of the Sherman Act. [**United States v. General Electric**, 358 F. Supp. 731 (S.D.N.Y. 1973)]])

Example: A consignment arrangement between an airline and travel agents for the sale of tickets was also upheld on grounds that the risk of loss (*i.e.*, the risk that the tickets would not sell) remained with the airline. [**Illinois Corporate Travel v. American Airlines**, 889 F.2d 751 (7th Cir. 1989), *cert. denied*, 495 U.S. 919 (1990)]

Compare: In **Simpson v. Union Oil Co.**, 377 U.S. 13 (1964), the Court all but overruled the *GE* case by striking down a "consignment" arrangement that was almost identical to that in *GE*. The Court distinguished *GE* on the grounds that (i) risk of loss due to nonsale passed to the retailers in *Simpson*, and (ii) *GE* was a patent case.

b. Unilateral refusals to deal [§275]

Manufacturers are free to announce "suggested retail prices," as long as they are merely suggested and the action is truly unilateral. But what if a seller announces that she will cease dealing with any customer who fails to adhere to the suggested retail price?

(1) Early view [§276]

In an early case, the Supreme Court decided that such an action was lawful as long as there was no "agreement" obligating the customer to resell at a specified price. The Court affirmed a person's right to choose those with whom she will deal and to announce in advance the circumstances under which she will refuse to deal. [**United States v. Colgate,** 250 U.S. 300 (1919)]

(2) Modern view [§277]

Some later cases have limited (but have not overruled) the *Colgate* case by finding *de facto agreements*. Any active exhortation of customers to adhere to suggested prices or any elaborate system of suspensions and reinstatements of retailers who fail to adhere and then agree to do so will constitute an agreement and unlawful resale price maintenance. [**FTC v. Beech-Nut,** 257 U.S. 441 (1923); **United States v. Parke, Davis & Co.,** *supra*, §259]

(a) Note—"agreement" need not involve plaintiff [§278]

In **Monsanto Co. v. Spray-Rite Service Corp.,** *supra*, §270, the Supreme Court held per se illegal an agreement between a manufacturer and several retailers who complained to the manufacturer about the price cutting activities of the plaintiff, another retailer. The manufacturer terminated the plaintiff, resulting in a lawsuit charging antitrust violations. The Court found that there was sufficient evidence of an *agreement regarding pricing* between the manufacturer and the complaining retailers.

1) But note

The *Colgate* rule still survives, and manufacturers are free to take *unilateral actions* to terminate discounting dealers. [*See* **Winn v. Edna Hibel Corp.,** 858 F.2d 1517 (11th Cir. 1988)] Unilateral terminations are most likely to survive antitrust scrutiny when the manufacturer clearly announces a termination policy and then adheres to that policy in all circumstances.

EXAM TIP　　　　　　　　　　　　　　　　　　　　**gilbert**

If you see an exam question where a manufacturer has set a price for resale of its product, you need to determine first if it is merely a *"suggested" price* as opposed to a required price. If it is not required by contract or enforced by the manufacturer in other ways, then it is probably *not* an antitrust violation. But if it is required in some way, then you must determine whether it is a minimum or maximum price being set. If it is a *minimum resale price*, it is a *per se violation*, but if you find it is a *maximum resale price*, you need to evaluate it under the *rule of reason* to determine its validity.

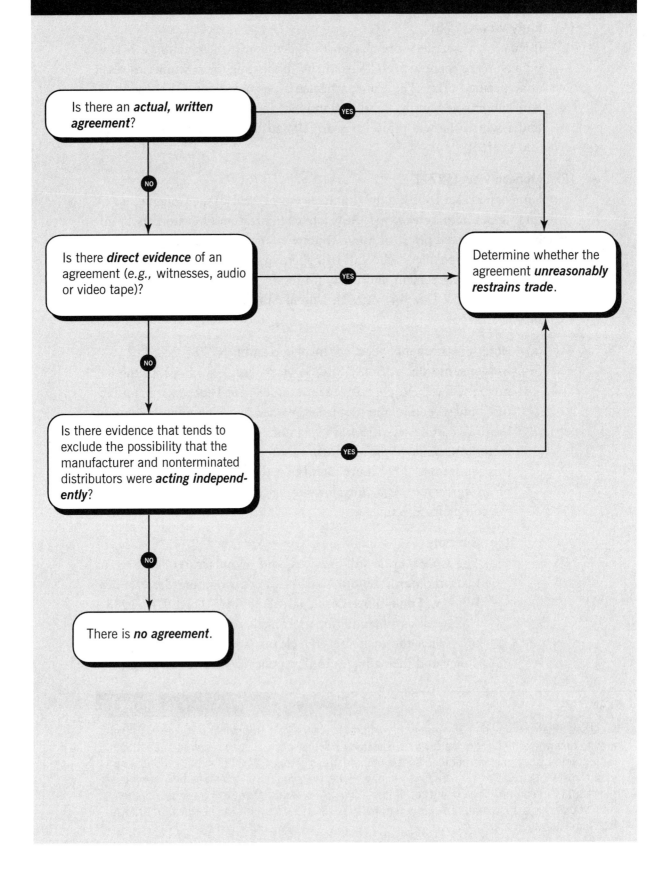

4. State Fair Trade Laws [§279]

Pressure to avoid price cutting among retailers marketing goods led to the Miller-Tydings Amendment in 1937 and the McGuire Act of 1952, which exempted from the Sherman Act (and the FTC Act) certain types of resale price maintenance agreements *if they were otherwise valid under state law.*

a. Repeal of fair trade [§280]

The Miller-Tydings Amendment and the McGuire Act in effect "passed the buck" to each state to determine whether resale price maintenance agreements on trademarked goods were legal. However, Congress in 1975 *repealed* this state power to authorize fair trade pricing—so that minimum resale price maintenance falls within the per se rules, *supra.*

> **e.g.** **Example:** A California statute requiring wine wholesalers to adhere to fair trade contracts or minimum price schedules set by producers violated section 1 of the Sherman Act. [**California Retail Liquor Dealers Association v. Midcal Aluminum, Inc.**, 445 U.S. 97 (1980); *and see* **324 Liquor Corp. v. Duffy**, 479 U.S. 335 (1987)—New York statute setting minimum retail prices for liquor invalid]

C. Exclusive Distributorships and Customer and Territorial Restrictions

1. Sole Outlets—Exclusive Distributors

a. Rule of reason applies [§281]

A contract in which the manufacturer appoints a distributor or dealer as her sole or "exclusive" outlet in a given region is subject to the rule of reason. In general, a manufacturer may lawfully pick and choose those with whom she will deal; therefore, she may choose to sell to certain buyers and not to others. However, the legality of any such arrangement may ultimately depend upon the extent of *interbrand* competition. If, for example, there is no interbrand competition (*i.e.*, the manufacturer has no competitors), *intrabrand* competition (*i.e.*, competition among the manufacturer's dealers) may be considered much more important, and thus a manufacturer's right to deal with whom she pleases is more restricted.

b. *Packard* case [§282]

The leading case in this area is **Packard Motor Car Co. v. Webster Motor Car Co.**, 243 F.2d 418 (D.C. Cir. 1957). In that case, Packard Motor Co., at the request of its largest dealer in Baltimore, terminated all other dealerships in that city. The jury found in favor of a terminated dealer, but the circuit court reversed, holding that a manufacturer can almost always make one dealer its sole outlet in a given area, even though this necessarily eliminates *intrabrand* competition.

c. Modern rule—*Business Electronics* [§283]

In **Business Electronics v. Sharp Electronics**, 485 U.S. 717 (1988), the Supreme Court found that although there had been an agreement between a manufacturer and a retailer to terminate another retailer for price cutting, that agreement was not illegal per se unless it included a specific agreement on prices to be charged by the retailer. The implication of *Business Electronics* is that *Packard*-type cases are to be evaluated under the **rule of reason**.

d. Market power required [§284]

Under the rule of reason inquiry, a claim that a television network violated the antitrust laws by distributing its signal only through a particular local station failed because the television network did not have market power. [**TV Communications Network v. Turner Network Television**, *supra*, §148]

2. Customer and Territorial Restrictions [§285]

While it may be lawful generally for a manufacturer to pick and choose *to whom* she will sell goods (*see* above), this does not mean that it is lawful for her to impose restrictions *on how the buyer can resell* those goods. Such restrictions are categorized as *vertical nonprice restraints*.

a. Former "*Schwinn* rule"—restrictions illegal per se [§286]

The Supreme Court formerly held that (like resale price maintenance) it was a per se violation of section 1 of the Sherman Act for a manufacturer to impose restrictions on its dealers as to the territory within which, or the customers to whom, a particular dealer may resell goods *purchased* from the manufacturer. [**United States v. Arnold Schwinn & Co.**, 388 U.S. 365 (1967)]

(1) Note

At the same time, the Court held that where goods were *consigned* by the manufacturer to the dealer (rather than sold), the *"rule of reason"* applied so that a restraint would be unlawful only if it "unreasonably" restricted competition. [**United States v. Arnold Schwinn & Co.**, *supra*]

b. Present law—"rule of reason" governs all such restrictions [§287]

In 1977, the Supreme Court overruled *Schwinn* and held that the *"rule of reason"* should be used to evaluate *all* nonprice vertical restrictions—whether customer, territorial, or location. [**Continental TV, Inc. v. GTE Sylvania, Inc.**, 433 U.S. 36 (1977); *and see* **Business Electronics v. Sharp Electronics**, *supra*]

(1) Rationale

The Court specifically rejected the "goods sold-goods consigned" distinction drawn in *Schwinn*, emphasizing that certain nonprice vertical restrictions may *foster interbrand competition* and thereby have redeeming competitive virtues, even though they reduce or eliminate *intrabrand competition*.

(2) *GTE Sylvania* as applied by lower courts [§288]

In applying the rule of reason, lower federal courts have focused on the totality of circumstances and have frequently stressed the distinction between intrabrand and interbrand competition drawn in *GTE Sylvania*. [*See, e.g.*, **Tunis Brothers Co. v. Ford Motor Co.**, 952 F.2d 715 (3d Cir. 1991), *cert. denied*, 505 U.S. 1221 (1992)—"The emphasis of antitrust theory is . . . upon protecting interbrand competition"]

Example: A manufacturer's threat to terminate a retailer for "transshipping" the manufacturer's merchandise (licensed sports apparel) to other retailers not specifically approved by manufacturer was not unlawful. The manufacturer's valid interests in the "quality and image it wishe[d] to project for its products" and in preventing counterfeiting were more than adequate to overcome any anticompetitive effects of the "no transshipment" policy. [**Trans Sport, Inc. v. Starter Sportswear, Inc.**, 964 F.2d 186 (2d Cir. 1992)]

Example: A brewer's nonprice territorial restrictions upon its wholesalers had a greater procompetitive effect on interbrand competition than their anticompetitive effect on intrabrand competition and therefore did not violate section 1. The court found that the purpose of the brewer's restrictions was "to increase its interbrand competitiveness by causing its wholesalers to distribute more effectively and efficiently." [**New York v. Anheuser-Busch, Inc.**, 811 F. Supp. 848 (E.D.N.Y. 1993)]

(3) Trend in favor of defendants [§289]

Many commentators and judges have noted a predominance of decisions in favor of defendants in rule of reason cases. This trend manifests itself in many subtle ways, including the manner in which the courts characterize certain defendants' actions. For instance, assume a manufacturer sells its products both directly to customers and indirectly through independent distributors. If the manufacturer terminates one distributor for underbidding the manufacturer and other distributors, should the case be treated as a horizontal conspiracy to allocate markets, which would be illegal per se, or as a vertical nonprice restraint, which is subject to the rule of reason? In **Smalley & Co. v. Emerson & Cuming, Inc.**, 808 F. Supp. 1503 (D. Colo. 1992), the court held it was a vertical restraint and granted the manufacturer's motion for summary judgment. [*Compare* **United States v. Topco Associates, Inc.**, *supra*, §226—Court found a similar arrangement horizontal and therefore illegal per se]

D. Tying Arrangements

1. Definitions

a. "Tying" and "tied" products [§290]

Under a "tying" arrangement, the seller refuses to sell product A (the "tying" product) to a customer unless the customer also agrees to buy product B (the "tied" product) from the seller. The seller is thus said to "tie" or condition the sale of the desired "tying" product to the purchase of the "tied" product. Buyers are thus "coerced" and suppliers "foreclosed."

b. Types of tying arrangements [§291]

The tying product and the tied product may be related in a variety of ways: they may be products that are used in fixed proportions (*e.g.*, nuts and bolts); the tied product may be designed to be used with the tying product (*e.g.*, software with a personal computer); or the tied and tying products may be usable together or separately (*e.g.*, seed and fertilizer). A tying arrangement may be contractual, in which a seller says that it will not sell the tying product unless the buyer will also purchase the separate tied product. Or, the tying arrangement may be technological, in which the seller physically integrates the tying product and tied product, so that anyone purchasing the tying product necessarily purchases the tied product simultaneously. [**United States v. Microsoft Corp.**, 253 F.3d 34 (D.C. Cir. 2001)]

c. Requirements for tying arrangement [§292]

There are four basic requisites for an illegal tie: (i) there must be *separate* tying and tied products; (ii) the sale must be *conditioned on* the arrangement or *due to coercion or force* by the seller; (iii) the seller must have sufficient *economic power* in the *tying* product market to restrain competition appreciably in the *tied* product; and (iv) the tying arrangement must affect *more than an "insubstantial" dollar volume of commerce* in the tied product market. [*See, e.g.*, **T. Harris Young & Associates, Inc. v. Marquette Electronics, Inc.**, *supra*, §151] Most circuits require that the tying seller have a direct economic interest in the sale of the tied product. [**Carl Sandburg Village Condominium Association v. First Condominium Development Co.**, 758 F.2d 203 (7th Cir. 1985)] Also, some circuits require that the plaintiff prove that the tying arrangement has an anticompetitive effect. [**United Farmers Agents Association v. Farmers Insurance Exchange**, 89 F.3d 233 (5th Cir. 1996)]

(1) Note

In addition to the *per se rule* against tying, a tying arrangement that does not violate the per se test can still violate the *rule of reason*.

ILLEGAL TYING ARRANGEMENTS—A CHECKLIST

FOR A TYING ARRANGEMENT TO BE ILLEGAL, THE FOLLOWING ELEMENTS MUST BE MET:

☑ *Separate* tying and tied products;

☑ The sale is **conditioned upon** the arrangement or due to **coercion** or **force** by the seller;

☑ The seller has sufficient **economic power** in the **tying** product market to restrain competition in the **tied** product; and

☑ The arrangement must affect a **substantial dollar volume of commerce** in the tied product market.

2. Reasons to Use Tying Arrangements

a. To extend market power [§293]

A firm may be able to use its monopoly power in the market for one product to create monopoly power or monopoly profits in its sales of another product by tying sale of the two products together. For instance, a firm selling a unique, patented product can force buyers to purchase a related product from that firm simply by tying sale of the patented product to purchase of the related product. Theoretically, the monopolist may be able to reduce or eliminate competition for the tied product and to create a monopoly for itself in the market for that product.

b. To protect products, image, or goodwill [§294]

A firm may try to protect its product, image, or business goodwill by a tying arrangement. For example, a firm may fear that its products will be serviced poorly by untrained or unauthorized operators, and to eliminate that risk it may refuse to distribute replacement parts to independent service providers. In the franchise context, a franchisor may require its franchisees to purchase tied products (such as ingredients, napkins, etc.) in order to ensure that all franchisees deliver a consistent product.

c. To engage in price discrimination or to evade other price controls [§295]

A tying arrangement may allow a firm to engage in price discrimination. For example, suppose a company has a patent on a very high speed, high quality color printer, but that the print cartridges used in the printer are not patented and are widely available from a number of suppliers. If the company leases the printer to all its users at the same rental rate but requires those users to purchase print cartridges from their company, it can effectively charge heavier users more for the lease of the printer, even though all leases are written at the same rental rate. Regulated firms can use tie-ins to evade price regulation. If, for example, a cable television firm's monthly service rates are set by statute, the firm might try to circumvent the price restriction by requiring its customers to "lease" converter boxes at unregulated, inflated rates.

d. To take advantage of efficiencies and economies of scale [§296]

Most products are, in fact, combinations of several separate products and services, any one of which might be viewed as capable of being sold separately. But does it make sense to say that car makers "tie" sales of their engines to sales of the rest of their cars? Do customers want to buy those "products" separately? The answer to these questions is clearly no, pointing up a critical tension between the law against tie-ins and economic reality. For a variety of reasons, it is probably more efficient and cost-effective to have the car's engine made and installed by the manufacturer, and there are infinitely more examples of efficiencies and economies of scale created by the assembly and sale of related products as a single, unified whole. Although courts do not generally acknowledge efficiencies or economies of scale as justifications for tie-ins, they do address the issue implicitly when they determine (as they must) whether the tying item and the tied item are *separate* products. The car/engine example seems an easy case, but other cases are not so clear (*e.g.*, cars and car stereos or cars and gasoline). [*See, e.g.*, **Town Sound & Custom Tops, Inc. v. Chrysler Motors Corp.**, 959 F.2d 468 (3d Cir.), *cert. denied*, 506 U.S. 868 (1992); *and see infra*, §306]

3. Statutory Prohibitions

a. Clayton Act section 3 [§297]

Section 3 of the Clayton Act provides that it is unlawful for any person to lease or sell *commodities* or fix a price therefor "on the condition [or] agreement . . . that the lessee or purchaser thereof shall not use or deal in the . . . commodities of a competitor . . . of the lessor or seller, *where the effect may be to substantially lessen competition* or tend to create a monopoly in any line of commerce."

(1) "Commodities" vs. other forms of property [§298]

Section 3 applies only to "goods" or "commodities," and *not* to services, intangibles, or real property.

(2) "Condition" or "agreement" [§299]

Though the statute refers to a "condition" or "agreement," a formalized arrangement is *not required*. Any leverage the seller has with the customer to foreclose the customer from dealing with seller's competitors will suffice.

(3) Note—coercion required [§300]

Where the customer voluntarily buys both products from the same source, and no element of coercion is present, the purchases cannot amount to a tying arrangement. [**Service & Training, Inc. v. Data General Corp.**, 963 F.2d 680 (4th Cir. 1992)] However, an illegal tie has been found where a buyer voluntarily took both products, because the seller had the requisite economic power or leverage and used it to induce purchase of the tied product. Despite the absence of any written contract, the court held that use of the seller's power could be inferred from (i) coercion; (ii) resolute enforcement of a policy to "influence" buyers to take both products; or (iii) widespread purchase of both products by buyers. [**Ungar v. Dunkin' Donuts of America, Inc.**, 531 F.2d 211 (3d Cir. 1976)]

b. Sherman Act section 1 [§301]

Section 1 of the Sherman Act also applies to tie-ins, and covers arrangements involving services, intangibles, or real property not covered by the Clayton Act provisions. [**Times-Picayune Publishing Co. v. United States**, *supra*, §194]

c. Statutory standards tend to converge [§302]

Section 3 of the Clayton Act was enacted to stop certain tie-in practices in their incipiency. Although section 3 is therefore arguably more restrictive than section 1 of the Sherman Act, today the standards applied are similar for both statutes. [*See, e.g.,* **Town Sound & Custom Tops, Inc. v. Chrysler Motors Corp.**, *supra*, §296]

d. FTC section 5 [§303]

Section 5 of the FTC Act also covers tie-ins that would be illegal under either the Clayton or Sherman Acts.

→ not correct

4. Tying Usually Illegal Per Se [§304] *→ not correct*

Although limited exceptions are recognized (*see* the "new industry" and "quality control" defenses, §§312-313), the oft-repeated rule is that tying arrangements are *illegal per se*, when the prerequisites of *separate products, coercion or force, market power*, and a *more than de minimis amount of commerce* are established. This result may be reached under either the Clayton or Sherman Acts. [**Jefferson Parish Hospital District No. 2 v. Hyde**, 466 U.S. 2 (1984)]

a. Note—special per se rule [§305]

While courts use the term "illegal per se" to describe tying arrangements, the per se rule in this context is *not the same* as it is in the context of horizontal price fixing agreements. In tying cases, the courts require a *detailed inquiry* into market definitions and the existence of market power, something they do not do in other "per se" cases.

EXAM TIP   **gilbert**

Keep this distinction in mind when you face a tying question on your exam. Although you should state in your answer that courts generally find tying agreements *illegal per se*, you should discuss each element of a tying claim, including market definitions and market power. Thus, your analysis will seem more analogous to the rule of reason than to the per se rule.

---

b. Elements of a per se tying plan

(1) Proving that tying and tied products are separate [§306]

To determine whether two products are in fact separate for tying purposes, courts do not focus "on the functional relation between them, but rather on the *character of demand* for the two items." [**Jefferson Parish Hospital District No. 2 v. Hyde**, *supra*, §304] There must be sufficient demand for the two products for firms to provide them separately. [**Eastman Kodak Co. v. Image Technical Services**, *supra*, §148] Although this is usually not a problem, there are cases where a defendant may credibly argue the product is a *single* one (*e.g.*, picture tube and television, or car and spare tire).

Example: In **United States Steel Corp. v. Fortner Enterprises (I)**, 394 U.S. 495 (1969), the Court rejected defendant's argument that its sale of *prefabricated homes* and *loans* for purchase of the homes and real estate development were a single product. While such an argument probably makes sense for most purchases where credit is extended by the seller, here the Court found that the credit could reasonably be viewed as a separate (and "tying") product because its terms were favorable and the amount was for more than purchase of the homes (the tied product), since real estate development and acquisition costs were also advanced.

Example: Autos and auto sound systems have been held to be separate products. [**Town Sound & Custom Tops, Inc. v. Chrysler Motors Corp.**, *supra*]

Example: Copier replacement parts and copier service can be separate products if evidence establishes that the two are, or have been, sold separately. [**Eastman Kodak Co. v. Image Technical Services**, *supra*]

(a) Distinguish

In the context of technological integration, it is sometimes difficult to determine whether there are separate products. If the integration of two formerly separate products creates a more efficient new product, the integration may not constitute tying. [**United States v. Microsoft Corp.**, *supra*, §291]

(2) Conditioning or coercion [§307]

Courts have split on what type of proof is required to establish that the defendant conditioned sale of the tying product on the buyer agreeing to purchase the tied product as well. Some courts hold that a written contract containing the condition is sufficient. [**Bell v. Cherokee Aviation Corp.**, 660 F.2d 1123 (6th Cir. 1981)] Others require proof of actual coercion, as opposed to sales pressure by the defendant. [**Bob Maxfield, Inc. v. American**

Motors Corp., 637 F.2d 1033 (5th Cir. 1981)] The conditioning or coercion element is probably satisfied if the bundled products are priced so that purchase of the products individually is not economically viable. [**Tricom, Inc. v. Electronic Data Systems Corp.,** 1996-1 Trade Cas. (CCH) ¶71,351 (E.D. Mich. 1996)]

(3) Proving market power

(a) Early cases [§308]

Proof of dominance in the tying product market was what was necessary in early cases. Examples include the patented salt machines to which were tied the purchase of salt [**International Salt Co. v. United States,** 332 U.S. 392 (1947)], and the copyrighted films to which were tied the purchase of inferior films [**United States v. Loew's Inc.,** 371 U.S. 38 (1962)]. Also, the land sold by the Northern Pacific Railway, which required the purchaser to ship goods on the Northern Pacific Railway [**Northern Pacific Railway v. United States,** 356 U.S. 1 (1958)] and Loew's copyrighted feature films [**United States v. Loew's Inc.,** *supra*] are examples of product uniqueness, which were *presumed* to give the seller market dominance.

(b) Modern trend [§309]

The Supreme Court apparently has shifted subtly the market power inquiry. Although early cases focused on the defendants' power in the market for the tying product, the Court now emphasizes *the power of defendants to force consumers to make choices* they would not make in a competitive environment. This test would seem to stress the ability of the defendants to influence decisionmaking in the market for the *tied* product. [*See* **Jefferson Parish Hospital District No. 2 v. Hyde,** *supra*]

(c) Note

The fact that a defendant has offered *unique terms* on the tying product is *not* sufficient in itself to show the requisite market power. For example, United States Steel offered no-interest loans (the tying product) to developers who purchased United States Steel prefabricated houses (the tied product). The Supreme Court held that such credit terms did not establish the company's market power in the credit field, but merely indicated a willingness to provide cheap financing in order to sell expensive homes. Thus, plaintiff had to show that United States Steel had some cost advantage over competitors before such terms would indicate market power. [**United States Steel Corp. v. Fortner Enterprises (II),** 429 U.S. 610 (1977)]

e.g. Example: Plaintiffs were a group of independent service organizations ("ISOs") which, although not affiliated with the seller/

manufacturer, attempted to compete with it in the servicing of its copiers. Plaintiffs claimed that the seller/manufacturer had impermissibly tied the servicing of its machines to the sale of replacement parts by limiting the availability of those parts to the ISOs. This policy effectively made it more difficult for the ISOs to compete in the servicing of the copiers. The Supreme Court affirmed the lower court's ruling that a genuine issue existed as to the seller/manufacturer's market power in the separate markets for **service and parts** for its machines, even though it had no such power in the market for the sale of copiers. [**Eastman Kodak Co. v. Image Technical Services**, *supra*, §148]

(4) Proving more than an insubstantial amount of commerce involved [§310]
The plaintiff must show that more than an insubstantial amount of commerce is involved. This requirement is usually satisfied by proof of a more than *de minimis dollar volume* involved; market share analysis generally is not required.

Example: Foreclosure of $500,000 in salt was sufficient commerce in **International Salt Co. v. United States**, *supra* §308; and $60,800 was found "not insubstantial" in **United States v. Loew's Inc.**, *supra*, §308.

(a) Note
In **United States Steel Corp. v. Fortner Enterprises (I)**, *supra*, §306, the Court said: "[T]he relevant figure is the total volume of sales tied by the sales policy under challenge, not the position of this total accounted for by the particular plaintiff who brings suit."

5. Defenses [§311]
Defendants may offer the following affirmative defenses to a tying claim:

a. "New industry" [§312]
Some lower courts have permitted a tie when "instituted in the launching of a new business with a highly uncertain future." The tie is justified as necessary to assure proper functioning of special equipment, etc. As the business becomes established, however, tying may no longer be justified. [**United States v. Jerrold Electronics**, 187 F. Supp. 545 (E.D. Pa. 1960)—cable television antenna manufacturer required installers to purchase service contract to assure proper functioning of system; held legal at outset, but not after business had become established]

b. "Quality control for protection of goodwill" [§313]
The defense that tying is necessary to protect goodwill *rarely succeeds*. The Supreme Court has stated: "The only situation . . . in which the protection of goodwill may necessitate the use of tying clauses is *where specifications for a*

substitute would be so detailed that they could not practicably be supplied." [**Standard Oil v. United States**, 337 U.S. 293 (1949); *but see* **Trans Sport, Inc. v. Starter Sportswear, Inc.**, *supra*, §288—protection of defendant's goodwill was a legitimate justification for a "no transshipment" policy imposed by defendant, a policy that resembled (and was alleged by plaintiff to be) an illegal tie-in]

c. Software products [§314]

The D.C. Circuit in *Microsoft* held that the per se rule against tying arrangements should not apply to platform software products, *e.g.*, computer operating systems, because it may chill efficient innovation. Tying arrangements based on platform software should be evaluated under the rule of reason. [**United States v. Microsoft Corp.**, *supra*, §291]

E. Exclusive Dealing—Requirements Contracts

1. Introduction [§315]

A buyer may agree to handle only the seller's products and not those of a competitor. Often such arrangements take the form of a buyer's agreement to purchase his "requirements" exclusively from the seller. To a certain extent, the effect is similar to "tying" arrangements; *i.e.*, the buyer has agreed not to use a competitor's goods. Like tying arrangements, exclusive dealing may be treated under either section 3 of the Clayton Act (if it involves the *sale of goods*) or section 1 of the Sherman Act.

2. "Quantitative Substantiality" Test [§316]

The Supreme Court has traditionally treated exclusive dealing arrangements more leniently than tying arrangements, formulating a "quantitative substantiality test." Under this approach, the requisite adverse effect on competition *is presumed* when a seller's exclusive dealing contracts foreclose a *substantial dollar volume of the market* (*e.g.*, a substantial number of outlets for his product in the case of a manufacturer selling to retailers). [**Standard Oil v. United States**, *supra*—contracts affecting $58 million of business are illegal, even though defendant had only 6.7% of the market]

a. Note

In *Standard Oil, supra*, the Supreme Court recognized that—unlike tying arrangements—requirements contracts may be advantageous to buyers as well as sellers (in the form of reduced selling costs, a secured source of supply at a fixed price, etc.). Moreover, exclusive dealing contracts may allow new competitors to enter the market. And the competitive impact of such contracts can be determined by considering their duration, the market position of the seller, etc.

b. Result

Even so, the Court felt that it was inappropriate to make such a complex economic inquiry on a case-by-case basis. On the other hand, validating such contracts "across the board" might defeat the preventative goals of Clayton Act section 3. Hence, the Court adopted an easy-to-apply *test* that merely asks whether the dollar amount involved in the contract is substantial. If it is, an *anticompetitive effect is presumed*.

3. "Market Share" Test [§317]

More recently, the Court suggested a second test that focuses on the *size of the market share foreclosed* by the contract. "A mere showing that the contract itself involves a substantial number of dollars is ordinarily of little consequence." A substantial market foreclosure is necessary. [**Tampa Electric v. Nashville Coal**, 365 U.S. 320 (1961)—upholding a 20-year requirements contract for coal, because less than 1% of the coal market was foreclosed, even though $120 million was involved]

4. Rule of Reason [§318]

Under either section 1 of the Sherman Act or section 3 of the Clayton Act, exclusive dealing arrangements today are evaluated under the rule of reason.

5. De Facto Exclusive Dealing [§319]

A market arrangement may be treated as exclusive dealing even though there is no *express* contractual requirement that the parties deal exclusively, if the clear effect of the transaction is that the parties will not deal with anyone else.

---

e.g. **Example:** Microsoft Corp. required computer makers to pay it a royalty on every computer they shipped, whether or not the Microsoft operating system was installed. This "per processor license" was an exclusive dealing arrangement, because as a practical matter no computer manufacturer would be willing to pay two license fees in order to install a competing operating system. [**United States v. Microsoft Corp.**, *supra*, §314]

Chapter Six:
Mergers and Acquisitions

CONTENTS

Chapter Approach

Chapter Approach

For antitrust purposes, mergers are typically classified as either *horizontal* (a merger involving two competitors), *vertical* (a merger between firms at different levels of the same industry, as where a manufacturer acquires a distributor or one of its suppliers), or *conglomerate* (any merger that is not horizontal or vertical, usually an acquisition by one company of another firm in an industry in which the acquiring company is not already participating). Although the chief concern of the courts is the same for all types of mergers (namely, to preserve competition within markets), different mergers threaten competition in different ways and therefore are analyzed as follows:

1. *A horizontal merger* directly reduces the number of competitors in the market in which the parties are engaged, and so the law focuses on whether the merger *raises the concentration of firms* in the industry to a level or in a manner that increases the likelihood of anticompetitive conduct by the remaining participants (*e.g.*, through the raising of barriers to entry or by facilitating collusion).

2. *Vertical mergers* raise the specter of *foreclosure of part of a market to potential competitors* (*i.e.*, if a supplier acquires one of its customers, or vice versa, it may be less likely that the supplier's competitors will be able to market their products to the customer). If the share of the market foreclosed is significant, and if other economic factors indicate that the merger will have anticompetitive effects, the merger may be struck down.

3. *A conglomerate merger* can sometimes violate the antitrust laws if it serves to *eliminate* an actual *or perceived potential competitor*, since the threat of new entry to a market is a disincentive to firms already in the market to raise prices to or near monopoly levels.

With regard to the three different kinds of mergers above, the Department of Justice and the Federal Trade Commission have issued joint Guidelines describing their enforcement stances. Note that these Guidelines do not change case law, but help the federal antitrust enforcement officials decide when to challenge proposed mergers. Because the government is in a far better position to challenge mergers than most private parties, the Guidelines are important. In general, the Guidelines approach merger law in much the same way as the courts, but there are a few variations.

Although some cases have held or suggested that a merger can violate the antitrust laws merely by *increasing the concentration* in the relevant market and the *market share* of the merged firms, more recent cases have held (and the enforcement arms of the government seem to concur) that market share and concentration are only two of many factors to be examined in determining illegality. Other factors to consider include the *ease of entry* into the market, *interchangeability of products* in the market, *trends toward or away from concentration,* and (in the view of the government, but not yet the courts) *efficiencies* created by the merger.

A. Clayton Act Section 7

1. Background [§320]

Early antitrust cases involved attempts to dissolve mergers under section 1 of the Sherman Act. However, in cases such as **United States v. Winslow**, 227 U.S. 202 (1914), the Court held that section 1 did not bar mergers absent a showing of overt anticompetitive acts. The difficulties the government faced in attempting to enjoin mergers under Sherman Act section 1 led Congress to enact section 7 of the Clayton Act [15 U.S.C. §18].

2. Original Limitations [§321]

As originally passed (in 1914), section 7 prohibited any corporation engaged in commerce from acquiring "the whole or any part of the *stock* of another corporation also engaged in commerce, where the effect of the acquisition *may* be to lessen competition between the corporation whose stock is so acquired and the corporation making the acquisition, or to restrain competition in any section of commerce, or to tend to create a monopoly."

a. But note [§322]

This covered only mergers by acquisition of *stock* (*i.e.*, it did not apply to mergers by purchase of the assets of another corporation). And it apparently covered only *horizontal* mergers among competitors—not vertical mergers among complementary entities. [*See* **Hartford-Empire Co. v. United States**, 323 U.S. 386 (1945)]

3. Celler-Kefauver Amendment and Subsequent Amendments [§323]

Consequently, section 7 was amended in 1950 (the Celler-Kefauver Act), in 1980, and in 1984 to make unlawful the acquisition by any "person" (defined in section 1 of the Clayton Act to include corporations) of "the stock . . . or the whole or any part *of the assets* of one or more persons *engaged in commerce*," where "in any line of commerce" in "any section of the country" the effect of acquisition *may* be "*substantially to lessen competition*, or tend to create a monopoly." The amendments expand section 7 to ensure coverage of vertical and conglomerate mergers (as well as horizontal mergers) and to include mergers by acquisition of assets (as well as stock).

a. Purposes of Act, as amended [§324]

The antimerger provisions of section 7 are intended to serve several purposes:

(1) *To ensure better market performance* by prohibiting increases in market concentration that might lead to less competitive market *structures* (*e.g.*, oligopoly);

(2) *To encourage internal growth and expansion*, which has the effect of increasing competition and competitors;

(3) *To preserve local control over industry*, by discouraging absentee corporate ownership of local businesses; and

(4) **To protect small businesses.** (*Note:* It is arguable that merger policy also harms small businesses by depriving them of a source of buyers for the business.)

EXAM TIP **gilbert**

When answering an exam question that addresses mergers, consider the *purposes* that the laws in this area seek to achieve (*i.e.,* better market performance, growth and expansion, local control over industry and the protection of small business) before determining whether the acquisition is unlawful.

---

b. Effect on section 1 of the Sherman Act [§325]

As a result of the amendments' broadening of section 7, section 1 of the Sherman Act is now practically irrelevant in its application to mergers.

B. Judicial Interpretation of Section 7

1. In General [§326]

Section 7 applies to three types of mergers: horizontal, vertical, and conglomerate. In applying the language of section 7 to these merger areas, the courts have centered on the meaning of three phrases: *"line of commerce," "section of the country,"* and *"may be substantially to lessen competition."*

2. Market Definition—"Line of Commerce" [§327]

Section 7 requires the same relevant product market analysis as for monopolization under Sherman Act section 2 (*see supra,* §§145-148). Here also, the emphasis has been on *interchangeability of products,* although less may be required to overturn a merger because of the prophylactic nature of section 7. [**United States v. Continental Can Co.,** 378 U.S. 441 (1964)—can manufacturer's acquisition of glass jar maker overturned, even though interchangeability of products was far from complete]

Example: This broad interpretation of "line of commerce" (or, as some have suggested, willingness to manipulate market definition) was illustrated in **United States v. Greater Buffalo Press, Inc.,** 402 U.S. 549 (1971), which invalidated the merger of several firms involved in printing comic supplements for newspapers. The Court found only one "line of commerce" involved, even though the firms were not direct competitors (some printed for newspapers that had their own comics, while others printed for syndicates engaged in sale of copyrighted comic strips). The Court noted, "There may be *submarkets* within one broad market for antitrust purposes . . . but submarkets are not a basis for disregard of a *broader line of commerce that has economic significance.*"

---

a. "Hypothetical monopolist" approach [§328]

The Department of Justice ("DOJ") and Federal Trade Commission ("FTC")

Merger Guidelines take a somewhat different approach to market definition. The Guidelines define a market by asking whether a hypothetical monopolist in the proposed market could profitably impose a *small but significant and nontransitory increase in price* ("SSNIP"). If a monopolist could raise prices by, say, 5% without a competitive response, the market has been defined correctly. But if consumers would turn to substitute products, or if new competitors would enter the market in response to the price increase, those products or competitors must be included in the market definition.

3. **Market Definition—"Section of the Country" [§329]**

Section 7 requires that the court define the geographic market in each case. The Supreme Court has treated "section of the country" as meaning the *"relevant geographic market"*—i.e., "the area where the effect of the merger on competition will be both *immediate and direct.*" [**United States v. Philadelphia National Bank**, 374 U.S. 321 (1963)]

a. **May be more than one relevant market [§330]**

In cases where the acquired firm markets its products on a local, regional, or national basis, the Court has acknowledged the existence of *more than one relevant market* for the products. [**United States v. Pabst Brewing Co.**, 384 U.S. 546 (1966)—lessening of competition in a three-state area held sufficient because this area was *one* "relevant market" for the product]

b. **Limitation [§331]**

However, more recently, the Court has seemed determined to apply a more rigorous, analytical definition of relevant geographical market. The Court has *refused* to determine the legality of a merger by measuring its effect on areas where the acquired firm is *not* in direct competition. [**United States v. Connecticut National Bank**, 418 U.S. 656 (1974)—in a case involving potential competition, the relevant geographic market was the localized area in which the acquired firm is in significant direct competition with other firms, albeit not in competition with the acquiring firm]

(1) **Note**

In **United States v. Marine Bancorporation**, 418 U.S. 602 (1974), the Court rejected a state-wide market definition in favor of a local definition that more accurately described where the acquired firm *actually* marketed its goods or services.

4. **Anticompetitive Effects Analysis—"May Be Substantially to Lessen Competition" [§332]**

Section 7 is concerned with attacking potential anticompetitive effects *before* they happen. Congress was concerned with probabilities, not certainties, and the Act was designed to have a *preventative*, not merely corrective, effect. [*See* **FTC v. Procter & Gamble Co.**, 386 U.S. 568 (1967)—invalidating merger merely because of *potential* lessening of competition in bleach market and because merger would create barriers to possible entry by newcomers into the bleach market]

a. **Potential lessening sufficient [§333]**

Section 7 applies whenever a "tendency" toward monopoly, or a *"reasonable likelihood"* of a substantial lessening of competition, is shown. [**United States v. Penn-Olin Chemical**, *supra*, §240] Bad acts or predatory conduct are not required.

b. **Must be probability of effect [§334]**

However, section 7 deals with *probabilities*, not "ephemeral possibilities." [**United States v. Marine Bancorporation**, *supra*—Court refused to assume that the merger of a bank in one city with other banks in the state would lead to state-wide bank oligopoly, where nothing in the record showed this was likely to occur]

c. **Harm must be within scope of Act [§335]**

The alleged harm to be created by the merger must be the sort that the antitrust laws were designed to prevent. Damages resulting merely from increased competition are not recoverable under the Clayton Act. [**Cargill, Inc. v. Monfort of Colorado, Inc.**, *supra*, §112]

5. **Justifications for Mergers [§336]**

This heavily prophylactic approach has jeopardized mergers having only a slight statistical impact on competition. As a result, there has been some attempt to create limited "exceptions" for mergers whose *net effect is pro-competitive:*

a. **"Small company doctrine" [§337]**

The Supreme Court by way of dictum recognized that two or more small companies might be allowed to merge in order to compete more effectively with larger, dominant firms in the relevant market. [*See* **Brown Shoe Co. v. United States**, 370 U.S. 294 (1962)]

(1) **But note**

This doctrine was apparently *rejected* (or at least severely limited) by the Court in the *Von's Grocery* case (*see infra*, §357).

b. **"Failing company doctrine" [§338]**

Other decisions indicate that a merger between a failing company and a competitor should be allowed, in the absence of any other purchasers. [**International Shoe Co. v. FTC**, 280 U.S. 291 (1930)]

(1) **But note**

For this defense to be available, the acquired company must be "in imminent danger of failure," it must have "no realistic prospect for a successful reorganization," and there must be "no viable alternative purchaser." [**Dr. Pepper/Seven-Up Companies v. FTC**, 991 F.2d 859 (D.C. Cir. 1993)]

(2) **Burden of proof [§339]**

The burden of proof is on those seeking refuge under the doctrine. [**Citizen Publishing Co. v. United States**, *supra*, §239]

c. Lack of competitive harm [§340]

While nominally it is the plaintiff's burden to show potential competitive harm from a merger, it is relatively easy to make out a prima facie case of potential harm. At this point, the burden shifts to the defendant to demonstrate that the merger will not in fact injure competition. [**United States v. General Dynamics Corp.,** *supra,* §166]

---

e.g. **Example:** In *General Dynamics, supra,* the government challenged the merger of two companies with 13% and 9% shares in a highly concentrated market for coal. The Court held that the merger was presumptively illegal because of the increase in concentration. However, it went on to hold that the defendants effectively rebutted this presumption by proving that the acquired company had all but run out of coal reserves, and therefore would not be an effective competitor in the future, even if the merger did not take place.

---

e.g. **Example:** Defendant, a national movie theatre chain, purchased all three of its competitors in the Las Vegas, Nevada market for first-run movies. While this gave it a market share of nearly 100%, entry by others later reduced that to roughly 50% of the market. The Ninth Circuit held that the acquisition was not illegal, because subsequent events had shown that the defendant was not able to maintain its market share. [**United States v. Syufy Enterprises,** 903 F.2d 659 (9th Cir. 1990)]

---

(1) Note

A private plaintiff does not have standing to challenge a merger if that plaintiff's injury stems from an increase in competition from the merged entity. [**Brunswick Corp. v. Pueblo Bowl-O-Mat Inc.,** 429 U.S. 477 (1977)]

d. Economic efficiencies [§341]

Historically, courts have been unreceptive to the argument that a merger increases the efficiency of the acquiring company. [*See* **FTC v. Procter & Gamble Co.,** *supra,* §332] More recently, however, courts have allowed defendants to offer proof of efficiencies resulting from a merger, if the efficiencies would "ultimately benefit competition and, hence, consumers." [**FTC v. University Health, Inc.,** 938 F.2d 1206 (11th Cir. 1991)]

(1) And note

The 1992 DOJ/FTC Horizontal Merger Guidelines contain a limited efficiency defense for horizontal mergers. (*See infra,* §377.)

6. Post-Acquisition Evidence [§342]

Generally, courts have not been hospitable to efforts to introduce post-acquisition evidence to show the lack of anticompetitive effects of a merger. This is so because the evidence is self-serving and the post-acquisition conduct is usually within the control of the merged companies. [*See, e.g.,* **United States v. Continental Can Co.,** *supra,* §327]

a. **But note**

Post-acquisition evidence *may be admissible* when it is *not* within the control of the merged companies and demonstrates fundamental changes in the pattern and structure of the industry which are probative of whether the merger lessened competition. [**United States v. General Dynamics Corp.**, *supra* §156; **United States v. Syufy Enterprises**, *supra*, §340]

THEORIES BY WHICH TO JUSTIFY MERGERS	**gilbert**
SMALL COMPANY DOCTRINE	While the exception has been *limited*, courts may allow for several small companies to merge in order *to effectively compete* with larger firms in the marketplace.
FAILING COMPANY DOCTRINE	If a company is in *imminent danger of failing*, with *no realistic prospect of reorganization*, a merger with a competitor may be allowed in the *absence of a viable alternative purchaser*.
LACK OF COMPETITIVE HARM	The defendant company may show that the proposed merger will *not, in fact, hurt competition*.
ECONOMIC EFFICIENCIES	In a recent trend, courts may permit mergers that increase the *efficiency of a company*, if that will *ultimately increase competition* and benefit consumers.

C. Horizontal Mergers

1. In General [§343]

"Horizontal mergers" are mergers between competitors—*i.e.*, companies performing similar functions in the production or distribution of comparable goods or services. Horizontal mergers can drive an industry toward monopoly or facilitate cartels by increasing industry concentration.

a. Bright line rules vs. totality of circumstances [§344]

The courts, wishing to streamline analysis of these cases, have attempted to establish bright line rules for *presumptive* (although not absolute) *illegality* based almost entirely upon market concentrations and the market shares of the merging firms. But the task has proved daunting. Similarly structured markets can behave very differently, and a panoply of factors can impact competition within any market. Consequently, useful bright line rules have proven elusive, and the modern trend seems to be to evaluate cases on the *totality of their circumstances*, with the government bearing greater responsibility to prove the anticompetitive effects of a challenged merger.

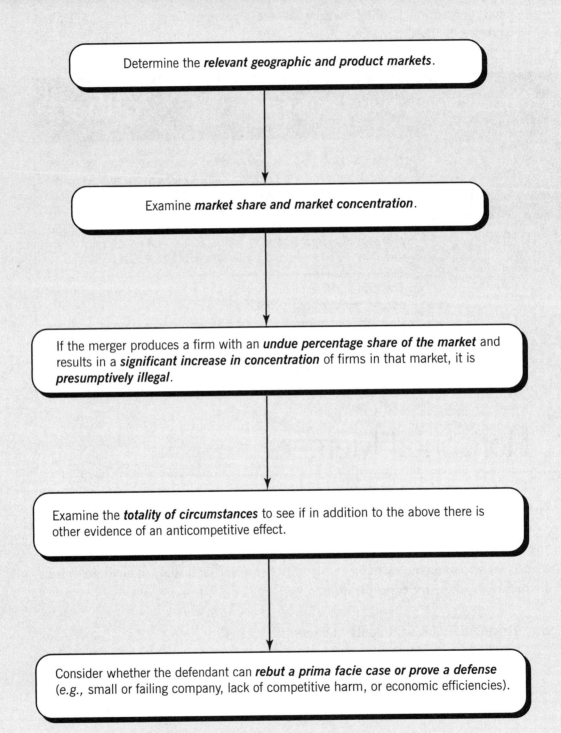

Determine the *relevant geographic and product markets*.

Examine *market share and market concentration*.

If the merger produces a firm with an *undue percentage share of the market* and results in a *significant increase in concentration* of firms in that market, it is *presumptively illegal*.

Examine the *totality of circumstances* to see if in addition to the above there is other evidence of an anticompetitive effect.

Consider whether the defendant can *rebut a prima facie case or prove a defense* (*e.g.*, small or failing company, lack of competitive harm, or economic efficiencies).

(1) **Analysis of market structure [§345]**

Courts focus primarily on two factors: (i) the *concentration of the subject market*, and (ii) the *market shares of the merging firms*. In general, the more concentrated the market and the larger the market share of the parties to the merger, the more likely the merger will be deemed illegal.

(a) **Mitigating factors [§346]**

Even in cases of presumptive illegality, however, courts will examine evidence mitigating the presumption. Additional factors that courts will consider include the *heterogeneity of products* in the market, *low barriers to entry, excess capacity, trends toward or away from market concentration* and (in the case of the 1992 Horizontal Merger Guidelines adopted by the DOJ and the FTC) *certain efficiencies* created by the merger, such as economies of scale and integration of operations. (*See infra*, §§372 *et seq.*)

(b) **Measure of market concentration [§347]**

There are different ways to measure market concentration. The DOJ's 1968 Merger Guidelines advocated use of the four-firm concentration ratio, which sums the market shares of the four largest firms in the relevant market. The 1992 Merger Guidelines, which are currently in use, rely on the Herfindahl-Hirschman Index ("HHI") to measure market concentration. (*See infra*, §377.) The HHI is the most commonly used measure of market concentration.

b. **Characterizing mergers [§348]**

Of the three types—horizontal, vertical, and conglomerate—horizontal mergers are generally most likely to be condemned because of their potential for direct impact upon competition by way of reduction of the number of competitors. However, it is not always a simple task to tell a horizontal merger from one of the other types. For example, in *Brown Shoe* (*see infra*), the merged companies manufactured different grades of the same product (*i.e.*, one made better quality, expensive shoes, and the other made lower quality, less expensive shoes). Although there is no hard and fast rule for making this determination, the inquiry focuses on the *elasticity of demand* between the two products. (*See infra*, §§597 *et seq.*)

c. **Mergers that eliminate perceived potential entrant [§349]**

The Supreme Court has recognized that a merger may violate section 7 because it eliminates a potential competitor that is perceived to be "waiting in the wings" to enter the market of the acquired company. [*See, e.g.*, **FTC v. Procter & Gamble Co.**, *supra*, §332; **United States v. Penn-Olin Chemical Co.**, *supra*, §333; **United States v. Falstaff Brewing Corp.**, 410 U.S. 526 (1973); **Tenneco, Inc. v. FTC**, 689 F.2d 346 (2d Cir. 1982)]

(1) **Theory supporting loss of potential competition [§350]**

The "wings effect" presupposes a market structure with some barriers to entry in the market of the *acquired firm*. Yet because the *acquiring firm* is perceived by those firms in the target market as having the means and potential for entry, the mere presence of that firm "waiting in the wings" causes the firms already in the market to make pricing and output decisions more competitively, so as not to encourage the firm in the wings to enter. If such a firm merges with a firm already in the market, the "wings effect" upon pricing and output decisions will vanish.

(2) Evidence required [§351]

A prima facie case may be established from evidence demonstrating that:

(i) *The acquiring firm had the necessary means to enter the market;*

(ii) *The existing firms in the market were influenced by the potential entry* (this would generally require proof of a less-than-competitive market structure); and

(iii) *The number of potential entrants was not so many* that the elimination of the acquired firm would be insignificant.

[**FTC v. Procter & Gamble Co.**, *supra*]

Example: Where a large soap manufacturer acquired a liquid bleach manufacturer, the Supreme Court held that the soap company was a potential entrant into the liquid bleach business and that *the merger thus destroyed whatever restraining effect its presence at the edge of the market might have had* on those already in it. [**FTC v. Procter & Gamble Co.**, *supra*]

Compare: In 1982, the Second Circuit reversed a decision of the FTC and refused to invalidate a merger between an industrial corporation and a manufacturer of replacement auto shock absorbers on grounds that barriers to entry in the shock absorber market were so high that the acquiring firm could not have been perceived as a potential competitor. [**Tenneco, Inc. v. FTC**, *supra*, §349]

---

2. *Brown Shoe* Analysis [§352]

In **Brown Shoe Co. v. United States**, *supra*, §337, the Supreme Court considered the application of section 7 in horizontal merger cases. The two parties to the merger in that case competed as shoe retailers in a number of local geographic markets. Though such areas were only a fraction of all the geographic markets, the merger was held unlawful under section 7. The Court stressed congressional intent to prevent oligopolies and to protect viable, small, locally owned businesses—even if this resulted in higher costs and prices from the maintenance of fragmented industries and markets. The Court examined *market share evidence* together with *economic and historical factors* that indicated a *trend toward concentration*. The Court also stressed the *lack of any affirmative justification* for the *Brown* merger.

3. **"Presumptive Illegality" Test of** *Philadelphia National Bank* **[§353]**

In **United States v. Philadelphia National Bank,** *supra,* §329, the Court invalidated a merger of two banks. In its opinion, the Court tried to simplify the test for legality of horizontal mergers: "A merger which produces a firm *controlling an undue percentage share* of the relevant market, *and* results in a *significant increase in the concentration* of firms in that market, is so inherently likely to lessen competition substantially that it must be enjoined in the absence of evidence clearly showing that the merger is not likely to have such anticompetitive effects." Thus, the Court adopted a test of "presumptive illegality" that focuses upon market structure.

a. **"Undue percentage share of relevant market" [§354]**

In *Philadelphia National Bank,* the Court held that *30%* of the relevant market constituted an "undue percentage" share of the market. However, the Court took pains to note that no inference of *legality* should be drawn simply because a merger results in less than 30% control of the market.

(1) **"Relevant market"**

Since the legality of horizontal mergers turns in large part on market share, definition of the "relevant market" is a crucial first step (*see supra,* §329).

(2) **But note**

Market share is only *one factor* in determining the legality of a merger. This was graphically illustrated in **United States v. Aluminum Co. of America,** 377 U.S. 271 (1964), where the Supreme Court stressed that the acquisition of even a very small competitor by a dominant competitor in a concentrated industry may violate section 7. In that case, the acquired firm (Rome Cable) held only 1.3% of the aluminum conductor market, but it was an *aggressive, innovative firm* whose absorption by Alcoa would have affected competition far more than its 1.3% of the market might indicate.

b. **"Increased concentration in the relevant market" [§355]**

The Court also focused on increased concentration in *Philadelphia National Bank,* emphasizing that the purpose of section 7 is "to put a halt to the rising tide of concentration in American business." In *Philadelphia National Bank,* concentration was increased by 33%.

(1) **Comment**

The source of the concentration is not important. Concentration is to be avoided, whether it results primarily from past mergers or from the challenged merger. [**United States v. Pabst Brewing Co.,** *supra,* §330]

c. **Modern trend—totality of circumstances [§356]**

In spite of the Supreme Court's efforts to set standards for presumptive illegality, some modern lower court decisions and the DOJ/FTC Horizontal Merger Guidelines have opted for a more circumspect approach, stressing that market concentration and market share data alone are *not* dispositive, and that other evidence of the anticompetitive effects of a given merger is essential to a finding of illegality. [*See, e.g.,* **United States v. Baker Hughes Inc.**, 908 F.2d 981 (D.C. Cir. 1990); *and see infra,* §377]

EXAM TIP	gilbert

What this means on an exam is that the totality of the circumstances approach requires you to use a highly flexible, fact-intensive inquiry. Thus, remember to consider all relevant factors and ***do not simply focus on the market share percentage***, but use the percentage as an indicator of the direction your answer should take.

---

4. **When Will Illegality Be Presumed? [§357]**

A 30% market share and a 33% concentration were sufficient in *Philadelphia National Bank* to presume illegality. Considerably less has been required in other cases.

Example: In **United States v. Von's Grocery**, 384 U.S. 270 (1966), the Court enjoined a merger between two Los Angeles grocery chains merely because of a trend toward chain store ownership in the area, even though there were no barriers to entry into the market (*i.e.*, there were numerous other competing chains), and even though the combined market share of the two merged companies was only 7.5% of the local grocery market, in a market structure where the largest firm in the area had only 8%, and the four-firm concentration ratio changed from 24.4% to 28.6% as a result of the merger. However, the *Von's Grocery* case has been heavily criticized by commentators on the grounds that it ignored the intensely competitive nature of the market.

Example: *General Dynamics, supra,* §342, also indicates that a prima facie case can be made with concentration levels less than those demonstrated in *Philadelphia National Bank*. The Court indicated in *General Dynamics* that the government had made its prima facie case by demonstrating that the merger resulted in a firm with approximately 11% of the market and an increase in the two-firm concentration ratio from 45% to 48.6%.

5. **Defendant's Burden of Proof [§358]**

Once a prima facie case has been made (*i.e.*, market share/concentration ratios satisfy the *Philadelphia National Bank* criteria), the defendant must rebut the prima facie case or prove it is entitled to a recognized defense (*see supra,* §§336 *et seq.*).

Example: In *General Dynamics, supra,* the defendant successfully rebutted the government's statistical case by demonstrating that the figures were misleading and that because of structural changes in the industry, the merger did not substantially lessen competition.

a. **Note**

Justifications or special defenses must be proven by the defendant. [**Citizen Publishing Co. v. United States**, *supra,* §239]

6. Effects of Guidelines [§359]

Horizontal Merger Guidelines adopted in 1992 by the DOJ and the FTC (*see infra*, §§372 *et seq.*) depart somewhat from the approach taken by the Supreme Court: (i) the Guidelines *measure market concentration differently* from the Supreme Court; and (ii) the Guidelines *require evidence of anticompetitive effects,* in addition to market share/concentration data, to establish illegality (as discussed *supra*, §355). The net effect of these positions may be a decrease in government prosecutions of illegal mergers, for the government's standards for illegality as expressed in the Guidelines are generally more stringent (*i.e.*, more presumptive of *legality*) than those employed by the Supreme Court.

D. Vertical Mergers

1. In General [§360]

"Vertical mergers" are those between companies standing in a supplier-customer relationship (*e.g.*, auto manufacturer merges with producer of transmissions used in its cars). A manufacturer's acquisition of its distributor represents a vertical merger. Vertical mergers have been attacked under merger law because they have the potential of foreclosing or squeezing unintegrated competitors, increasing entry barriers, and limiting future competition.

2. Application of Section 7 [§361]

In determining the legality of vertical mergers under section 7, courts focus on the following factors:

(i) *First, the relevant geographic and product markets* are determined.

(ii) *Next, the probable effect* of the merger is considered by measuring the *share of the market* that may be foreclosed.

(iii) *If a significant share of the market is foreclosed or potential competition is eliminated*, the court must then consider any *economic and historical factors* peculiar to the case, including any *trend toward concentration* in the industry, *barriers to new entry* created by the merger, and the *nature* and *purpose* of the merger.

> **Example:** *Brown Shoe* (*supra*, §352) illustrates the test applied. The Court there invalidated the vertical portion of a merger in which the acquiring firm manufactured only about 4% of the shoes in the country, and the acquired firm had only about 1.6% of the retail shoe sales. The Court felt that the anticompetitive effects of the merger would be "more than de minimis." Accordingly, the Court examined the economic and historical factors involved and invalidated the merger, stressing Brown Shoe's *history* of expansion by merger into the retail market, the *trend toward concentration* and vertical integration in the industry, and the *lack of any persuasive justification* for the acquisition.

Determine **relevant geographic and product markets**.

Determine **probable effect of merger** by measurement of market share.

If a significant share of the market is foreclosed, or competition is eliminated, consider **economic and historical facts**, including:

- Industry trend toward concentration

- Barriers to new entry

- Nature of merger

- Purpose of merger

> **e.g.** **Example:** The same reasoning applies where a large *buyer* attempts to capture its *seller* or supplier. Thus, in **Ford Motor Co. v. United States**, 405 U.S. 562 (1972), the acquisition by a major auto manufacturer of a large spark plug and battery maker was held a violation of section 7, on the ground that it would *foreclose* other companies *from selling* spark plugs and batteries to the auto manufacturer (a foreclosure of 15%). Divestiture was required.

a. Recent trends [§362]

More recently, courts have shied away from the "de minimis foreclosure" test applied in *Brown Shoe*. Modern courts tend to apply a rule of reason type analysis to vertical mergers, asking whether the merger will have *significant anticompetitive effects* in either the upstream or the downstream market.

b. Defenses [§363]

For reasons analogous to those discussed in the previous chapter (*see supra*, §287), vertical mergers between a manufacturer and its distributors may produce significant efficiency gains. For that reason, courts may be more receptive to efficiency defenses in the vertical context than in horizontal cases.

E. Conglomerate Mergers

1. Introduction [§364]

Conglomerate mergers include all types of mergers that are *not classified as horizontal or vertical mergers*. When relevant market definitions are too narrow to classify a merger as horizontal, the merger may be analyzed under conglomerate merger doctrine as a "product or market extension" merger.

2. Reasons for Concern [§365]

To be sure, conglomerate mergers increase wealth and corporate power in the hands of fewer and fewer firms, but section 7 is concerned with the "lessening of competition." Unless some such anticompetitive effect is possible, the merger cannot be illegal under section 7. There are some circumstances, however, in which a merger between firms not in a vertical or horizontal relationship may adversely affect competition. [**FTC v. Consolidated Foods Corp.**, 380 U.S. 592 (1965)]

a. Merger may lessen or eliminate potential competition [§366]

There are two ways in which a merger may lessen potential competition in a relevant market:

(1) *The merger may eliminate a perceived potential entrant*; or

(2) *The merger may eliminate an actual potential entrant.*

Determine the **relevant geographic and product markets.**

Examine whether there are any anticompetitive **effects** such as

- A **lessening or elimination of potential competition**

- **Increased barriers to entry** or an **opportunity for anticompetitive practices**

- **Increased potential for anticompetitive reciprocity**

b. **Merger may make powerful firms even more powerful [§367]**
This "unfair advantage" may occur because the merger:

(1) *Increases barriers to entry* into a particular industry; or

(2) *Increases the opportunity for anticompetitive practices*, such as prediction or practices leading to price rigidity.

c. **Merger may increase the potential for anticompetitive reciprocity**

(1) **Nature of "reciprocity" [§368]**
Suppose a trucking firm buys substantial quantities of boxes to use in packing goods for shipment. It might say to a box company, "We will buy boxes from you *only if* you ship all of your own deliveries on our truck line." An agreement that expressly conditioned the trucking firm's purchase of boxes on the box company's exclusive use of their trucking service might be a restraint of trade violating Sherman Act section 1, if the competitors of both companies were foreclosed thereby.

(2) **Potential reciprocity as a result of conglomerate merger [§369]**
Suppose instead that a large auto manufacturer that purchases huge quantities of office stationery acquires a paper mill that sells paper to stationery manufacturers. Thereafter, the auto manufacturer might condition its purchases of stationery from a stationery company on that stationery company's agreement to purchase all of its raw paper from the paper mill, the auto manufacturer's new subsidiary. In the case of one proposed merger involving such "potential reciprocity," the Supreme Court held that the reciprocity was "one of the congeries of anticompetitive practices at which the antitrust laws are aimed," because it would introduce "an *irrelevant and alien factor into the choice* among competing products" (*i.e.*, by the stationery firm, in the foregoing example). [**FTC v. Consolidated Foods Corp.**, 380 U.S. 592 (1965)]

(a) **Criticism**
Some authorities argue that potential reciprocity in trading should *not* render a merger illegal because the two trading partners would not agree to trade unless each benefited. Note, however, that this criticism does not change the fact that *competitors* of the trading partners would be foreclosed.

F. Joint Ventures

1. **In General [§370]**
A joint venture exists when two independent entities combine their resources in

order to create a new product, manufacturing system, distribution network, etc. In **United States v. Penn-Olin Chemical Co.**, *supra*, §349, the Supreme Court held that joint ventures were subject to the same analysis under section 7 as more conventional mergers. The Court recognized that the joint venture eliminates potential competition. (*See supra*, §351.) Joint ventures are also treated under section 1 of the Sherman Act (*see supra*, §240).

2. Reasons for Concern [§371]

Joint ventures can create efficiencies but when entered into between actual or potential competitors, joint ventures create anticompetitive risks. The agreements at issue in **Broadcast Music, Inc. v. CBS**, *supra*, §208, and **NCAA v. Board of Regents**, *supra*, §147, may be considered types of joint ventures. The joint venture in *BMI* was upheld because it created a new product (the blanket license) and, therefore, was seen as efficient and procompetitive. While the overall joint venture in *NCAA* created the product of college football and was seen as procompetitive, the specific provision limiting the number of televised games unreasonably restrained trade and was held to violate section 1 of the Sherman Act.

e.g. Example: The Chicago Bulls basketball team challenged the National Basketball Association's ("NBA") restrictions on the team's right to sell its games to the "superstation" WGN, a Chicago television station broadcasting nationally over a myriad of cable systems. Because, as the court found, the NBA is a joint venture and not a single entity, its efforts to block the sale of games by the Bulls to WGN constituted a violation of section 1 of the Sherman Act. The court likened the NBA's actions to those of a cartel, attempting to curtail output without adequate competitive justification. [**Chicago Professional Sports Limited Partnership v. National Basketball Association**, 961 F.2d 667 (7th Cir.), *cert. denied*, 506 U.S. 954 (1992)]

G. Department of Justice/Federal Trade Commission Merger Guidelines

1. History of the Guidelines [§372]

The Justice Department first issued Merger Guidelines in 1968. The Guidelines were revised in 1984 and again in 1992, although the 1992 revisions relate only to horizontal mergers. The 1992 Guidelines were issued jointly by the Department of Justice and the Federal Trade Commission.

2. Significance of Merger Guidelines [§373]

The Merger Guidelines do not change substantive law and are not binding on the courts or the FTC. [**Olin Corp. v. FTC**, 986 F.2d 1295 (9th Cir. 1993)] However, the FTC has expressly adopted the Horizontal Merger Guidelines, and its enforcement policies relative to vertical and conglomerate mergers closely track those of the Justice Department. Moreover, the Merger Guidelines have more practical significance than the Vertical Nonprice Restraint Guidelines because private parties' abilities to challenge mergers are extremely limited. Few private parties have standing to sue to prevent or dissolve a merger, and at the time a merger is consummated, there are usually no damages to collect. Consequently, the government's role in preventing and unwinding anticompetitive mergers is far more significant than that of private parties.

a. Private enforcement—*Cargill* [§374]

The Supreme Court's decision in **Cargill, Inc. v. Monfort of Colorado, Inc.,** *supra*, §335, probably increased somewhat the barriers to private enforcement of section 7 of the Clayton Act, when it held that losses or injuries from increased competition as a result of a merger could not form the basis for relief.

(1) But note

If successful in challenging mergers under section 7, private parties are entitled to divestiture (among other remedies). [**California v. American Stores Co.**, *supra*, §95]

3. Horizontal Merger Guidelines [§375]

Like the courts, the DOJ and the FTC focus on market shares and market concentrations in evaluating horizontal mergers. But the Guidelines do not stop there. Rather, they indicate a number of other factors to be taken into account, and they imply that the burden is on the government to prove the anticompetitive effect of a merger by demonstrating both an objectionable market structure and independent evidence of a negative impact on competition. The Guidelines consider whether a merger will allow the merged firm to unilaterally behave in an anticompetitive manner and whether the post-merger marketplace will be more susceptible to anticompetitive concerted action.

a. Defining the relevant market [§376]

Although they employ an approach that is somewhat different from that used by the courts, the Guidelines still focus on the interchangeability of various products in defining relevant product and geographic markets. (*See supra*, §328, discussing the Guidelines' "hypothetical monopolist" test.)

b. Measuring market concentration [§377]

Most courts determine market concentration by calculating the Herfindahl-Hirschman Index ("HHI"). The HHI of a given market is computed by adding the *squares* of the market shares of every firm in the market. (Thus, if a market consists of five firms having respective market shares of 40%, 25%, 15%, 12%, and 8%, its HHI is $(40 \times 40)+(25 \times 25)+(15 \times 15)+(12 \times 12)+(8 \times 8)=2658$.) Whether the government will challenge a merger depends at least in part on the post-merger HHI. The Guidelines also consider the amount of increase in the HHI pre-merger and post-merger.

(1) *If the post-merger HHI is less than 1000*, under the 1992 Guidelines, the government is unlikely to challenge the merger.

(2) *If the post-merger HHI is between 1000 and 1800*, the government is unlikely to challenge a merger that produces an increase in the HHI of 100 points or less. If the increase exceeds 100 points, the government will take into account a variety of related factors (*see* below) in deciding whether to challenge.

(3) *The government is more likely to challenge mergers that produce a post-merger HHI in excess of 1800 and an increase in HHI in excess of 100 points*, although related factors can overcome even this presumption. If the post-merger HHI is greater than 1800, but the merger adds only 50 - 100 points, the government may challenge, depending on the related factors. If the merger adds less than 50 points to the HHI, the government is unlikely to challenge the merger.

c. **Additional factors in evaluating mergers [§378]**
As noted, the government routinely takes account of factors other than market concentration in deciding whether to assail a particular merger. These include:

(1) *Ease of entry into the relevant market,* on the theory that firms in the market are less likely to extract monopoly profits successfully if potential competitors can enter the market and compete with relative ease;

(2) *Adequacy of irreplaceable raw materials* (*e.g.*, when a firm in a mining industry appears to have a sizeable market share when in fact it has substantially depleted its reserve [*See, e.g.*, **United States v. General Dynamics**, *supra*, §358]);

(3) *Excess capacity of firms in the market*;

(4) *Trends toward increased concentration*; and

(5) *Particular efficiencies created by the merger,* such as economies of scale, integration and specialization of operations, and lowering of aggregate costs. In 1997, the 1992 Merger Guidelines were amended to provide for a more meaningful efficiency defense, including whether the proposed merger can *increase overall competition* by allowing the merged firm *to lower cost, improve quality, enhance service, or create new products.*

4. **Vertical Merger Guidelines [§379]**
Last issued in 1984, the Vertical Merger Guidelines focus principally on three dangers of vertical mergers: *barriers to entry, danger of collusion,* and *opportunities to avoid rate regulation.*

a. Barriers to entry [§380]

The Justice Department indicates that it will challenge a vertical merger if:

(1) *The market is already so vertically integrated* that new entrants would be forced to enter *two markets* (*e.g.*, production *and* distribution) to compete effectively;

(2) *Forcing potential competitors to enter two levels* rather than one *increases the costs of entry*; and

(3) *The subject market is not competitive.* The DOJ bases its determination of competitiveness on the HHI, and will not challenge a merger unless it affects at least one market with an HHI of 1800 or more.

b. Collusion [§381]

The DOJ is more likely to challenge a merger in a concentrated market (HHI of 1800 or more) if the merger increases the danger of collusion. The HHI should not change as a result of the merger because if the merger is truly vertical, the firms were not competing in the same market, and a merger therefore will not increase market concentration.

c. Avoidance of rate regulations [§382]

The DOJ will challenge a merger that provides "substantial opportunities" for firms to cheat on or avoid rate regulations.

d. Vertical Merger Guidelines in practice [§383]

The Guidelines provide merging firms with substantially more room to maneuver than the case law does. The FTC, however, has not adopted the Guidelines, and continues to challenge vertical integration in limited circumstances.

5. Conglomerate Merger Guidelines [§384]

Although the Guidelines (reissued in 1984) track the case law on conglomerate mergers by threatening to challenge mergers that eliminate actual potential entrants or perceived potential entrants, the DOJ does not commonly attack conglomerate mergers. As with vertical mergers, the Guidelines stress market concentration (HHI over 1800) and the existence or nonexistence of barriers to entry as major factors in the decision to challenge or not challenge a particular union.

H. Pre-Merger Notification

1. In General [§385]

Under the Hart-Scott-Rodino Antitrust Improvements Act of 1976, certain merging firms are required to *notify* the DOJ in advance of consummation of their transaction and to *wait* a period of time before closing (30 days for most deals; 15 days for mergers by tender offer), to allow the government to evaluate the transaction and its effects upon competition.

2. Applicable Mergers [§386]

The statute applies only to mergers that satisfy one of two tests: As a result of the acquisition, the acquiring firm would hold an aggregate total amount of the voting securities and assets of the acquired person either:

(i) In excess of $200 million; *or*

(ii) Between $50 million and $200 million *if* one of the following three tests is satisfied:

    i. The acquiring party has total assets or annual net sales of $100 million and is acquiring voting securities or assets of a person engaged in manufacturing that has annual net sales or total assets of $10 million;

    ii. The acquiring party has total assets or annual net sales of $100 million and is acquiring voting securities or assets of a person not engaged in manufacturing that has total assets of $10 million; *or*

    iii. The acquiring party has total assets or annual net sales of $10 million and is acquiring voting securities or assets of a person with annual net sales or total assets of $100 million or more.

Chapter Seven: Price Discrimination— The Robinson-Patman Act

CONTENTS

Chapter Approach

Chapter Approach

Broadly speaking, the Robinson-Patman Act prevents discrimination in the price charged competing purchasers, unless there is justification for the price differential. However, firms may wish to sell the same product to different customers at different prices for a number of reasons. The antitrust laws do not concern themselves with these situations unless the *price discrimination harms competition*.

When analyzing a claim of price discrimination, be sure that the following can be shown: A firm *sold* the *same product* (*not a service or mixed sale*) to different purchasers *at different prices*, and *competition in a relevant market was harmed* thereby. Keep in mind that the injury sustained may be in the market occupied by the discriminating firm, or in the market occupied by that firm's customers, or in the market occupied by the customers' customers. Then consider whether any *defenses* apply. Even harmful price discrimination may be justified by cost-based factors, by changing market conditions, or by the need of the discriminating firm to meet competition in a particular submarket.

A. Economic Analysis of Price Discrimination

1. Necessary Conditions for Price Discrimination

a. Market power [§387]
Generally, only a firm with some power over price has the ability to engage in price discrimination. In competitive markets with homogeneous products, no firm has the power to price discriminate. Only in markets with a few sellers or *differentiated products* can firms charge different prices to different buyers for the same product.

b. Differences in elasticity of demand [§388]
A seller with market power can price discriminate by charging a higher price to those customers with inelastic demand for the product, while offering a lower price to buyers with more elastic demand. Differences in elasticity of demand usually reflect different incomes and the availability of close substitutes.

c. Ability to identify and separate buyers by elasticity of demand [§389]
Only if buyers can be separated easily (by geography, by age, by income) and prevented from reselling can price discrimination succeed. Unless buyers are

separated or prevented from *reselling*, an arbitrageur could buy at the lower price and resell at the higher price. Thus, price discrimination is much easier with services than goods, since it is difficult to resell a service. (The Robinson-Patman Act does not apply to services. *See infra*, §406.)

2. Seller's Incentive to Discriminate in Price [§390]

If the necessary conditions are present, a seller can increase its total revenues, and hence its profit, by charging higher prices to those customers who are willing to pay more for the product. There are usually some costs of practicing price discrimination (*i.e.*, the cost of identifying and separating buyers), which partially offset these higher profits.

3. "Price Discrimination" Defined [§391]

In economic terms, price discrimination occurs when identical or similar products are sold at prices that have different ratios to the marginal cost of producing the products. If two items have the same marginal cost, then different prices are, *ipso facto*, *discriminatory*. On the other hand, if two items have different marginal costs, identical prices would be *evidence* of price discrimination.

4. Effects of Price Discrimination

a. Positive effects [§392]

Price discrimination can potentially have at least three positive economic effects:

(1) *It may provide an incentive* for a seller to increase output. Remember that a firm with market power has an incentive to restrict output because it has a downward sloping marginal revenue curve. By price discriminating, the firm can increase sales by offering additional units of output by lowering its price to some—but not all—of its customers.

(2) *Price discrimination may allow a firm to cover total costs* and thus enable it to offer a *new product* which it could otherwise not do. Consider a prospective law journal with costs and demand such that at the profit-maximizing *single* price, the publisher would lose money. By charging one price to libraries and a lower price to law students and faculty, the firm is able to earn a profit.

(3) *In oligopolistic markets*, there is some evidence that firms are *more likely to compete in terms of price* if they are able to price discriminate. Such a price reduction—even if only to some customers—may provoke more competition in the industry than would otherwise exist.

b. Negative effects [§393]

Price discrimination is also likely to have adverse economic effects of three main types:

(1) *While price discrimination may allow firms to just cover costs*, it may also *enable a firm to earn excess profits*. In that event, it is very difficult to weigh the efficiency gains (from expanded output) against the equity losses (from the transfer of income from consumers to the producer).

(2) *Price discrimination can be used as a predatory pricing practice* to harm competitors in a particular market. A multi-region (or multi-product) firm can eliminate a small, single-region (or single-product) firm by charging a low price (below average cost) in that region, while charging a higher price elsewhere to cover the loss. The small firm that is driven from the market is said to suffer *primary line injury*.

(3) *Price discrimination may injure competitors who are forced to pay a higher price* than the buyer(s) who receives "preferential treatment," *i.e.*, a lower price. In particular, it is thought that large buyers (*i.e.*, chain stores) could use their monopsonistic power to force lower prices from their suppliers, thereby harming smaller buyers (*i.e.*, single retail outlets). Of course, if price differences reflect differences in the cost of supply (*i.e.*, large volume shipments), lower prices are not discriminatory. The firm that is at a competitive disadvantage because its competitor is receiving preferential treatment is said to suffer *secondary line injury*. (That firm's customers are said to suffer *tertiary line injury* if they compete with the customers of the buyer who received preferential treatment.)

CONSEQUENCES OF PRICE DISCRIMINATION	gilbert
POSITIVE EFFECTS	**NEGATIVE EFFECTS**
Provides an incentive to *increase seller output* and increase sales	Potential to harm smaller buyers *forced to pay a higher price*, injuring competition
Allows firms to *cover costs* and therefore enables *new product development*	May not just enable firms to cover costs, but also to *earn excess profits*
May encourage firms to *compete in terms of price* in an oligopolistic market	Can be used as a *predatory practice* to harm competitors and eliminate small firms

5. Purposes of Robinson-Patman Act [§394]

The Act is intended to protect small, independent businesses from injury caused by discriminatory pricing. Section 2 of the Clayton Act (the original legislation) was aimed at preventing primary line injury caused by geographic price discrimination by sellers. The Robinson-Patman amendments were enacted to ensure that sellers would not treat small businesses differently from larger scale businesses at the same competitive level. The "chain store bill" thus sought to eliminate the ability of large businesses or chains to use their mass purchasing scale to extract favorable, discriminatory treatment from sellers.

B. Elements of a Prima Facie Robinson-Patman Violation

1. In General [§395]

Under section 2(a) of the Clayton Act (the Robinson-Patman Act), it is unlawful for any person:

(i) *Engaged in commerce*

(ii) *To discriminate in price between different purchasers*

(iii) *Of commodities of like grade and quality,*

(iv) *Where the effect may be to substantially lessen competition* in any line of commerce, or tend to create a monopoly, or

(v) *To injure, destroy, or prevent competition* with any person who either grants *or* knowingly receives the benefits of such discrimination, *or* with the customers of either of them.

Both the *seller* who *offers* and the preferred *buyer* who *knowingly receives* discriminatory prices are guilty of violating the Act. [**FTC v. Fred Meyer, Inc.**, 390 U.S. 341 (1968)]

2. "Engaged in Commerce" [§396]

This "jurisdictional" element requires that "at least one of the two transactions which, when compared, generate a discrimination . . . cross a state line." [**Gulf Oil Corp. v. Copp Paving Co.**, *supra*, §78] The Supreme Court has thus construed the Act's jurisdictional requirements strictly, rejecting the broader "affecting commerce" test applied to the Sherman Act.

3. "Discriminate in Price Between Different Purchasers"

a. "Purchase" required [§397]

The "discrimination" must be in connection with a "purchase," *i.e.*, a sales transaction. Leases and consignments are *not* covered by section 2(a). There must be *at least two purchases.* [**Terry's Floor Fashions, Inc. v. Burlington Industries, Inc.**, 763 F.2d 604 (4th Cir. 1985)]

b. Contemporaneous sales required [§398]

The sales at different prices must be *fairly contemporaneous*—as determined

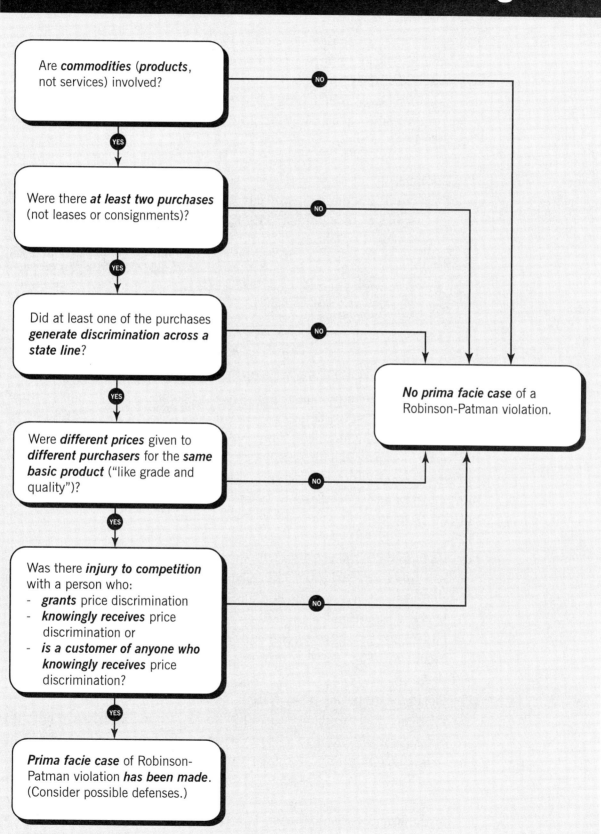

Are **commodities** (**products**, not services) involved?

NO → No prima facie case

YES ↓

Were there **at least two purchases** (not leases or consignments)?

NO → No prima facie case

YES ↓

Did at least one of the purchases **generate discrimination across a state line**?

NO → No prima facie case

YES ↓

Were **different prices** given to **different purchasers** for the **same basic product** ("like grade and quality")?

NO → No prima facie case

YES ↓

Was there **injury to competition** with a person who:
- **grants** price discrimination
- **knowingly receives** price discrimination or
- **is a customer of anyone who knowingly receives** price discrimination?

NO → No prima facie case

YES ↓

Prima facie case of Robinson-Patman violation **has been made**. (Consider possible defenses.)

No prima facie case of a Robinson-Patman violation.

by market conditions. [**Atlanta Trading Corp. v. FTC**, 258 F.2d 365 (2d Cir. 1958); **Dairyland Power Cooperative v. AMAX, Inc.**, 700 F. Supp. 979 (W.D. Wis. 1986)]

c. Indirect price discrimination covered [§399]

The Act also prohibits indirect price discrimination that results from *discriminatory terms other than price*, such as preferential credit terms. Moreover, price discrimination has been found where *quantity discounts* were theoretically open to all but, as a practical matter, were closed to small buyers. [**FTC v. Morton Salt Co.**, 334 U.S. 37 (1948)]

(1) But note

If a quantity discount is justified by cost *differences in shipping* the goods, it is not illegal. (*See infra*, §§419-422.)

EXAM TIP   **gilbert**

On an exam, don't just look for a difference in prices charged. Remember to check for *indirect price discrimination*. Although different prices for different buyers is the most obvious way to violate Robinson-Patman, *preferential credit terms*, *special discounts*, and *freight charges* (see *below*) may violate the Act.

---

d. Freight charges and price discrimination covered [§400]

The Robinson-Patman Act also applies to a difference in the "mill net return" (*i.e.*, *profit* differential) as a result of similar sales. There is no price discrimination where a manufacturer sells "f.o.b. mill" or otherwise forces the buyer to pay the freight or delivery charges, provided that the price at the seller's location is uniform and available to all buyers on a nondiscriminatory basis. *However*, "price discrimination" may occur where the price charged includes delivery, or is computed with reference to some freight "basing point."

(1) Uniform delivered price [§401]

A manufacturer who sells goods at a uniform delivered price (which includes transportation) may be guilty of discriminating in price against those buyers closest to his plant. His costs of delivery are much less as to such purchasers, so he is in effect forcing them to pay "phantom freight." [**Corn Products v. FTC**, 324 U.S. 726 (1945)]

(2) Single freight basing point system [§402]

Likewise, if all merchandise is sold "f.o.b. Chicago" (the base point), this may operate discriminatively *if* the commodities are actually shipped *from some other point* (*e.g.*, Kansas City). In such a case, the purchasers in or near Kansas City are paying "phantom freight" from Chicago. On facts such as these, the Supreme Court condemned the price scheme as violative of the Robinson-Patman Act. [*See* **Corn Products v. FTC**, *supra*; **FTC v. Cement Institute**, *supra*, §257—cement manufacturers quoted identical prices at any given point in United States, so that a buyer who was closer to the source of supply could not obtain cement at a lower price]

(3) Zone pricing system [§403]

The result may be the same even with a "zone pricing system"—*e.g.*, all buyers within 100 miles of Chicago pay one price—where a buyer in Town X (98 miles from Chicago) is actually supplied from a seller in that same town and otherwise could have purchased for much less because no freight would be involved.

(4) Note—Sherman Act [§404]

Delivered pricing schemes may also be attacked under the Sherman Act if they are part of price fixing conspiracies. [*See, e.g.*, **Sugar Institute, Inc. v. United States**, 297 U.S. 553 (1936)]

e. Wholesaler-retailer distinction considered [§405]

Although "wholesalers" and "retailers" may appear to be at different levels of distribution, a seller may violate the Robinson-Patman Act by selling at different prices to the two groups in cases where, as a practical matter, the two groups compete. [**Texaco, Inc. v. Hasbrouck**, 496 U.S. 543 (1990)]

Example: "Functional discounts," purportedly related to the performance of certain additional distributional functions by the wholesaler to a supplier, have been found to violate the Robinson-Patman Act if, in fact, they do not compensate wholesalers for actual services rendered. They also violate the Act when the receiving "wholesaler" is actually owned or controlled by retailers who compete with retailers that do not receive a discount. [**Texaco, Inc. v. Hasbrouck**, *supra*]

(1) Note

In such circumstances, the members of the wholesale buying group have been called "indirect purchasers" or, in some cases, have been deemed "actual purchasers."

4. "Commodities of Like Grade and Quality"

a. "Commodities" [§406]

The requirement of "commodities" means *tangible articles* and *excludes services and intangibles* from coverage under the Robinson-Patman Act. [**Tri-State Broadcasting v. UPI**, 369 F.2d 268 (5th Cir. 1966)]

(1) Mixed sales [§407]

Mixed sales, such as *construction contracts,* are likewise not covered—although there may be price discrimination as to building materials supplied under the contract. [**Ideal Plumbing Co. v. Benco, Inc.**, 529 F.2d 972 (8th Cir. 1976)]

This is worth remembering: Mixed sales often include sale of **goods or other tangible articles** along with services; so be sure to consider whether there is illegal price discrimination as to the goods.

(2) Lawful price discrimination [§408]

As stated, intangibles are not covered by Robinson-Patman, and thus price discrimination in sales is not unlawful. Examples of such intangibles include:

(a) *Mutual fund shares* [**Baum v. Investors Diversified Services**, 409 F.2d 872 (7th Cir. 1969)];

(b) *Patent licenses* [**LaSalle Street Press v. McCormick & Henderson, Inc.**, 293 F. Supp. 1004 (N.D. Ill. 1968), *modified*, 445 F.2d 84 (7th Cir. 1971)];

(c) *Real estate leases* [**Export Liquor Sales v. Ammex Warehouse**, 426 F.2d 251 (6th Cir. 1970), *cert. denied*, 400 U.S. 1000 (1971)];

(d) *Cellular telephone service and systems* [**Metro Communications Co. v. Ameritech Mobile Communications, Inc.**, 984 F.2d 739 (7th Cir. 1993)]; and

(e) *Printing of comic books* [**First Comics, Inc. v. World Color Press, Inc.**, 884 F.2d 1033 (7th Cir. 1989), *cert. denied*, 493 U.S. 1075 (1990)].

(3) Other antitrust laws [§409]

Price discrimination in services and intangibles may still violate the *Sherman Act* if it constitutes a *restraint of trade or an attempt to monopolize.* [*See, e.g.,* **Brooke Group Ltd. v. Brown & Williamson Tobacco Corp.**, *supra*, §175] Or, it may constitute an *unfair method of competition* within the meaning of section 5 of the *FTC Act.*

b. "Like grade or quality" [§410]

Generally, if two products have physical differences that affect their acceptability to buyers, the products are not of "like grade or quality."

(1) But note

Mere differences in the brand name or label under which the product is sold are *not* sufficient to justify price discrimination. [**FTC v. Borden**, 383 U.S. 637 (1966); **Hartley & Parker, Inc. v. Florida Beverage Corp.**, 307 F.2d 916 (5th Cir. 1952)—"Four Roses under any other name would still swill the same."]

5. **"Injure Competition with Any Person Who Grants Such Discrimination" [§411]**
The Act permits recovery for three different kinds of injury. The language here quoted aims at *primary line* injury. Generally, what must be shown is a *substantial and sustained drop in price* in a local area by a large competitor, with the *intent or known effect* of destroying, injuring, or "disciplining" a smaller-scale rival. [**Indian Coffee Corp. v. Procter & Gamble Co.**, 752 F.2d 891 (3d Cir.), *cert. denied*, 474 U.S. 863 (1985)]

> **Example:** Predatory price cuts *below cost* in a local area is an example of such injury. [**Moore v. Mead's Fine Bread Co.**, 348 U.S. 115 (1954); **Utah Pie Co. v. Continental Baking Co.**, 386 U.S. 685 (1967)]

a. **But note—must injure competition [§412]**
Below-cost predatory pricing is not illegal if it does not harm *competition*, even if it does harm one of the competitors in the relevant market. [**Brooke Group Ltd. v. Brown & Williamson Tobacco Corp.**, *supra*]

> **Example:** In *Brooke Group*, two cigarette manufacturers engaged in a fierce price war over generic cigarettes, ending, according to the plaintiff, with the defendant selling its generic cigarettes at a loss. The Supreme Court upheld lower court rulings granting the defendant judgment as a matter of law, because the predatory pricing, even if successful in damaging the *plaintiff*, could not have harmed *competition in the relevant market*. The Court determined that the defendant could never have ascended to a market position in which it could have set prices high enough to *recoup* its losses sustained in the predatory pricing scheme. Therefore, the defendant could not have harmed competition, and therefore was not in violation of the law.

b. **Requirements for predatory pricing claim [§413]**
Because primary line price discrimination cases are frequently based on claims of predatory pricing, the standards for proving a predatory pricing claim under the Sherman Act are relevant here, including proof of pricing below a relevant measure of cost. [**William Inglis & Sons Baking Co. v. Continental Baking Co.**, 942 F.2d 1332 (9th Cir. 1991)—primary line price discrimination claim failed because plaintiff could not prove that defendant's prices fell below cost, properly measured; *see supra*, §§174-176, *and see infra*, §§419-422—discussing appropriate measures of cost]

6. **"Injure Competition with Any Person Who Knowingly Receives Price Discrimination" [§414]**
This language aims at *secondary line* injury, which accounts for the majority of Robinson-Patman Act cases. Very little beyond a difference in price is required to establish such injury. Competitive injury may be *inferred* from the discrimination itself. [**Texaco, Inc. v. Hasbrouck**, *supra*, §405; *and see* **Standard Motor Products,**

Inc. v. FTC, 265 F.2d 674 (2d Cir. 1959)]—injury has been inferred from price differences to competitors with low profit margins operating under highly competitive conditions] However, this inference may be *rebutted* by the defendant. [**Texaco, Inc. v. Hasbrouck,** *supra*]

Example: A vendor who sells at a lower price to a wholesaler than to a retailer is guilty of price discrimination if the wholesaler passes the lower price on to controlled retail subsidiaries; *i.e.,* price discrimination charges *cannot* be avoided simply by incorporating a captive subsidiary. [**Perkins v. Standard Oil Co.,** 395 U.S. 642 (1969)—Standard Oil sold to plaintiff at a higher price than it charged Signal Oil, a wholesaler; Signal passed its lower price on to oil dealers in competition with plaintiff]

---

a. **Temporary discrimination [§415]**

However, *no injury* will be found or presumed if the discrimination is only *temporary,* so that any injury is insubstantial. [**American Oil Co. v. FTC,** 325 F.2d 101 (7th Cir. 1963)—gas company lowered wholesale price to one station during 17-day price war; rival station 15 miles away alleged injury because it did not receive a similar concession]

b. **Other sources available [§416]**

Also, there is *no injury* where it appears that the "nonfavored" buyer *could have purchased the goods from another source at the same price* charged by the discriminating seller to the "favored buyer." [**Tri-Valley Packing Association v. FTC,** 329 F.2d 694 (9th Cir. 1964); **Caribe BMW, Inc. v. Bayerische Motoren Werke Aktiengesellschaft,** 821 F. Supp. 802 (D.P.R. 1993)]

7. **"Injure Competition with Customers of Any Person Who Knowingly Receives Price Discrimination" [§417]**

The Act also aims at *tertiary line injury,* which may be suffered by a customer of a buyer who was discriminated against, when that customer must then compete with customers of buyers who received favorable treatment from a seller. The standards for tertiary line price discrimination are similar to those in secondary line cases.

C. Defenses to a Prima Facie Violation of Robinson-Patman Act

1. **Effect of Discrimination Is De Minimis [§418]**

In addition to asserting affirmative defenses, it may be possible to rebut a prima facie violation by demonstrating that the effect of the seller's price discrimination upon each buyer's business operation is *de minimis.* [**Minneapolis-Honeywell Regulator Co. v. FTC,** 191 F.2d 786 (7th Cir. 1951), *app. dismissed,* 344 U.S. 206 (1952)—refusing

TYPES OF INJURY TO COMPETITION UNDER ROBINSON-PATMAN ACT

gilbert

TYPE OF INJURY	DEFINITION	STANDARD
PRIMARY LINE	Injury to competitor of person who **grants** price discrimination	Must be **substantial and sustained drop** in price in local area by large competitor; Must be **intent or knowledge of effect** of injuring smaller-scale rival; and Must **harm competition**.
SECONDARY LINE	Injury to competitor of person who **knowingly receives** price discrimination	**Difference in price** usually enough to infer injury to competition; but **May be rebutted** by defendant.
TERTIARY LINE	Injury to competitor of **customer** of person who knowingly receives price discrimination	**Basically the same as with secondary line**

to find Robinson-Patman Act violation because the effect of discriminatory prices charged to different purchasers for temperature control units was trivial on the resale price charged by those purchasers for oil burners that incorporated the controls]

2. Cost Differential [§419]

Section 2(a) expressly provides that "nothing herein contained shall prevent differentials which make only *due allowance* for differences in the cost of manufacture, sale, or delivery resulting from the differing methods or quantities in which such commodities are sold or delivered."

a. Effect [§420]

Proving a cost justification establishes an *absolute defense* to a prima facie violation of the Robinson-Patman Act.

(1) But note

This defense is difficult to rely upon in practice, because of the expense involved in compiling the necessary evidence and because of the FTC's restrictive interpretation of the defense. To be valid, quantity discounts must be documented by *actual* cost savings due to the quantity sold, not merely by a generalized assertion that larger deliveries are more economical.

EXAM TIP   **gilbert**

If a valid cost justification defense is rare in practice, it will not likely be a correct answer on an exam. Be cautious in deciding that this defense is applicable and be sure that *actual cost savings* do exist.

---

b. Limitation [§421]

Even if quantity discounts *are* sufficiently supported by cost savings to the seller, where the number of buyers who qualify for the discount is so few that allowing the discount would be unjust or would promote a monopoly, the FTC is empowered to fix and establish quantity limits on purchases. [Section 2(a); *and see* **FTC v. Morton Salt Co.**, *supra*, §399—largest quantity discount, although theoretically available to all, was really limited to five large grocery chains and enabled them to sell at retail below the price of competitive stores who purchased salt from independent wholesalers]

c. Computing "cost differential" [§422]

A seller may *classify* customers into *reasonable categories* based on the average costs of selling to the customers in each group, and then charge all customers in each group an appropriate price. The reasonableness of the category depends on the *homogeneity of the group*. The groups must be composed of "members of such self-sameness as to make the averaging of costs of dealing with the group a valid and reasonable indicium of the cost of dealing with any specific group member." [**United States v. Borden Co.**, 370 U.S. 460 (1962)]

> **Example:** In **United States v. Borden Co.**, the dairy had classified its cus-
> tomers into five classes: chain stores and four classes of independent gro-
> cers. The dairy attempted to justify different prices for the different classes
> based on comparative costs such as trucking expenses, bad debts, returned
> milk, and drivers' and clerical time, and the volume of purchases. However,
> the Court held that the classifications lacked sufficient homogeneity; some of
> the independents purchased amounts comparable to or greater than the chains.

(1) And note

Where the defendant "classified" customers into two groups, one of which
had 2,000 members and the other only one member, the court had no trouble
rejecting the classification as insufficient. [**Allied Accessories & Auto Parts
v. General Motors Corp.**, 825 F.2d 971 (6th Cir. 1987)]

3. Changing Conditions [§423]

Section 2(a) also provides that "nothing herein shall prevent price changes from time
to time in response to changing conditions affecting the market for, or the market-
ability of, the goods concerned, such as (but not limited to) actual or imminent deterioration of perishable goods, obsolescence of seasonal goods, distress sales under
court process, or sales in good faith in discontinuance of business in the goods concerned."

a. But note

This defense is rarely used and is confined to *temporary* situations caused by the
physical nature of the commodity. [*See, e.g.*, *In re* **American Oil Co.**, 60 F.T.C.
1786 (1962), *vacated on other grounds*, 325 F.2d 101 (7th Cir. 1963)—defense
not applicable to a price war situation; *but see* **Comcoa, Inc. v. NEC Telephones,
Inc.**, 931 F.2d 655 (10th Cir. 1991)—jury verdict in favor of defendants upheld
on grounds of changing conditions defense]

4. Meeting Competition in Good Faith [§424]

Section 2(b) provides that a seller may rebut a prima facie case of price discrimination
by showing that her lower price was "made in good faith to meet an equally low price
of a competitor." Where the defense is relied upon, the price difference must meet the
following *requirements:*

a. Reasonable belief [§425]

The seller must show that, at the time she made the price concession, she pos-
sessed facts that "would lead a *reasonable and prudent person* to believe that the
granting of a lower price would in fact meet the equally low price of a competitor." [**FTC v. Staley**, 324 U.S. 746 (1945)]

(1) Note

"Good faith" is the key; sellers need not communicate price verification information with each other in order to establish the meeting-competition defense. [**United States v. United States Gypsum Co.,** *supra,* §215]

(a) Rationale

This interpretation of the Act's requirements avoids conflicts with the Sherman Act, which seeks to limit communication of pricing information among competitors (particularly when the industry is highly concentrated or oligopolistic) in order to avoid price stabilization and rigidity.

> **Example:** Customer complaints that the seller needed to lower prices in order to be competitive were sufficient to trigger a good faith reduction, even though the customers did not quote specific prices from competitors. [**Great Atlantic & Pacific Tea Co. v. FTC,** 440 U.S. 69 (1979)]

b. Same (not lower) price [§426]

The price concession must only *meet* (rather than beat) the competitive price for a similar product.

(1) Seller's competitor [§427]

The seller's price concession must be made to meet a price offered by *the seller's* competitor. A seller cannot justify a price concession on the ground that it enabled the *customer* to meet his own competitor's better price. [**FTC v. Sun Oil,** 371 U.S. 505 (1963)]

(2) Same quality product [§428]

The seller cannot grant a price concession in order to meet the price of a lower quality product sold by a competitor. [**Callaway Mills Co. v. FTC,** 362 F.2d 435 (5th Cir. 1966)]

c. Response to individual [§429]

Generally, the price difference must be a response to an *individual* situation— and not itself a pricing system, such as base-point pricing. [**FTC v. Staley,** *supra*] However, there is no requirement that the lower price be set on a customer-by-customer basis rather than an area-wide basis. [**Falls City Industries v. Vanco Beverage, Inc.,** 460 U.S. 428 (1983)]

d. Other factors [§430]

There is *no requirement* that the price discrimination result from lowering rather than raising prices. In addition, the defense is available both to those who meet a competitor's lower price to retain an older customer and to those who do so to gain new customers. [**Falls City Industries v. Vanco Beverage, Inc.,** *supra*]

REQUIREMENTS OF GOOD FAITH DEFENSE— A CHECKLIST **gilbert**

TO REBUT A PRIMA FACIE CASE OF PRICE DISCRIMINATION, A SELLER MAY SHOW:

☑ *Reasonable belief* that price would meet the equally low price of a competitor;

☑ The price concession *must be equal to* (not lower than) the seller's competitive price for a product *of equal quality*; and

☑ The price difference must be *in response to an individual situation*.

5. Availability of Discount [§431]

Where the seller offers a discounted price only to those who meet certain conditions, but as a practical matter *any purchaser could meet the conditions* and therefore take advantage of that discounted price, the price is not discriminatory. [**Bouldis v. U.S. Suzuki Motor Corp.**, 711 F.2d 1319 (6th Cir. 1983)]

D. Prohibitions on Indirect Price Concessions

1. In General [§432]

Section 2(c), (d), and (e) of the Robinson-Patman Act prohibit indirect price discrimination in the form of brokerage or other payments to the seller's customers, and services and facilities supplied by the seller. Practices banned by these subsections are *illegal per se* (*i.e.*, no competitive injury need be shown and no cost-justification defense is permitted). The purpose is to force price concessions to be made directly, so that their effect can be judged more accurately.

2. "Brokerage" [§433]

The language of section 2(c) is not easy to understand. In somewhat simplified form, the statute provides that: "It is unlawful for any person to pay, grant, or receive any brokerage or allowance in lieu thereof except for services rendered in connection with the sale or purchase of goods, either to the other party to such transaction or to an agent of any party to such transaction other than the person by whom such commission is so granted or paid." (As Justice Frankfurter once said, "Precision of expression is not an outstanding characteristic of the Robinson-Patman Act.") The examples below help clarify section 2(c).

Example: Large Buyer demands a price concession from Seller. Instead of getting the concession directly, Buyer persuades Seller to pay a "brokerage fee" to a third party, who turns it over to Buyer. This is unlawful under section 2(c).

Seller ("any person") is paying a "brokerage" to the third party, an agent of Buyer, and the payment is not for any "services rendered in connection with the sale."

Example: Suppose Buyer decides to deal directly with Seller, and demands a price concession from Seller equal to the brokerage fee Seller would normally have paid to the third party. This is also unlawful under section 2(c), since it is an "allowance in lieu of brokerage."

Compare: Buyer might be entitled to the allowance if *she* performed services that the third party ordinarily performed in connection with the transaction (*e.g.*, prepared documents, arranged transportation, etc.).

Example: Buyer demands a price concession from Seller, who normally sells through Broker. Seller is unwilling at first to grant such a concession, but consents after Broker agrees to lower his brokerage fee for transactions with Buyer. This is also unlawful under section 2(c); Broker is "any person" who has granted an "allowance in lieu of brokerage." [**FTC v. Henry Broch,** 363 U.S. 166 (1960)] A seller and his broker can agree on any brokerage fee they wish, *but once agreed*, they cannot lower it to meet the demand of a favored buyer unless the reduced charge is justified by some difference in the brokerage services rendered to that buyer.

3. **"Discriminatory Allowances or Services" [§434]**
Section 2(d) and (e) forbid compensation to customers of the seller or the furnishing of services (such as promotional advertising) to customers unless the compensation or services are "available on proportionally equal terms to all other customers competing in the distribution of such products . . . ."

a. **Competitive relationship [§435]**
Literally, section 2(e) requires proportional treatment of *all* purchasers, but this has been construed as requiring that the purchasers be in some competitive relationship.

(1) **But note**
A retailer who buys through a wholesaler may be considered the "customer" of the original supplier and hence entitled to proportionate treatment with other direct retail customers of the supplier. [**FTC v. Fred Meyer, Inc.,** *supra,* §395]

b. **Cost justification no defense [§436]**
Cost justification for a discriminatory rendering of services or allowances, or a showing of no competitive injury, will *not* constitute a defense for the seller. [**FTC v. Simplicity Pattern,** 360 U.S. 55 (1959)]

c. **Distinguish—meeting competition defense [§437]**

However, the meeting competition defense *is* available under section 2(d) and (e), although it is difficult to prove. [**Exquisite Form Brassiere v. FTC**, 301 F.2d 499 (D.C. Cir.), *cert. denied*, 369 U.S. 888 (1962)]

d. **May provide allowances, services if on equal basis [§438]**

Moreover, the Act permits the furnishing of special facilities, services, or "allowances" to all buyers "on proportionally equal terms."

Example: A seller may lawfully set up schedules under which she will provide these services or other allowances—depending on dollar volume of business, number of customers reached, etc.—but they must be "practically" available to all competing customers. [*See* **Alan's of Atlanta v. Minolta Corp.**, 903 F.2d 1414 (11th Cir. 1990)]

---

(1) **But note**

A seller may not use an artificial schedule that favors only certain purchasers. [*See* **Elizabeth Arden, Inc. v. FTC**, 156 F.2d 132 (2d Cir. 1946), *cert. denied*, 331 U.S. 806 (1947)—manufacturer provided a free demonstrator-clerk but only at "selected" retail outlets, those being the outlets that had previously "cooperated" to manufacturer's satisfaction]

E. Buyer's Inducement or Receipt of a Discriminatory Price

1. **In General [§439]**

Section 2(f) makes it unlawful for "*any* person . . . *knowingly* to *induce* or *receive* a discrimination in price which is prohibited by this section." Thus, a *buyer* may be held to violate section 2 if he knowingly induces or receives a price discrimination unlawful under section 2(a). [**FTC v. Fred Meyer, Inc.**, *supra*]

2. **Knowledge Required [§440]**

It must be shown that the buyer *knew* the price obtained was discriminatory, *i.e.*, that the methods by which he was served and the quantities that he purchased were such that any cost defense by the seller would be unsuccessful. But this burden of proof may be discharged by evidence of "trade experience" of the buyer. [**Automatic Canteen v. FTC**, 346 U.S. 61 (1953)]

3. **Buyer's Liability Limited by Defenses Available to Seller [§441]**

If a seller cannot be held liable for a Robinson-Patman Act violation (*e.g.*, the seller has a "meeting competition" defense), then a buyer cannot be held liable. [**Great Atlantic & Pacific Tea Co. v. FTC**, *supra*, §425—buyer not liable under section 2(f) when *seller* would have had a good faith meeting competition defense, even though *buyer knew* that seller did not meet, but in fact substantially beat, competitor's price]

4. Allowances or Services [§442]

Although section 2(f) speaks only to "price discrimination," a buyer who knowingly induces or receives discriminatory *allowances or services* (within the meaning of section 2(d) and (e)) is also chargeable with unfair competition under section 5 of the FTC Act (*see* below). [**Grand Union Co. v. FTC**, 300 F.2d 92 (2d Cir. 1962)]

F. Exemptions

1. Sales to Government [§443]

Sales to the federal government, states, or municipalities have been held exempt from the provisions of the Robinson-Patman Act.

a. Limitation—government as market participant [§444]

However, there is *no exemption* for purchases by state and local government agencies for the purpose of reselling in the retail market in competition against private enterprise. [**Jefferson County Pharmaceutical Association v. Abbott**, 460 U.S. 150 (1983)]

2. Sales to Nonprofit Institutions [§445]

The Nonprofit Institutions Act [15 U.S.C. §13c] *exempts* purchases by nonprofit institutions from the provisions of the Robinson-Patman Act.

3. Export Sales [§446]

By its own terms, the Robinson-Patman Act applies only to "commodities . . . sold for use, consumption, or resale within the United States . . . or other place under the jurisdiction of the United States." [15 U.S.C. §13(a)] Thus, export sales are *excluded*.

G. Damages

1. Basis of Recovery—Actual Injury [§447]

A violation of section 2(a) does not entitle the plaintiff to "automatic damages" in the amount of price discrimination, because proof of a section 2(a) violation establishes only that some injury may have occurred. Therefore, the plaintiff must *prove actual injury caused by the price discrimination* in order to recover damages under section 4 of the Clayton Act. [**J. Truett Payne v. Chrysler Motor Corp.**, *supra*, §121]

Chapter Eight:
"Unfair Methods of Competition"

CONTENTS

Chapter Approach

Chapter Approach

This chapter discusses the Federal Trade Commission Act, which to some extent overlaps the Sherman and Clayton Acts. It gives the FTC powers similar in many respects to those of the Justice Department in enforcing the antitrust laws. Indeed, the FTC's authority is so extensive that it is effectively empowered to *fill in gaps* in the Sherman and Clayton Acts and to reach conduct or market conditions that *violate neither the letter nor the spirit* of those Acts. The FTC has rule-making authority and can impose a wide range of penalties and remedies.

A. Federal Trade Commission Act Section 5

1. Prohibits Unfair Competition and Deceptive Practices [§448]

Section 5 of the Federal Trade Commission Act prohibits *"unfair methods of competition,"* and *"unfair or deceptive acts or practices in or affecting commerce."* [15 U.S.C. §45]

2. FTC Has Exclusive Enforcement Authority [§449]

The Federal Trade Commission Act vests the FTC with the *exclusive* authority to enforce section 5 of the Act. There is *no private right of action* under the Act.

3. Scope of FTC Authority [§450]

The FTC is empowered to prohibit anticompetitive conduct *and* to protect consumers from deceptive practices. The latter area has received considerable attention by the FTC in recent years (*e.g.*, children's television advertising, fair packaging and labeling, "corrective advertising"), but it does not directly concern antitrust.

B. Anticompetitive Practices Covered by Section 5

1. Violations of the Clayton Act [§451]

The FTC has *concurrent* authority (with the DOJ and injured private parties) to enforce the Clayton Act, including the Robinson-Patman price discrimination amendments.

2. ### Violations of the Sherman Act [§452]

    The FTC is not expressly charged with the authority of enforcing the Sherman Act—as it is with the Clayton Act. However, section 5 of the FTC Act has been read so broadly that *any violation of Sherman Act section 1 or 2 would also be a violation of section 5* of the FTC Act—thus allowing the FTC to issue cease and desist orders to control such conduct. [**FTC v. Sperry & Hutchinson Co.**, 405 U.S. 233 (1972)]

3. ### Violations of the "Spirit" of the Sherman and Clayton Acts [§453]

    Moreover, the Supreme Court has held that section 5 is *not* confined to acts illegal at common law or prohibited under other antitrust laws.

    a. ### Potential violations [§454]

        For example, section 5 authorizes the FTC to intervene even *before* an actual violation takes place—*i.e.*, "to stop in their incipiency acts and practices which, when full blown, would violate" the Sherman or Clayton Act. [**FTC v. Motion Picture Advertising Service**, 344 U.S. 392 (1953)]

        Example: The FTC overturned an agreement between Texaco and Goodrich, whereby Texaco would promote the sale of Goodrich tire, battery, and accessory items to Texaco's independent dealers. The FTC found no "tying" or overt coercion in such promotions, but found that the *dominant position* of Texaco over its dealers created a *"strong potential for stifling competition."* The agreement was *"inherently coercive"* and thus an "unfair method of competition." [**FTC v. Texaco, Inc.**, 393 U.S. 223 (1968)]

        ---

    b. ### "Gaps" in Sherman and Clayton Acts [§455]

        Likewise, the FTC has authority to issue cease and desist orders to control conduct that might not be expressly covered in the Sherman or Clayton Acts; *i.e.*, the Commission can "fill in the gaps" left in those laws. [*See* **Grand Union Co. v. FTC**, *supra*, §442—FTC action against *buyer* for "knowingly receiving allowances" in violation of Clayton Act §2(d) upheld as an "unfair method of competition" under FTC §5, even though the terms of §2(d) apply only to sellers]

EXAM TIP	gilbert
If you conclude that a scenario on an exam will not create a violation of the Sherman or Clayton Acts, remember to consider the *gap-filling role of the FTC Act* before determining the action is valid.	

4. ### Conduct that Violates Neither the "Letter" Nor the "Spirit" of Sherman and Clayton Acts [§456]

    Finally, the FTC may find that conduct is an "unfair method of competition" under section 5 based on *public values found outside the antitrust laws*, and even though the conduct violates *neither* the "letter" nor the "spirit" of other antitrust laws.

> **e.g. Example:** The FTC may validly find practices to be a violation of section 5 (*i.e.,* an "unfair method of competition") even though such practices have been held to be *lawful* under state law. [**FTC v. Sperry & Hutchinson Co.,** *supra,* §452—S & H attempted to suppress trading stamp exchanges trafficking in its stamps]

a. Effect

The FTC therefore has *quasi-legislative power* in determining "fairness" and "unfairness" in business activity. The FTC may act "*like a court of equity,* considering public values beyond those enshrined in the letter or encompassed in the spirit of the antitrust laws." [**FTC v. Sperry & Hutchinson Co.,** *supra*]

b. FTC standards of "unfairness" [§457]

While specific standards are elusive, the FTC has described various factors it will consider in determining whether a practice not covered by the letter or spirit of other laws is nonetheless "unfair":

(1) *Whether the practice offends public policy,* as established by statutes, the common law, or otherwise (*i.e.,* whether it is at least within the penumbra of some common law, statutory, or other established concept of unfairness);

(2) *Whether it is immoral, unethical, oppressive, or unscrupulous;* and/or

(3) *Whether it causes substantial injury* to consumers, competitors, or others in business. [29 Fed. Reg. 8324, 8355 (1964)]

c. Comment [§458]

The *Sperry* decision has been quite controversial. More recently, courts have tried to confine the FTC's discretion within the general policy guidelines of the antitrust laws. For example, the Second Circuit overturned an effort by the FTC to make independent price signalling illegal, on the grounds that the FTC's decision was inconsistent with antitrust policy. [**E. I. duPont de Nemours & Co. v. FTC,** *supra,* §258]

C. Section 5 as a Source of Rule-Making Power

1. Authority to Issue Rules of Business Conduct [§459]

The FTC has asserted that its power to prevent "unfair methods of competition" and "unfair or deceptive trade practices" authorizes it to promulgate *substantive rules of business conduct—i.e.,* to define what is and is not "unfair" conduct in particular businesses. This substantive rule-making power by the FTC was *upheld* in **National**

Petroleum Refiners' Association v. FTC, 482 F.2d 672 (D.C. Cir. 1973), *cert. denied*, 415 U.S. 951 (1974), in which the FTC rule requiring gasoline stations to post octane numbers on gas pumps was upheld.

2. Legislation Confirms Authority [§460]

The Magnuson-Moss Warranty-Federal Trade Commission Improvement Act of 1975 [15 U.S.C. §57a] specifically authorized the FTC to issue substantive rules governing unfair or deceptive trade practices. Any rules promulgated are subject to review by the courts of appeals.

D. FTC Remedies

1. Varied Remedies [§461]

The FTC has a wide range of remedies available to enforce its statutory authority including cease and desist orders, civil penalties, and preliminary injunctions (*see supra*, §§136-141).

Chapter Nine: Intellectual Property Rights and Their Antitrust Implications

---

CONTENTS

Chapter Approach

Chapter Approach

Obvious tension exists between the antitrust laws and the patent system because the antitrust laws encourage competition, while the patent laws provide the right to exclude competitors in some circumstances. The limited monopoly provided by the patent laws (exclusive right within the United States for up to 20 years) is believed to be necessary in order to encourage technological progress through invention. At least in one respect, then, the antitrust and patent laws are compatible; *i.e.*, both seek to maximize consumer satisfaction. Not surprisingly, a considerable body of law has been developed to define and harmonize the relationship between the antitrust and patent laws.

To a lesser extent, courts have also considered a similar conflict between the antitrust laws and other forms of intellectual property. Copyright, trade secret, and trademark laws all grant some form of exclusive rights to their owners, and these exclusive rights must also be harmonized with antitrust.

In general, the use, licensing, or acquisition of intellectual property does not violate the antitrust laws. However, there are exceptions:

(i) A pattern of acquiring *all intellectual property rights in a field* can violate section 7 of the Clayton Act;

(ii) Licensing practices can restrain trade if they are *unnecessarily restrictive or discriminatory*; and

(iii) Competing firms can *improperly "pool"* their patents.

A. Economic Justifications for Patents

1. **Economic Theories—In General [§462]**
   Four theories have been advanced to justify the granting of intellectual property rights:

   (i) *The natural rights theory*—what one invents or creates is inherently one's own property;

   (ii) *The reward theory*—inventors should receive compensation for the benefits they render to society;

   (iii) *The exchange for secrets theory*—patents and copyrights discourage persons from keeping new ideas secret, thus increasing the wealth of ideas that eventually get into the public domain; and

(iv) *The profit-incentive theory*—protection of new ideas acts as an incentive to develop those ideas.

The profit-incentive theory is the fundamental and accepted justification for patents and the one recognized in the Constitution ("to promote the Progress of Science and Useful Arts"). [**Mercoid Corp. v. Mid-Continent Co.,** 320 U.S. 661 (1944)]

2. **Rationale for Profit-Incentive Theory [§463]**

An invention is a peculiar economic product. While the costs of development may be great, "ideas" are susceptible to being appropriated by others without compensation to the inventor, unless the ideas are somehow protected. If no protection is afforded and "free riding" is permitted, then there will be little incentive to devote resources to the development of new and useful ideas. Unless the idea can be kept secret (often impossible), it will be available to everyone—including competitors of the inventor (if any)—without any need for the investment of further resources on their part.

   a. **Remedy**

   Given this situation, there are two ways to create an incentive to invent: (i) give direct governmental grants to inventors of useful ideas; or (ii) give an inventor the legal right *to appropriate* the invention, with the owner free to sell it, rent it, or use it for his exclusive benefit. The intellectual property laws adopt the second method. The principal difficulty with the first method is one of valuation. For the second method, valuation is simple: As with real property, a patent's value is determined by market forces.

   b. **Note**

   The intellectual property laws represent Congress's judgment that the *benefits to be derived* from increased incentives to invent *outweigh the burden* of the temporary misallocation of resources that a patent monopoly may cause. This balance can be adjusted by lengthening or shortening the period of the intellectual property right, or by broadening or narrowing its scope.

3. **Limits on Intellectual Property Rights [§464]**

Intellectual property rights are limited in three basic ways:

   a. **Powers granted [§465]**

   Generally, the intellectual property laws do not provide the owner with complete control over the invention. Instead, they provide only certain rights. For example, the patent owner can prevent others from making, using, or selling the invention. The copyright owner can prevent others from copying, modifying, or performing the copyrighted work, but cannot prevent others from using the work or reselling a particular copy.

   b. **Scope [§466]**

   Intellectual property rights protect only certain, defined aspects of an invention. In the patent laws, for example, those aspects are legally defined by the *claims* of the patent. In the copyright laws, the scope of protection is limited by the rule that ideas cannot be appropriated, only a particular expression.

c. Duration [§467]

Intellectual property rights are of *limited duration*. They expire either after a certain length of time (patent and copyright laws), or upon the occurrence of a particular event (trademark and trade secret laws).

B. The Patent System

1. Patent Grant

a. United States Constitution [§468]

Article 1, section 8, clause 8 provides that the Congress shall have power "to promote the Progress of Science and Useful Arts, by securing for limited Times to Authors and Inventors the exclusive Right to their respective Writings and Discoveries."

b. The Patent Act [§469]

The Patent Act implements the above congressional power and allows the person who invents or discovers any *new and useful* process, machine, manufacture, or composition of matter, or any new and useful improvement thereof, to obtain a patent granting the *right to exclude others from making, using, selling, offering for sale, or importing* the invention in the United States for a period of up to *20 years* from the filing of the patent application, provided the invention is *not* such as would be *obvious* to a person having ordinary skill in the particular art. [35 U.S.C. §§101, 103, 154]

(1) Novelty [§470]

A patent will be denied if:

(i) *Before its invention* by the applicant, it was *known or used* by others in the United States or patented or *described in a publication* anywhere (including foreign countries); or

(ii) *More than one year before the date of the application*, it was patented or described in a publication anywhere or in public use or sale in the United States; or

(iii) *The invention* was made in this country *by another* who had not abandoned, suppressed, or concealed it before the applicant's invention thereof.

[35 U.S.C. §102]

(2) Utility [§471]

In interpreting the requirement of utility, the Supreme Court has required that an invention be "refined and developed" to the point where "specific benefits exist in currently available form." [**Brenner v. Manson**, 383 U.S. 519 (1966)]

(3) "Nonobviousness" [§472]

The nonobviousness requirement is contained in 35 U.S.C. section 103, which requires that the invention not be "obvious to one of ordinary skill in the art." [*See* **Graham v. John Deere Co.**, 383 U.S. 1 (1966)]

(4) Power of exclusion, not use [§473]

A patent merely gives a right to *exclude* others from making, selling, or using the invention. [35 U.S.C. §154] It does *not* give the right to *use* the invention. For example, if a company has a patent on pencils (*the dominant patent*) and an inventor has a patent on pencils with erasers (*the subservient patent*), the company cannot make pencils with erasers without infringing the inventor's patent; and the inventor cannot make pencils with erasers either—since to do so would infringe the company's patent. Thus, the two patents are *blocking*: To make such pencils, one of the parties will have to license the other, and they may in fact cross-license each other.

2. Patent Procedure

a. Application [§474]

A prospective patentee submits to the United States Patent Office an application containing a *specification* (*i.e.*, a written description of the invention and the manner of making and using it in full, clear, concise, and exact terms so that any person skilled in the art could make and use it) and a *drawing* thereof. [35 U.S.C. §§111-113]

b. Patent Office review [§475]

The Patent Office examines the application and *issues a patent* if the applicant is entitled thereto. Otherwise, the Patent Office notifies the applicant that the claim is *rejected*, stating the reasons for rejection. If the applicant persists, with or without an *amendment* (which cannot introduce new matter into the invention), the application is reexamined. [35 U.S.C. §§122, 123]

c. Interferences [§476]

Whenever application is made for a patent that would interfere with that of any pending applicant, the Patent Office gives a notice of interference. The question of priority of invention is then determined by a board of patent interferences. [35 U.S.C. §135]

3. **Rights of Patentees**

a. **Effect of patent [§477]**

The Patent Act in effect gives patents the status of personal property, in that the holder is entitled to transfer the patent and protect it in the same manner as any other property interest.

b. **Use by patentee [§478]**

The patentee may exploit the patent herself by excluding others from use.

(1) **No duty to use [§479]**

There is no general duty to use a patent. The patentee may elect to do nothing with the invention—*i.e.*, to "suppress it." [*See* **Continental Paper Bag Co. v. Eastern Paper Bag Co.**, 210 U.S. 405 (1908); **Special Equipment v. Coe**, 324 U.S. 370 (1945)]

(a) **But note**

Arguably this conflicts with the constitutional objective "to promote science and useful arts." [*See* **Vitamin Technologists, Inc. v. Wisconsin Alumni Research Foundation**, 146 F.2d 941 (9th Cir. 1944), *cert. denied*, 325 U.S. 876 (1945)]

(b) **And note—compulsory licensing statutes [§480]**

Also, in a *few limited areas*, Congress has enacted legislation requiring licensing: atomic energy [42 U.S.C. §2183]; plants [7 U.S.C. §2404]; and air pollution [42 U.S.C. §7608].

c. **Assignments, licenses, etc. [§481]**

The patentee may *assign* the patent outright to another; or may *license* another to use the patented process, either exclusively or in conjunction with others, in the whole or any part of the United States. [35 U.S.C. §261]

(1) **Licensee may challenge patent validity [§482]**

At one time, one who had been granted a license to use the patent was estopped to challenge the validity of the patent (*i.e.*, so that he could not refuse to pay royalties on this ground). However, the Supreme Court has held to the contrary, *allowing* a licensee to defend an action for royalties by asserting the invalidity of the patent. [**Lear, Inc. v. Adkins**, 395 U.S. 653 (1969)]

(a) **Rationale**

Public interest in permitting full and free competition in the use of ideas is important. The licensee may be the only one with enough economic incentive to challenge the patentability of the inventor's discovery.

(b) But note
The Supreme Court did *not* hold that the royalty agreement itself was unenforceable (*i.e.*, compensation may be due for disclosing even an unpatented idea).

(2) Abuse [§483]
A licensee may also challenge a patent on grounds of "abuse" (*see* below). [**Sola Electric v. Jefferson Electric**, 317 U.S. 173 (1942)]

4. Infringement Actions

a. Direct infringement [§484]
The patentee is entitled to sue for damages, injunctive relief, or both, anyone who makes, uses, sells, offers for sale, or imports the patented invention without the patentee's consent. [35 U.S.C. §154] Such use constitutes an "infringement" of the patent—*whether or not it is intentional.*

b. Contributory infringement actions [§485]
Contributory infringement actions, where someone aids another in the infringement of the patent, require some degree of *scienter.*

(1) Contributory infringers
One who *actively induces infringement* of a patent by another is himself liable as an infringer. One who sells an unpatented component of a patented invention or material, for use in a "patented combination" or process, is liable as a contributory infringer only if it appears that he *knew* (i) that the component had only limited use in a patented combination or process, and was not suitable for other use; and (ii) that the combination was patented, and the use for which he is providing a component was an infringement thereon. [**Aro Manufacturing Co. v. Convertible Top Co.**, 377 U.S. 476 (1964)]

(2) Distinguish
However, if the unpatented component is a common staple item capable of "substantial noninfringing use," its supplier will *not* be held a "contributory infringer."

5. Defenses to Infringement Actions

a. Invalidity [§486]
An infringer can always defend on the ground that the patent itself is *invalid.* Although a patent issued by the United States Patent Office is presumed valid, the infringer can overcome the presumption by showing that the invention was not original, that another has priority, etc.

b. Patent misuse [§487]
An infringer can also defend on the ground that the patentee has *misused* or

abused the patent (*e.g.*, through an attempt to "tie" an unpatented commodity to it in violation of the Clayton Act). [**Morton Salt Co. v. G.S. Suppiger Co.**, 314 U.S. 488 (1942)] However, the Supreme Court has held that by enacting section 271 of the Patent Act, Congress intended to limit the patentee's liability for patent misuse. [**Dawson Chemical Co. v. Rohm & Hass Co.**, 448 U.S. 176 (1980)—fact that the patent holder distributed instructions for its patented process only to purchasers of an unpatented chemical did not constitute misuse or illegal tying, and could not be used as a defense against an allegation of contributory infringement]

(1) Note

The "patent misuse" doctrine is an equitable defense based upon the "unclean hands" of the patentee. While the concept of "misuse" *includes antitrust violations*, it may also include other conduct by the patentee that may be found to be inequitable. When "misuse" is found, the court will not enforce the patent.

(2) And note

A patentee can regain the right to enforce the patent or can rebut the misuse defense only by demonstrating that the "misuse" has been *abandoned* and that the consequences of the misuse have dissipated. [**Morton Salt Co. v. G.S. Suppiger Co.**, *supra*] As a practical matter, "abandonment" has been difficult to prove.

c. Fraud [§488]

Fraudulent procurement or enforcement of a patent constitutes an equitable defense to a patent infringement suit. [**Precision Instrument Manufacturing Co. v. Automotive Maintenance Machinery Co.**, 324 U.S. 806 (1945)]

(1) Note

Such fraud may also provide an affirmative basis for relief under the antitrust laws, if the other elements of an antitrust claim can be shown. [**Walker Process Equipment, Inc. v. Food Machinery & Chemical Corp.**, 382 U.S. 172 (1965)]

SUMMARY OF DEFENSES TO INFRINGEMENT ACTIONS — gilbert

INVALIDITY OF PATENT	To overcome a presumption of validity, infringer may show that the invention was *not original* or that *another has priority*.
PATENT MISUSE	Infringer may show the patentee has *abused or misused the patent* (*e.g.*, antitrust violations, other inequitable conduct).
FRAUD	Infringer may raise an equitable defense based on *fraudulent procurement or enforcement* of the patent.

C. Copyrights

1. **The Copyright Act [§489]**

   The Copyright Act grants protection to *original works of authorship* that fall within the subject matter of copyright—typically literary and creative works. Copyright protection gives the copyright owner the exclusive rights to *copy, adapt, distribute, perform, and display* her works. [17 U.S.C. §§102, 103, 106]

   a. **Copyright subject matter [§490]**

      Subject matter eligible for copyright protection includes literary works, works of art, musical compositions, dramatic works, and sound recordings. [17 U.S.C. §102(a)] Computer programs qualify as "literary works" protectable under the Act. [**Apple Computer v. Franklin Computer,** 714 F.2d 1240 (3d Cir. 1983)]

   b. **Fixation [§491]**

      To receive copyright protection, works must be "*fixed in a tangible medium of expression*" from which they can be perceived, either directly or with the aid of a machine. [17 U.S.C. §102]

   c. **Originality [§492]**

      A work of authorship must possess at least a *modicum of originality* to qualify for copyright protection. Works such as telephone books, which merely compile data in a completely predictable fashion, are not protectable. [**Feist Publications, Inc., v. Rural Telephone Service Co.,** 499 U.S. 340 (1991)]

   d. **Idea-expression dichotomy [§493]**

      Copyright protection extends only to the original *expression* in a work. Ideas themselves cannot be the subject of copyright, and thus they may be freely copied. [**Baker v. Selden,** 101 U.S. 99 (1879)]

2. **Procedure [§494]**

   Copyright protection is *automatic* once a work meets the criteria listed above. Government approval is not necessary for copyright protection. Nor need the copyright owner comply with any "formalities" (such as notice of copyright). However, copyright owners must *register* their works with the Copyright Office before bringing suit for infringement. [17 U.S.C. §411]

3. **Rights of Copyright Owner [§495]**

   The copyright owner has the exclusive right to prevent others from doing the following things:

   (i) *Copying* the work;

   (ii) *Adapting* the work to a new form (also referred to as making a "derivative work");

(iii) *Distributing* copies of the work;

(iv) *Performing* a dynamic work *publicly*; and

(v) *Displaying* a static work *publicly*.

[17 U.S.C. §106]

a. Limits on exclusive rights [§496]

The exclusive rights listed above are limited by a number of provisions that grant certain rights to users of copyrighted works, such as the fair use doctrine [17 U.S.C. §107], the library exception [17 U.S.C. §108], and the teacher's exception [17 U.S.C. §110].

4. Infringement Actions [§497]

The copyright owner is entitled to sue, for damages and injunctive relief, anyone who violates any of the exclusive rights set forth in section 106 (*see* above).

a. Substantial similarity [§498]

Because direct evidence of copying is often difficult to come by, courts will find infringement if the plaintiff can show that the defendant had *access* to the plaintiff's work and that the works were *substantially similar*. [**Gaste v. Kaiserman**, 863 F.2d 1061 (2d Cir. 1988)]

b. Scienter [§499]

As with patent infringement, intentional copying is not required. Copyright infringement is a *strict liability offense*. However, proof of inducement or contributory infringement may require intent in some cases. (*See supra*, §485.) Also, although copyright violation is a strict liability offense, the plaintiff must still show copying. If an author *independently* comes up with a copyrightable expression that another author has already copyrighted, the former has not infringed and may copyright her own expression. In contrast, once an inventor patents her work, that patent is enforceable against the world; independent creation is no defense to patent infringement.

5. Defenses to Infringement Actions

a. Fair use [§500]

Certain violations of the exclusive rights of copyright are excused as "fair uses," generally because they are done for public benefit, are not commercial in nature, or do not injure the plaintiff's market for the copyrighted work. Fair use is a fact-specific, case-by-case inquiry. [17 U.S.C. §107]

b. Copyright misuse [§501]

Like patent misuse, copyright misuse is an equitable doctrine that operates to bar a copyright owner from enforcing her right if she has misused the copyright, generally by violating the *antitrust laws* or otherwise extending the reach of the copyright monopoly. [**Lasercomb America v. Reynolds**, 911 F.2d 970 (4th Cir. 1990)]

D. Relationship of Intellectual Property to Antitrust Laws

1. Monopolization [§502]

Intellectual property rights are *legal monopolies* granted by statute. Thus, a valid patent or other intellectual property right can be a defense to a charge of monopolizing under section 2 of the Sherman Act, if the market monopolized is covered by the intellectual property right.

a. Limitation of legal monopoly [§503]

In some cases, however, even a legal monopoly may not be allowed:

(1) Monopolization by patent acquisition [§504]

Acquiring a patent is an "acquisition of an asset" within the meaning of section 7 of the Clayton Act, which can be enjoined if the effect may be "to substantially lessen competition and tend to create a monopoly." [**United States v. Lever Bros.**, 216 F. Supp. 887 (S.D.N.Y. 1963)]

(2) Compulsory licensing as a remedy [§505]

Note that, as a *remedy* for past violations of the antitrust laws (especially section 2 of the Sherman Act), the *courts may break up the "legal monopoly" (patent); i.e.*, courts may order *compulsory licensing* of present and future patent rights to all comers at reasonable royalty rates (and occasionally on a royalty-free basis). [*See* **United States v. Glaxo Group, Ltd.**, 410 U.S. 52 (1973)]

(3) Exclusive licensing [§506]

Where an intellectual property owner has assigned or licensed her rights exclusively to one party, courts will normally treat the license as *equivalent to a sale of the intellectual property right*, potentially subject to section 2 of the Sherman Act and section 7 of the Clayton Act.

b. Refusal to deal as monopoly conduct [§507]

In some cases, the owners of intellectual property rights have refused to license their rights or to sell patented products in order to reduce competition in the market for servicing equipment. Courts have split on whether such refusals violate antitrust laws. The First Circuit held that a purported monopolist's refusal to license its intellectual property is presumptively valid. [**Data General Corp. v. Grumman Systems Support Corp.**, 36 F.3d 1147 (1st Cir. 1994)] The Ninth Circuit agreed, but held that this presumption could be overcome if the reason given for the refusal to deal was pretextual. [**Image Technical Services, Inc. v. Eastman Kodak,** 125 F.3d 1195 (9th Cir. 1997)—facts showed only a few of the relevant parts were patented and manager who refused to sell Kodak parts to competing service providers did not know that some of these parts were protected by patents] Disagreeing with the Ninth Circuit, the Federal Circuit refused to consider evidence of pretext and endorsed a broad right by intellectual property owners to decline to license. [*In re* **Independent Service Organizations Antitrust Litigation ("Xerox"),** 203 F.3d 1322 (Fed. Cir. 2000)]

2. Restraints of Trade Found in Certain Patent Licensing Practices [§508]

The "legal monopoly" created by the patent grant extends only as far as the patentee's own use or reasonable exploitation of the invention. It does *not* permit her to "extend" her monopoly by anticompetitive behavior in the licensing or distribution of the patented product.

a. Introduction [§509]

Licensing is generally to be encouraged because it permits the intellectual property owner to market her property efficiently. However, licensing and cross-licensing—and the agreements concluded in such licenses—can also operate as restraints of trade, with significant anticompetitive effects which go beyond securing the full economic benefits of the patent grant for the patentee. Recognizing this fact, the courts have developed a common law on what licensing practices by the patentee constitute an "abuse" of the patent grant and violate the policies of the antitrust laws.

EXAM TIP   **gilbert**

Most of the cases in this chapter involve the patent laws, because patent laws most commonly grant rights that can effect a legal monopoly. But for exam purposes, remember that the rules discussed in this chapter are broadly applicable to the licensing of *any form of intellectual property right*.

---

b. Restrictions on licensee [§510]

In general, once the patentee (or her licensee) has *sold* a patented product, the purchaser is free of the patent monopoly, and may use or resell the product anywhere in the United States without infringing the patent. The patentee has extracted all the monopolistic profits to which she is entitled. [**Adams v. Burke,** 84 U.S. 453 (1873)]

(1) Resale price restrictions [§511]

In the famous *General Electric* case [**United States v. General Electric,** *supra,* §274], the Supreme Court held that a patentee *could by agreement* restrict the price for which a *licensee* could sell the patented product.

(a) Rationale

The patent grant created the right to exclude others from "making, using, or *selling*" and the patentee could, therefore, license the right to sell the patented product on any condition "normally and reasonably adapted to serve as a pecuniary reward for the patent monopoly." The Court reasoned that the patentee, among other things, might want to protect her own market from price competition by her licensee.

(b) Restrictions [§512]

The *General Electric* case has been highly criticized as an unreasonable extension of the patent grant. The scope of the decision has therefore been restricted:

1) *The patentee cannot agree with a licensee to fix the price* of *unpatented* products made by a patented machine. [**Cummer-Graham v. Straight Side Basket Corp.,** 142 F.2d 646 (5th Cir. 1944)]

2) *Nor can the patentee restrict the persons to whom, or the terms on which,* the licensed products, once sold by the licensee, may be *resold* by others. [**United States v. Univis Lens Co.,** 316 U.S. 241 (1942)]

3) *The owners of two patents may not cross-license* the patents and *fix the prices* to be charged by themselves and their licensees for the respective products, or *divide up territories,* or agree to *boycott* other products. [**United States v. Line Materials Co.,** 333 U.S. 287 (1948)]

4) *One court has held* that *General Electric* does *not apply* to the grant of *multiple* licenses. [**Newburgh Moire Co. v. Superior Moire Co.,** 237 F.2d 283 (3d Cir. 1956)]

(2) Use restrictions [§513]

When the patented invention has several separate uses or applications, the Supreme Court has held that the patentee *can* properly limit a licensee to one or more such uses and grant such rights exclusively or nonexclusively. [**General Talking Pictures Corp. v. Western Electric,** 305 U.S. 124 (1938)]

(a) Effect

Use restrictions may allow the patentee to engage in price discrimination. The elasticity of demand for the patented product or process may vary considerably among different uses. (For example, in *General Talking Pictures,* above, the patentee separated the use of its patented amplifier into the commercial field and home radios.) The patentee can then charge a higher royalty for the use where the elasticity of demand is lower.

(3) Territorial restrictions [§514]

By statute, a patentee may restrict her licensee to any territory she wishes. [35 U.S.C. §261]

c. Grant-back clauses or patent accumulation [§515]

It is not illegal per se to include in the patent license a covenant requiring the licensee to assign to the licensor any improvement patents developed by the licensee. [**Transparent-Wrap Machine v. Stockes & Smith,** 329 U.S. 637 (1947)] However, these practices have been found to violate the Sherman Act where they *unduly* restrain or monopolize trade.

d. Attempts to "extend" patent monopoly [§516]

Attempts to "extend" the patent monopoly may violate the antitrust laws:

(1) Exclusive dealing [§517]

A patentee who requires that distributors agree *not to sell* products that compete with the patented product may be guilty of "abusing" the patent. [**F.C. Russell Co. v. Consumers Insulation,** 226 F.2d 373 (3d Cir. 1955)]

(2) Tying arrangements [§518]

Likewise, a patentee cannot extend her monopoly by forcing customers to buy nonpatented goods from her if they wish to obtain the patented goods—*i.e.*, an illegal "tie." [**International Salt Co. v. United States,** *supra*, §309; *and see supra,* §§304-307]

(a) Market power [§519]

Allegations of tying involving intellectual property are subject to the normal rules governing tying arrangements (*see supra,* §§297 *et seq.*). While some early cases held that an intellectual property right *automatically* conferred market power, the more recent trend has been to require proof of market power in these cases, just as in other tying cases.

(b) Non-staple products [§520]

Where a product has no purpose except in connection with a patented machine, it is not "tying" for the patentee to control the sale of the product as well as the machine itself. [**Dawson Chemical v. Rohm & Haas,** *supra,* §487]

(3) Extension of term [§521]

A royalty agreement or contract that extends beyond the expiration date of the patent is *unlawful*. [**Brulotte v. Thys Co.,** 379 U.S. 29 (1964)]

(4) Royalties as percentage of sales [§522]

The Court has invalidated a patent licensing agreement whereby the patentee required royalties to be paid on both patented *and unpatented* articles. "The patentee may not use the patent's leverage to extend the monopoly to derive a benefit *not attributable to use* of the patent's teaching." [**Zenith Radio Corp. v. Hazeltine Research, Inc.**, 395 U.S. 100 (1969)]

(a) But note
When a "total sales" approach is used for the convenience of *both* the patentee and licensee, a violation will not be found.

(5) Block-booking [§523]
Nor will the courts permit a royalty structure that forces a licensee to pay for a *group* of patents, where he in fact wishes to use only a single patent (called "block-booking"). The same result applies where the patentee refuses on request to charge a different rate for use of individual patents in the group, or charges an unreasonably high rate for the sought-after patent. [*See* **Zenith Radio Corp. v. Hazeltine Research, Inc.**, *supra*] Block-booking is most commonly discussed in the context of copyright owners who refuse to license one film or group of films unless the licensee agrees to purchase a license for another (unwanted) film or group of films. Generally seen as a species of tying arrangement, courts condemn such block-booking as per se illegal. [*See, e.g.,* **United States v. Paramount Pictures, Inc.**, 334 U.S. 131 (1948); **United States v. Loew's, Inc.**, 371 U.S. 38 (1962); **MCA Television Ltd. v. Public Interest Corp.**, 171 F.3d 1265 (11th Cir. 1999)]

(6) Reciprocal dealing [§524]
It is possible that a monopolist may violate the Sherman Act by refusing to sell a desired product to a patent holder unless that patent holder agrees to license its patent to the monopolist. [*See* **Intergraph Corp. v. Intel Corp.**, 195 F.3d 1346 (Fed. Cir. 1999)—rejecting the argument based on the facts of the case; *compare* **Betaseed, Inc. v. U & I, Inc.**, 681 F.2d 1203 (9th Cir. 1982)—defendant firm with monopoly power in the market for processing sugar beets conditioned processing on the plaintiff's agreement to buy seeds from the defendant]

e. Patent pools—settlement of patent disputes [§525]
Sometimes parties to a patent infringement suit settle by forming a patent "pool," whereby the patents are cross-licensed and royalties are divided in an agreed-upon manner.

(1) *Cracking Case* [§526]
The famous 1931 *Cracking Case* [**Standard Oil v. United States**, 283 U.S. 163 (1931)] involved an improved process for the refining of gasoline. No exclusive method existed for cracking gasoline. The four defendant firms in the *Cracking Case* each secured patents, and conflicts developed among them. Infringement suits were filed and interferences begun. In settlement of the disputes, the parties agreed to release each other from liability for past infringement and give each the right to sublicense at a royalty fixed by

agreement—with the royalties to be divided in an agreed-upon manner (a patent pool). The government did not challenge the cross-licensing itself, but claimed that the pooling of royalties was illegal per se. The Court held that the pool was a *"legitimate settlement of disputes"* according to the value of patent claims. The government also attacked the fixing of royalties in the agreement, but the Court held that this was a legitimate incident of the patent monopoly, since the defendants together did *not* have monopoly power over the market for either gasoline or "cracked" gasoline.

(a) But note
A patent pool with minimum set royalties has been held illegal when it involved *all the manufacturers* in the industry. [**United States v. New Wrinkle,** 342 U.S. 371 (1951)]

(2) Settlements involving pharmaceutical patents [§527]
Under the provisions of the 1984 Hatch-Waxman Act, the first drug company to apply to manufacture a generic version of an established patented drug (called a *"pioneer drug"*) receives a 180-day period of exclusive marketing rights. In some cases, the pioneer drug company has sued the generic drug manufacturer for patent infringement and, to settle the infringement suit, has paid the manufacturer of the generic version of the drug not to sell its drug during the 180-day period. This arrangement leaves the pioneer drug company with the same market power that it enjoyed before its patent expired. Some courts have held such agreements to be per se unlawful. [*In re* **Cardizen CD Antitrust Litigation,** 332 F.3d 896 (6th Cir. 2003)] Others have rejected per se condemnation, instead requiring the application of rule of reason analysis to determine whether such settlement terms unreasonably restrain trade. [**Valley Drug Co. v. Geneva Pharmaceuticals, Inc.,** 344 F.3d 1294 (11th Cir. 2003)]

3. Enforcing Intellectual Property Rights [§528]
Obtaining and enforcing intellectual property rights against infringers is commonly alleged to be an effort to monopolize a market. However, such antitrust claims rarely succeed.

a. Fraudulent procurement [§529]
A patentee who obtains his patent by defrauding the Patent Office may violate section 2 of the Sherman Act, but only if all the normal elements of a monopolization claim can be made out. [**Walker Process Equipment, Inc. v. Food Machinery & Chemical Corp.,** *supra*, §488]

b. Anticompetitive litigation [§530]
The owner of a valid intellectual property right may be liable for monopolization if he brings a *sham infringement lawsuit* in an effort to harass a competitor. Once again, the other elements of a section 2 claim must also be established. [**Handgards, Inc. v. Ethicon, Inc.,** 601 F.2d 986 (9th Cir. 1979)]

(1) Limitation—antitrust immunity [§531]

This rule is significantly limited by the antitrust petitioning immunity doctrine, which provides that a party filing a lawsuit cannot be liable for bringing the suit unless it is demonstrated to be a "sham"—meaning that it is *both objectively baseless* (filed without probable cause) *and improperly motivated* (filed in order to harass, rather than in expectation of judicial relief). [**Professional Real Estate Investors, Inc. v. Columbia Pictures Industries Inc.,** 508 U.S. 49 (1993)]

4. Justice Department Guidelines [§532]

In 1995, the DOJ and the FTC issued joint Guidelines concerning the licensing of intellectual property. The new Guidelines contain a number of important changes in antitrust enforcement policy:

a. Market definition [§533]

While markets in intellectual property cases are normally defined in the same way as in any antitrust case, the Guidelines raise the possibility that the relevant market may be a market not for goods or services, but for intellectual property itself (a *technology market*), or for research and development in the future (an *innovation market*).

b. No special treatment [§534]

The Guidelines indicate the government's intention to treat intellectual property in the same way as any other property for antitrust purposes. This reverses the governing rule during the 1980s, when the government took a "hands-off" attitude toward intellectual property licensing.

c. Rule of reason [§535]

The Guidelines acknowledge the potential pro-competitive benefits of intellectual property licensing, and generally apply the rule of reason to transactions involving intellectual property. Furthermore, the Guidelines create an "antitrust *safety zone*" by refusing to challenge licensing arrangements unless the parties to the arrangement have a market share greater than 20%.

Chapter Ten:
Exemptions from the Antitrust Laws

CONTENTS

Chapter Approach

Certain businesses, industries, or practices are exempted from the antitrust laws. The basic types of exemptions you should consider are:

(i) Exemptions *required by the Constitution*, *e.g.*, by the First Amendment or Commerce Clause (these are discussed in chapters II and IV as well as in this chapter);

(ii) Exemptions *expressly created by statute*, *e.g.*, the exemption for export associations under the Webb-Pomerene Export Trade Associations Act; and

(iii) Exemptions *implied by the statutorily created regulatory structures*; *e.g.*, the Securities Exchange Act.

Note that the courts are loathe to expand these exemptions and are careful not to create new ones without justification. Thus, you should greet most claims of antitrust exemption with skepticism and carefully examine whether the facts of the case fit into the narrow framework of the particular exemption.

A. Background

1. In General [§536]

The antitrust laws are designed to promote competition as a means of ensuring efficient and fair use and allocation of resources. However, some businesses or industries have been exempted from the prohibitions of the antitrust laws.

2. Rationale for Exemptions [§537]

Industries are usually exempted for two reasons: (i) the exempted industries are regulated by other governmental agencies charged with protecting the public's interest (*e.g.*, air, motor, rail, and interstate water carriers, insurance companies, and stock exchanges) *or* (ii) the exempted industries are thought to require the special protection that cartelization may provide (*e.g.*, agricultural organizations, export trade associations, and labor unions).

a. Criticism of exemptions

Many authorities believe that a number of the existing exemptions are no longer economically justified—that the regulating agencies have become protectors of the status quo, often to the detriment of the consumer, and that the economy would be better off if the force and discipline of the marketplace were allowed to intervene.

3. Types of Exemptions [§538]

Exemptions may be *constitutionally mandated*, *expressly granted* by Congress, or *implied by courts* from regulatory schemes created by Congress or implied to avoid conflicts between federal antitrust laws and state laws or practices.

a. Exemptions are strictly construed and hesitantly created [§539]

The courts are hesitant to create or expand exemptions. Thus, specific exemptions granted by Congress are narrowly confined to the language of the statute [*see, e.g.,* **National Broiler Marketing Association v. United States**, 436 U.S. 816 (1978)]; and parties claiming exemptions by implication bear a heavy burden of justification [**Federal Maritime Commission v. Seatrain Lines, Inc.**, 411 U.S. 726 (1973)].

b. Implied antitrust immunity [§540]

Implied antitrust immunity can be justified only by a convincing showing of a *clear repugnancy* between the antitrust laws and the regulatory system at issue. Even substantial industry regulation does not necessarily indicate an intent to repeal the antitrust laws with respect to every action taken within that industry. [**Otter Tail Power Co. v. United States**, *supra*, §190] Implied immunity is much clearer where the regulatory agency is empowered to regulate the allegedly unlawful conduct.

---

e.g. **Example:** Blue Cross's refusal to permit a newly constructed hospital to participate in its standard health care agreement constituted an unlawful refusal to deal and was not exempt from the antitrust laws, even though a federal statute had appointed a local organization to oversee new hospital construction and the plaintiff hospital had not received construction approval. Blue Cross's actions were not immune because the regulatory body did not require or formally request Blue Cross not to deal with unapproved hospitals. [**National Gerimedical Hospital & Gerontology Center v. Blue Cross of Kansas City**, 452 U.S. 378 (1981)]

B. Agricultural Organizations

1. Express Antitrust Immunity [§541]

Section 6 of the Clayton Act provides:

Nothing contained in the antitrust laws shall be construed to forbid the existence and operation of . . . agricultural, or horticultural organizations, instituted for purposes of mutual help and *not having capital stock or conducted for profit*, or to forbid or restrain individual members of such organizations from lawfully carrying out the legitimate objects thereof; nor shall such organizations or the members thereof be held or construed to be illegal combinations or conspiracies in restraint of trade under the antitrust laws.

a. Capper-Volstead Act [§542]

With the Capper-Volstead Act, Congress extended this exemption to capital stock agricultural cooperatives comprised of "persons engaged in the production of agricultural products as farmers, planters, ranchmen, dairymen [or] nut or fruit growers . . . ." [7 U.S.C. §291]

b. Fisherman's Cooperative Marketing Act [§543]

The Fisherman's Cooperative Marketing Act extends the exemption to fishing, fish processing, and fish marketing cooperatives. [15 U.S.C. §521]

2. Scope of Exemption [§544]

Like most other exemptions from the antitrust laws, this one is narrowly construed.

a. Agricultural production [§545]

The exemption extends only to the conduct of *"persons engaged in agricultural production."* Thus, it has been held *not* to exempt the activities of firms or persons operating packinghouses (this is not "production" of farm products). [**Case-Swayne Co. v. Sunkist Growers, Inc.**, 389 U.S. 384 (1967); *and see* **United States v. Hinote**, 823 F. Supp. 1350 (S.D. Miss. 1993)—catfish processor not entitled to an exemption merely because it had acquired an interest in a catfish farm]

b. Mixed association [§546]

Nor does the exemption cover the activities of an association consisting in *part* of persons engaged in "production" and in part of persons *not* so engaged. [**United States v. Borden Co.**, 308 U.S. 188 (1939)]

> **Example:** The Court denied exempt status to a broiler chicken nonprofit marketing and purchasing cooperative, in which nine of the 75 members did not own breeder fowl. Although the nine were vertically integrated into other processing stages of the broiler industry, their failure to raise their own breeder fowl took them outside the term "farmers" as used in the Capper-Volstead Act. [**National Broiler Marketing Association v. United States**, *supra*, §539]

EXAM TIP   **gilbert**

On an exam, remember how narrowly construed the agricultural producer exemption is. Unless the party seeking the exemption is defined *as a farmer, planter, etc.,* it is unlikely that he will qualify for the exemption.

---

c. Coercive activities [§547]

Even if the organization qualifies, the exemption does *not* legalize activities that are *coercive*—*e.g.*, boycotts aimed at forcing nonmembers to join the co-operative.

> **e.g. Example:** Price fixing by a cooperative was permitted because it was covered by the exemption, but a boycott to force nonmembers to adhere to the prices established by the cooperative was not within the scope of exemption and thus was illegal. [**Maryland & Virginia Milk Producers Association, Inc. v. United States,** 362 U.S. 458 (1960)]

> **cf. Compare:** An agreement by cooperative members to fix prices and boy-cott a competing cooperative was exempt from antitrust scrutiny, be-cause price fixing was the sort of "joint marketing activity" contemplated by the Capper-Volstead Act. [**Alexander v. National Farmers Organization,** 687 F.2d 1173 (8th Cir. 1982)]

3. Remedy for Illegal Conduct [§548]

Section 2 of the Capper-Volstead Act empowers the Secretary of Agriculture to issue *cease and desist orders* when an exempt organization is found to be monopolizing or restraining trade, to the extent that the price of any agricultural product is unduly enhanced.

a. But note

This does *not* give the Secretary of Agriculture primary or exclusive jurisdiction over such organizations. They can still be sued under the antitrust laws for exceeding the exemption granted [**United States v. Borden Co.,** *supra*], or for monopolizing or attempting to monopolize under section 2 of the Sherman Act [**Case-Swayne Co. v. Sunkist Growers, Inc.,** *supra*].

C. Interstate Water, Motor, Rail, and Air Carriers

1. Express Shipping Act Exemption [§549]

Section 15 of the Shipping Act of 1916 [46 U.S.C. §814] gives the Federal Maritime Commission ("FMC") the power to approve agreements among water carriers relat-ing to rates and other matters, and the agreements so approved are exempt from the antitrust laws. For example, the FMC has jurisdiction to review labor contracts that were alleged to be anticompetitive. [**Federal Maritime Commission v. Pacific Mari-time Association,** 435 U.S. 40 (1978)]

a. But note

The Act has been interpreted as exempting only those agreements that create ongoing rights and responsibilities among water carriers (and hence require continuing FMC supervision). Thus, FMC approval of a merger or acquisition of assets agreement imposing no ongoing responsibilities will **not** shield the water carriers involved from antitrust liability. [**Federal Maritime Commission v. Seatrain Lines, Inc.**, *supra*, §539]

2. Motor, Rail, and Air Carriers—Revoked Exemptions [§550]

Under the former Interstate Commerce Act and the Federal Aviation Act, the Interstate Commerce Commission and the Civil Aeronautics Board had powers similar to those of the Federal Maritime Commission to regulate trucking, rail and air transportation, and rates charged by firms in those industries. However, the deregulatory winds of the 1980s swept away these regulatory schemes. The Interstate Commerce Act was repealed in 1980, and the Civil Aeronautics Board was dissolved in 1985. As a result, these previously regulated industries are, for the most part, now subject *to the full force of the antitrust laws.*

3. Note—Federal Agency Action or Oversight Does Not Necessarily Create Exemption [§551]

There are many other kinds of federal agency approvals and regulatory structures that do **not create an exemption** from antitrust liability.

Examples: The Federal Power Commission approval of the merger or acquisition of assets of a natural gas company does not create an exemption [**California v. Federal Power Commission**, 369 U.S. 482 (1962)]; the Federal Communications Commission approval of an exchange of television stations does not create an exemption [**United States v. Radio Corp. of America**, 358 U.S. 334 (1959)]; and the Commodities Exchange Act and regulation of commodities exchange rules by the Commodity Futures Trading Commission do not confer antitrust immunity on the Chicago Board of Trade and its officers [**American Agriculture Movement, Inc. v. Board of Trade**, 977 F.2d 1147 (7th Cir. 1992)].

---

a. And note

The fact that electric power companies are subject to regulation by the Federal Power Commission (under the Federal Power Act) has been held **not** to bar a government antitrust suit. The Court found no intention in the Act to exempt power companies from the antitrust laws. [**Otter Tail Power Co. v. United States**, *supra*, §540]

D. Export Trade Associations

1. Express Antitrust Exemption—Webb-Pomerene Act [§552]

Section 2 of the Webb-Pomerene Export Trade Associations Act [15 U.S.C. §§61 *et seq.*] exempts from the Sherman Act those agreements or acts occurring in the course of export trade by an association of producers formed *solely* for the purpose of engaging in *export* trade. To qualify for protection under the Webb-Pomerene Act, an association must file a written statement and annual reports with the Federal Trade Commission. [15 U.S.C. §65]

a. Limitation [§553]

However, such activities are not exempt if they have the effect of restraining trade *within* the United States; nor are any agreements or activities that artificially or intentionally enhance or depress prices within the United States exempt.

(1) Note

Furthermore, the Supreme Court has held that an export association was not exempt from the antitrust laws when its sales to a foreign nation were *paid for by U.S. foreign aid payments*. Congress did not intend to exempt what, in effect, were *purchases by the U.S. government*. [**United States v. Concentrated Phosphate Export Association, Inc.,** 393 U.S. 199 (1968)]

b. Purpose of Act [§554]

The purpose of the Webb-Pomerene Act was to allow American competitors to group together in order to compete with foreign cartels in the world market. That purpose is now less important, as foreign cartels have disappeared and *American* firms now dominate international trade. Furthermore, as a matter of economics, an association of producers with any substantial degree of market power cannot agree together on the amount they will export without thereby affecting the level of domestic supply (and the level of domestic prices), and hence such activities would rarely be exempt (*see* above). [*Compare* **United States v. United States Alkali Export Association,** 86 F. Supp. 59 (S.D.N.Y. 1949)]

(1) Note

Webb-Pomerene does not apply only to American firms. [**International Raw Materials, Ltd. v. Stauffer Chemical Co.,** 978 F.2d 1318 (3d Cir. 1992), *cert. denied*, 507 U.S. 988 (1993)—association of soda ash exporters did not lose Webb-Pomerene exemption simply because many members of the association were subsidiaries of foreign corporations]

2. Express Antitrust Exemption—Export Trading Company Act [§555]

Because of Webb-Pomerene's limitations, few trade associations availed themselves of the Act's exemption. In 1982, Congress passed the Export Trading Company Act ("ETCA"), which provides a much stronger antitrust exemption for qualifying companies.

a. Commerce Department registration [§556]

To obtain ETCA immunity, an exporter must apply for and receive a certificate from the Commerce Department. The Commerce Department must certify that the proposed export activities will not have anticompetitive effects in the United

States. [15 U.S.C. §4013] The Commerce Department has *broad discretion* in the granting of such certificates. [**Horizons, International v. Baldridge,** 811 F.2d 154 (3d Cir. 1987)]

b. Replaces antitrust laws [§557]

Companies that obtain such a certificate are not liable under the general antitrust laws. They cannot be held criminally liable under the antitrust laws for conduct that is specified in a valid certificate issued pursuant to the ETCA. [15 U.S.C. §4016] However, they may be sued (for only single damages) by private parties if they violate the special standards set out in section 4013 of the Act.

E. Bank Mergers

1. Express Antitrust Exemption [§558]

Bank and savings association mergers are exempt from private enforcement of section 7 of the Clayton Act and section 1 of the Sherman Act by virtue of special legislation [12 U.S.C. §1828(c)] passed in 1966 in response to the Supreme Court ruling in **United States v. Philadelphia National Bank,** *supra,* §352.

a. Requirements for merger [§559]

This legislation requires that merging depository institutions obtain the approval of appropriate governmental authorities, and further requires such authorities to obtain reports from the Attorney General on any anticompetitive factors that may be involved. The Attorney General may attack any such merger in a judicial proceeding within 30 days of its approval by the governmental authorities.

b. Limitation [§560]

However, in any proceeding instituted by the Attorney General, the merger shall be upheld—even if competition will be substantially lessened thereby—if the anticompetitive effects are "clearly outweighed" by the public interest effect of the transaction in meeting "the convenience and needs of the community to be served." [12 U.S.C. §1828(c)(5)(B), (7)(B); *and see* **United States v. Phillipsburg National Bank & Trust Co.,** 399 U.S. 350 (1970)]

(1) But note

The Supreme Court has read this exemption *narrowly*, holding that if the bank merger is shown to have an anticompetitive effect, the parties are required to show that there is *"no other alternative"* (to the merger) to meet the convenience and needs of the community to be served. [**United States v. Third National Bank,** 390 U.S. 171 (1968)]

F. Insurance

1. **Express Antitrust Exemption Dependent on State Regulation [§561]**

   The *McCarran-Ferguson Act* [15 U.S.C. §§1011 *et seq.*] provides that federal antitrust laws are not applicable to the *business of insurance* to the extent that the business is *regulated by state law*. However, state regulation cannot render lawful any act or agreement to *boycott, coerce, or intimidate*.

2. **States' Regulatory Legislation [§562]**

   Today, every state has legislation regulating the insurance business, so that the aspects of insurance that are subject to federal antitrust laws are greatly reduced.

   a. **State permitted to regulate [§563]**

      The state that must be regulating is the state where the business activities of the insurance company have operative force. [**Traveler's Health Association v. FTC,** 298 F.2d 820 (8th Cir. 1962)]

      Example: A company doing mail order business in a state in which it is *not* licensed *will* be subject to federal regulation (despite the enactment in many states of the Uniform Unauthorized Insurers False Advertising Process Act).

3. **Exemption Narrowly Construed [§564]**

   The term "business of insurance" has been narrowly construed to *not exempt* from the antitrust laws the activities of an insurance company that merely reduce costs rather than spread risk. The statutory language "exempts the 'business of insurance' and not all 'business of insurance companies.'" [**Group Life & Health Insurance Co. v. Royal Drug Co.,** 440 U.S. 205 (1979)—refusing to find an exemption for retail price agreements between Blue Shield and participating pharmacies that limited the markup that the pharmacies would charge Blue Shield policy holders]

   Example: The creation by an insurance company of a "peer review" committee to review doctors' charges and determine whether they are "reasonable and customary" was held to be not exempt from antitrust scrutiny. The Court reasoned that it was not part of the business of spreading risk, did not involve the policy relationship between insurer and insured, and involved committee members who were not in the "business of insurance." [**Union Labor Life Insurance Co. v. Pireno,** 458 U.S. 119 (1982)]

   a. **Connection to foreign companies [§565]**

      Domestic insurers do not forfeit McCarran-Ferguson immunity merely because they agree to act with foreign reinsurers not subject to state regulation. [**Hartford Fire Insurance Co. v. California,** *supra,* §235]

4. "Boycotts" Not Exempt [§566]

Consistent with the Supreme Court's narrow construction of exemptions, the Act's use of the term "boycott" has been broadly construed to enlarge the activities that will be subject to antitrust scrutiny. [**St. Paul Fire & Marine Insurance Co. v. Barry**, 438 U.S. 531 (1978); **Hartford Fire Insurance Co. v. California**, *supra*]

G. Stock Exchanges

1. Implied Antitrust Exemption [§567]

Stock exchanges registered under the Securities Exchange Act of 1934 are permitted to fix minimum brokerage commission rates which all members must charge. Although the 1934 Securities Exchange Act contains no express exemption from the antitrust laws, the Supreme Court *has implied* one because application of the antitrust laws to commission rates would "unduly interfere . . . with the operations of the Securities Exchange Act." [**Gordon v. New York Stock Exchange**, 422 U.S. 659 (1975)]

a. Note

Similarly, the Court has held that an implied exemption from the antitrust laws was necessary for the regulatory framework of the Investment Company Act. [**United States v. National Association of Securities Dealers, Inc.**, 422 U.S. 694 (1975)]

b. Rationale and limits

Implied immunity in these cases appears to be based on the fact that government regulation and the application of the antitrust laws were *necessarily incompatible* in a particular case. There is no reason to believe implied immunity will extend to cases in which it is possible to apply both government regulation and the antitrust laws. [*See* **Silver v. New York Stock Exchange**, *supra*, §236— Sherman Act applied to NYSE membership rules]

H. Labor Unions

1. In General [§568]

There are actually two labor exemptions. The first is specifically codified in section 6 of the Clayton Act [15 U.S.C. §17]. It protects the activities of labor unions acting unilaterally and in their own interests (*e.g.*, in the process of organizing workers). The second is a nonstatutory exemption implied by the seemingly contradictory congressional policies "favoring collective bargaining . . . and free competition." [**Ehredt Underground, Inc. v. Commonwealth Edison Co.**, 830 F. Supp. 1083 (N.D. Ill. 1993)—*quoting* **Connell Construction Co. v. Plumbers & Steamfitters Local Union**,

421 U.S. 616 (1975)] The nonstatutory exemption protects certain collective bargaining agreements from assault under the antitrust laws. It also applies to employer conduct that takes place "during and immediately after a collective-bargaining negotiation" that "grew out of, and was directly related to, the lawful operation of the bargaining process," that "involved a matter that the parties were required to negotiate collectively," and that "concerned only the parties to the collective-bargaining relationship." [**Brown v. Pro Football, Inc.**, 518 U.S. 231 (1996)]

2. Limitations [§569]

The scope of exempt activities is limited.

a. Relation to nonlabor groups [§570]

Labor unions cannot combine with nonlabor groups to create monopolies and to control the marketing of goods and services. [**Allen Bradley Co. v. Local 3**, 325 U.S. 797 (1945)]

> **Example:** Although a union can properly demand a uniform wage scale throughout an industry, the union is not exempt from the antitrust laws where it agrees with one set of employers to impose a certain wage scale on other employers in order to disadvantage or destroy the latter. [**United Mine Workers of America v. Pennington**, 381 U.S. 657 (1965)]

> **Compare:** An agreement between a stage actors' union and theatrical agents that established a licensing system for approved agents and prohibited union members from using nonlicensed agents was a lawful agreement between a union and a labor group, because of the essential role agents played in procuring employment for union members. [**H.A. Artists & Associates, Inc. v. Actors' Equity Association**, 451 U.S. 704 (1981)]

b. Agreement limiting employer's dealing with third parties [§571]

A union-employer agreement that limits the discretion of the employer to deal with third parties is exempt *only if* it protects a *legitimate interest of labor union members*. [**Local 189 Amalgamated Meat Cutters v. Jewel Tea**, 381 U.S. 676 (1965)—butchers' union contracts with grocery-employers could properly impose uniform marketing hours for meat on grocers]

> **Example:** A "union-subcontractor" clause that prohibits union contractors from awarding contracts to nonunion subcontractors violates the Sherman Act and thus is not exempted. [**Connell Construction Co. v. Plumbers & Steamfitters Local Union**, *supra*] Unions attempting to enforce such clauses may therefore be held liable for damages to contractors injured thereby.

> **Example:** An alleged conspiracy between a union local and nonlabor entities to force an employer to enter into a collective bargaining agreement was

sufficient to prevent application of both the statutory and nonstatutory exemptions. [**Ehredt Underground, Inc. v. Commonwealth Edison Co.,** *supra,* §568]

Example: The efforts of a group of local trade unions to force nonunion employers out of the construction market were similarly unprotected by the statutory exemption. [**Altemose Construction Co. v. Building & Construction Trades Council,** 751 F.2d 653 (3d Cir.), *cert. denied,* 475 U.S. 1107 (1985)]

---

(1) And note

Even if the union enters into a combination in its legitimate self-interest, it may still face liability under the antitrust laws if the *means* it uses to achieve its legitimate goal are themselves anticompetitive. [**Connell Construction Co. v. Plumbers & Steamfitters Local Union,** *supra*]

I. Professional Baseball

1. Exemption by Stare Decisis [§572]

There has been a long-established judicial exemption from the antitrust laws for professional baseball.

a. *In* **Federal Baseball Clubs v. National League,** 259 U.S. 200 (1922), a member of the Federal League sued the National and American Leagues for treble damages under the Sherman Act. The Court held that baseball was not in "interstate commerce" and affirmed judgment for the antitrust defendants.

b. *In* **Toolson v. New York Yankees, Inc.,** 346 U.S. 356 (1953), the Court expressed reluctance to overrule *Federal Baseball Clubs,* above, noting that the leagues had relied on the earlier case and that Congress had not acted to overturn the decision. Hence, the Court held that baseball was not within the scope of the federal antitrust laws.

c. *In* **Flood v. Kuhn,** 407 U.S. 258 (1972), the Court recognized that, in fact, baseball "is a business and is engaged in interstate commerce" but nevertheless held that the baseball exemption—although it is "an aberration" and an "anomaly"— was entitled to the benefits of *stare decisis.*

2. Note—No Exemption for Other Sports [§573]

No other professional sport operating in interstate commerce, such as football, boxing, basketball, hockey, etc., is exempt. [*See, e.g.,* **Radovich v. National Football League,** 352 U.S. 445 (1957); **Haywood v. National Basketball Association,** 401 U.S. 1204 (1971); **McNeil v. National Football League,** 790 F. Supp. 871 (D. Minn. 1992); **Chicago Professional Sports Limited Partnership v. National Basketball Association,** *supra,* §371]

J. "State Action" Exemption

1. Deference to State Regulatory Schemes [§574]

A state-created regulatory scheme that is a *clearly articulated system* of regulation and is *affirmatively designed* to displace antitrust law is outside the reach of the antitrust laws under the "state action" exemption. [**Parker v. Brown**, 317 U.S. 341 (1943); **New Motor Vehicle Board v. Orrin W. Fox Co.**, 439 U.S. 96 (1978)] This is true even though the conduct in question may have anticompetitive effects. To qualify for protection under the state action exception, the challenged restraint must satisfy two elements: it must be "*clearly articulated and affirmatively expressed as state policy*," and "the policy must be '*actively supervised*' by the state itself." [**California Retail Liquor Dealers Association v. Midcal Aluminum, Inc.**, 445 U.S. 97 (1980)]

a. Clearly articulated state policy required [§575]

The more clearly expressed and rigidly imposed a state policy is, the more likely it is to bestow antitrust immunity upon regulated parties. But compulsion (as opposed to mere authorization) is no longer deemed necessary.

Example: Rate bureaus made up of common carriers operating in four states were authorized by the states to propose collective rates. These rate-making activities were immune under state action doctrine because the states had clearly articulated a decision to displace competition with regulated pricing. [**Southern Motor Carriers Rate Conference, Inc. v. United States**, 471 U.S. 48 (1985)]

Compare: A Michigan state commission approved (as part of the overall rate structure) the practice of a private electric utility in providing residential customers with free light bulbs. The United States Supreme Court held that approval of the utility's rates was not sufficient to exempt the "giveaway" because (i) light bulbs are not regulated, (ii) no clearly articulated state policy supported the light bulb program, and (iii) state participation was not so substantial that it would be unfair to hold the utility responsible for its conduct. [**Cantor v. Detroit Edison**, 428 U.S. 579 (1976)]

b. "Active supervision" required [§576]

The state must adequately supervise the regulatory scheme for the "state action" exemption to apply. [**California Retail Liquor Dealers Association v. Midcal**

Aluminum, Inc., *supra*, §280] However, application of this requirement has been uneven.

---

e.g. Example: A committee appointed by the state supreme court to administer bar examinations and the admission of candidates to the bar is exempt from the Sherman Act under the state action doctrine because the state supreme court retained plenary authority over bar admissions. [**Hoover v. Ronwin,** 466 U.S. 558 (1984)]

---

cf. Compare: Physician peer review boards authorized but not overseen by state agencies or courts are *not* exempt under the state action doctrine. [**Patrick v. Burget,** 486 U.S. 94 (1988)] And title insurance rates set by title insurance companies and then confirmed or vetoed by a state agency are not exempt as state action because of the lack of direct state involvement in the rate-making scheme. The state action exemption is intended to assure active, deliberate state participation in regulatory structures, and the mere potential for state regulation is not sufficient to justify antitrust immunity. [**Federal Trade Commission v. Ticor Title Insurance Co.,** 504 U.S. 621 (1992)]

---

c. **Limitation—governmental functions [§577]**

The "state action" exemption applies only to governmental functions, *not to nongovernmental functions* performed by the state.

---

e.g. Examples: The federal antitrust laws applied to an alleged conspiracy by three municipally owned utilities to prevent expansion by a private power company. [**Lafayette v. Louisiana Power & Light Co.,** 435 U.S. 389 (1978)] Also, municipal stadium and airport authorities and an airport commissioner were not exempt when they conspired with brewers to exclude a brand of beer previously sold at those facilities. [**Duke & Co. v. Foerster,** 521 F.2d 1277 (3d Cir. 1975)]

---

cf. Compare: Where the state action exemption applies and the state's action is immune (*i.e.*, a governmental function is involved), an individual cannot be liable for conspiring with the government. [**City of Columbia v. Omni Outdoor Advertising,** 499 U.S. 365 (1991)]

---

2. **Action of a Municipality [§578]**

The "state action" exemption exempts only *state* action—not the action of a municipality, unless the state is intimately involved. Thus, a "home rule" municipality that imposed a construction moratorium on expansion by a cable television company, which held a nonexclusive franchise from the city, violated the Sherman Act and was not entitled to immunity under **Parker v. Brown,** *supra*, §574. No immunity existed because: (i) the city's action did not constitute action of the state itself, despite the legislative powers granted it by the state; and (ii) the city's action was not taken pursuant to a clearly articulated and affirmatively expressed state policy.

[**Community Communications Co. v. City of Boulder,** 455 U.S. 40 (1982); *and see* **Hertz Corp. v. City of New York,** 1 F.3d 121 (2d Cir. 1993)—municipal regulation of car rental rates based only on broad "home rule" authority invalid]

a. **Distinguish—clear state delegation [§579]**
Where the state has in fact clearly delegated to municipalities the power to control a particular area of commerce, that delegation is sufficient to immunize conduct by local governments—and no continuing state supervision of the municipality is required. [**Southern Motor Carriers Rate Conference, Inc. v. United States,** *supra*, §575] Municipalities are treated differently from private parties in this respect.

b. **Immunity from damages [§580]**
The Local Government Antitrust Immunity Act of 1984 provides that municipalities and government officials are not liable in damages for violations of the antitrust laws, even if the state action doctrine does not shield them from injunctive relief. [15 U.S.C. §§35-36]

c. **Authorization by state [§581]**

> **Example:** Once a state has expressly and specifically authorized a municipality to regulate a particular market, state supervision is no longer necessary to preserve the state action exemption. [**Town of Hallie v. City of Eau Claire,** 471 U.S. 34 (1985)]

> **Example:** A municipality's decision to adopt rezoning ordinances restricting billboards was exempt under the state action doctrine because the state had authorized the municipality to regulate construction and land use to promote health, safety, morals, and the general welfare. [**City of Columbia v. Omni Outdoor Advertising,** *supra*]

EXAM TIP   **gilbert**

Although state action is immune from the antitrust laws, remember that a *municipality* (e.g., city or town) is **not** equivalent to the state. The municipality's action will be immune only if the court can find "state action" in the form of a *clear delegation of power* to the municipality, and mere "home rule" powers is not enough. You will have to analyze the facts carefully to make a determination whether there has been a delegation of power.

K. Concerted Action by Competitors Designed to Influence Governmental Action

1. **_Noerr-Pennington_ Doctrine [§582]**

Efforts by individuals or groups to petition the government are protected by the _antitrust immunity doctrine._ Under this doctrine, such activities are not illegal, _even if they are undertaken for anticompetitive purposes._ [**Eastern Railroad Presidents Conference v. Noerr Motor Freight,** 365 U.S. 127 (1961)—no violation of Sherman Act where complaint charged defendants had engaged in concerted public relations campaign to foster adoption of laws that would be adverse to plaintiffs' business; _and see_ **United Mine Workers of America v. Pennington,** _supra,_ §570]

a. **Rationale**

In determining the coverage of the Sherman Act, the Court in _Noerr_ relied heavily on the _right of petition_ recognized in the Bill of Rights, and the dangers inherent in any restriction of political activities given the First Amendment interests involved.

b. **Scope of doctrine [§583]**

The _Noerr-Pennington_ doctrine is not limited to attempts to influence legislators. It has been extended to attempts to influence _administrative agencies_ and the _courts_ (by instituting judicial proceedings, etc.). "The right of access to the courts is but one aspect of the right of petition." [**California Motor Transport v. Trucking Unlimited,** 404 U.S. 508 (1972)] The doctrine has also been held to extend to joint efforts to influence foreign governments. [**Coastal States Marketing, Inc. v. Hunt,** 694 F.2d 1358 (5th Cir. 1983); _but see_ **Occidental Petroleum Corp. v. Buttes Gas Oil Co.,** 331 F. Supp. 92 (C.D. Cal. 1971), _aff'd,_ 461 F.2d 1261 (9th Cir.), _cert. denied,_ 409 U.S. 950 (1972)]

(1) **But note—does not apply to private body [§584]**

The Supreme Court has refused to apply the _Noerr-Pennington_ doctrine to an attempt to influence a _private body_ that effectively dictates government policies and standards. [**Allied Tube & Conduit Corp. v. Indian Head, Inc.,** 486 U.S. 492 (1988)]

Example: In _Allied Tube,_ the private body in question was the National Fire Protection Association ("NFPA"). NFPA set and published product standards and codes related to fire protection which were widely used by governmental agencies nationwide in setting building codes and similar regulations. Plaintiff, a maker of plastic electrical conduit, proposed to NFPA that it permit the use of plastic conduit in addition to steel conduit, which had been approved and in use nationally for years. A group of steel conduit manufacturers and other steel industry members agreed to defeat the proposal by packing the annual meeting with new NFPA members whose task would be to vote down plaintiff's proposal. The Supreme Court held that the *Noerr-Pennington* doctrine did not protect the steel conduit manufacturers from antitrust liability. Distinguishing the case from *Noerr*, the Court noted that NFPA could not be viewed as a "quasi-legislative" body simply because of its influence on government standards.

(2) And note—coercion not covered by doctrine [§585]
In **FTC v. Superior Court Trial Lawyers Association**, *supra*, §232, the Supreme Court suggested that the *Noerr-Pennington* doctrine did not extend to horizontal agreements intended to *coerce* the government into paying higher prices to the "petitioners."

2. Limitations [§586]
However, there may be situations in which an "attempt to influence governmental action" is nothing more than harassment of a competitor or a "mere sham," and in such cases the courts might well find an unlawful combination in restraint of trade.

Example: In **California Motor Transport v. Trucking Unlimited**, *supra*, the Court *upheld* a cause of action under the Sherman Act based on claims that a group of truckers was attempting to monopolize the California market by instituting state and federal proceedings to resist every application for operating rights by would-be competitors, and by using its resources to oppose, delay, and defeat such applications. The Court held that such activity constituted an attempt to *interfere* with the would-be competitors' *right of access* to the agencies and courts, which would enable them to compete; and that such *purposeful interference* was *not* protected under *Noerr-Pennington*, *supra*.

a. Exception
For litigation to constitute a "sham," depriving plaintiff of *Noerr-Pennington* immunity, the lawsuit must be *both* "*objectively baseless and improperly motivated.*" [**Professional Real Estate Investors, Inc. v. Columbia Pictures Industries, Inc.**, *supra*, §531] And only if the litigation is objectively baseless "in the sense that no reasonable litigant could realistically expect success on the merits" may a court inquire into the subjective motivation of the complainant, to decide whether the lawsuit "conceals 'an attempt to interfere directly' with a competitor's business relationships" by using the lawsuit itself (rather than its outcome) as "'an anticompetitive weapon.'" [**Professional Real Estate Investors, Inc. v. Columbia Pictures Industries, Inc.**, *supra*—quoting *Noerr*, *supra*]

b. And note
The *Noerr-Pennington* doctrine does *not* shield the actions of a defendant in conspiring with the agency of a foreign government while engaged in private commercial activities to restrain competition in *foreign* commerce. [**Continental Ore Co. v. Union Carbide & Carbon**, 370 U.S. 690 (1962)—upholding cause of action under Sherman Act where American manufacturer was alleged to have conspired with Canadian corporation to exclude plaintiff from obtaining vanadium in Canada (Canadian corporation was owned by Canadian govern-

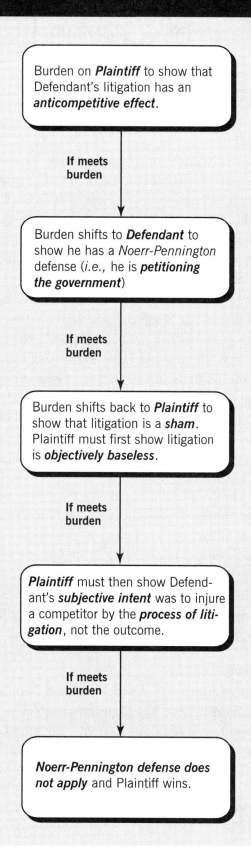

Burden on **Plaintiff** to show that Defendant's litigation has an **anticompetitive effect**.

If meets burden

Burden shifts to **Defendant** to show he has a *Noerr-Pennington* defense (*i.e.*, he is **petitioning the government**)

If meets burden

Burden shifts back to **Plaintiff** to show that litigation is a **sham**. Plaintiff must first show litigation is **objectively baseless**.

If meets burden

Plaintiff must then show Defendant's **subjective intent** was to injure a competitor by the **process of litigation**, not the outcome.

If meets burden

Noerr-Pennington defense does not apply and Plaintiff wins.

ment, but had been granted discretionary authority and was engaged in business activities)]

L. Rejection of "Learned Profession" Exemption

1. In General [§587]

The Supreme Court has held that Congress did **not** intend any sweeping "learned profession" exclusion from the Sherman Act. The fact that professional services (*e.g.,* medical, legal, or engineering services) may differ significantly from other business services, and, accordingly, the nature of the competition is such that services may vary, does not mean that the learned professions are exempt from per se rules or rule of reason analysis under the antitrust laws. [**National Society of Professional Engineers v. United States**, *supra*, §222] However, the Court has given inconsistent signals on the application of antitrust laws to learned professions, such as doctors, lawyers, and engineers. In some cases, the Court has suggested that the fact that concerted action is among members of a learned profession counsels against application of the per se rule and subjects the challenged restraint to *rule of reason* analysis. [**Federal Trade Commission v. Indiana Federation of Dentists**, 476 U.S. 447 (1986); **National Society of Professional Engineers v. United States**, *supra*] In other cases, the Court has held that agreements among members of learned professions are susceptible to *per se* condemnation. [**Arizona v. Maricopa County Medical Society**, 457 U.S. 332 (1982); **Federal Trade Commission v. Superior Court Trial Lawyers Association**, 493 U.S. 411 (1990)]

2. Minimum Fee Schedules for Attorneys Illegal [§588]

In holding that minimum fee schedules for legal services enforced by state bar disciplinary action constituted price fixing in violation of Sherman Act section 1, the Court further ruled that "the fact that the state bar is a state agency for some limited purpose does not create an antitrust shield, at least where the anticompetitive activities were not compelled by direction of the State acting as a sovereign." [**Goldfarb v. Virginia State Bar**, *supra*, §217]

a. Attorney boycott

Similarly, the Court condemned a concerted boycott among attorneys to not represent indigent clients unless the government increased compensation as per se illegal. [**Federal Trade Commission v. Superior Court Trial Lawyers Association**, *supra*]

3. Engineers' Ethical Code Provision Prohibiting Competitive Bidding Illegal [§589]

The Court found that the National Society of Professional Engineers' ("NSPE") ethical code provisions against competitive bidding constituted an agreement among competitors to refuse to discuss prices with potential customers and as such was clearly anticompetitive and in violation of section 1 of the Sherman Act. In such circumstances, the NSPE, like any other defendant whose agreement or conduct is plainly anticompetitive, may not seek to justify the restraint by claiming that it was adopted to foster public health and safety or safer products and services. Such arguments must be directed to Congress. [**National Society of Professional Engineers v. United States,** *supra*]

a. Note

Under the rationale of *National Society of Professional Engineers*, the ethical codes and professional standards of many professional associations may be vulnerable to antitrust attack.

4. Exception for State Action [§590]

A restraint upon attorney advertising imposed by a state supreme court in exercising state power over the supervision and practice of law is ***not*** subject to attack under the antitrust laws, since the Sherman Act does not encompass sovereign state actions. [**Bates v. State Bar of Arizona,** 433 U.S. 350 (1977); *and see supra,* §574] *But note*: The restriction on lawyer advertising was found unconstitutional because it interfered with free speech.

Chapter Eleven:
Appendix—Competition as an Economic Model

CONTENTS

(The authors wish to thank Professor Robert G. Harris, University of California School of Business Administration, for his helpful assistance in the preparation of this section.)

A. Basic Economic Analysis

1. Introduction [§591]

To understand the antitrust laws, it is important to understand the meaning of "competition," because protecting competition is the primary goal of the federal antitrust laws. In fact, many of the antitrust laws come into play only where "the effect . . . [of the specified conduct] may be substantially to lessen competition . . . in any line of commerce." [*See, e.g.,* Clayton Act §§2, 3, 7] This in turn requires an elementary understanding of how the price system affects the rationing of resources and the distribution of income in a market economy. This Appendix discusses the basic tools of economic analysis, the traditional classification of market structures, and the impact of market structures upon resource allocation. This knowledge of economic principles and institutions will be helpful in assessing court decisions and antitrust policies.

2. Demand Concepts

a. Measure of demand [§592]

A *demand schedule* equates the quantity of a particular good consumers are willing to buy at each respective price. A *demand curve* is a graphic representation of a demand schedule, with the price shown on the vertical axis and the quantity demanded at each price shown on the horizontal axis. (*See Figure 1* (*infra*), which illustrates a hypothetical demand curve for widgets.) Demand has the following characteristics:

(1) Consumer goods [§593]

The principal factors that determine demand for consumer goods are: consumer tastes, income of consumers, and the price of other goods or services.

(2) Goods, services used to produce other goods, services [§594]

The principal factors determining the demand for goods or services used in the production of other goods or services would include: demand for the final good or service, the productivity of the good or service in making the final product, and the productivity and cost of other goods or services that could be substituted for the good or service in question.

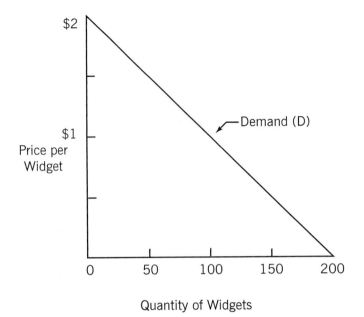

FIGURE 1—Industry Demand Curve for Widgets

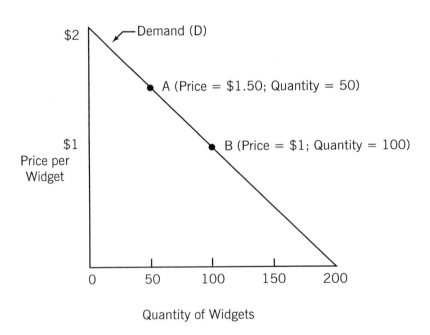

FIGURE 2—Elasticity of Demand

(3) Slope of demand curve [§595]

The demand curve is downward sloping, because, as a general rule, the higher the price of a good, the less of that good buyers are willing to purchase.

(4) "Industry demand" [§596]

Economic analysis generally distinguishes the demand for a given good or service (called "industry demand") from the demand for a good or service produced or supplied by a particular business firm or enterprise. The industry demand is simply the *sum* of the demands for goods or services of all the individual firms in any industry.

b. Elasticity of demand [§597]

"Elasticity" is a measure of the responsiveness of the amount of goods demanded to changes in the price of the good or service. Price elasticity of demand is defined as "the percentage change in quantity taken, divided by the percentage change in price, when the price change is small."

Example: In *Figure 2* (opposite), assume that the price of widgets changes from $1.50 to $1.00. In response to this price change, the demand curve illustrates that consumers will buy more widgets at the lower price (100 rather than 50). The elasticity is equal to the percentage change in quantity [(50 - 100) ÷ 50 = -100%] divided by the percentage change in price [(1.50 - 1.00) ÷ 1.50 = 33% = -3]. Note that elasticity is negative, meaning that a price increase causes a decrease in quantity demanded.

---

(1) Factors determining elasticity [§598]

Factors determining elasticity of demand include the availability of close substitutes for the good or service, the number and variety of uses to which the good or service can be put, and the price of the good or service relative to the buyer's income.

(2) "Elastic" vs. "inelastic" [§599]

Demand is considered *elastic* if a small change in price causes a large change in quantity demanded. *Inelastic* demand is a situation in which the quantity demanded is unresponsive to price changes.

(3) Graphic representation [§600]

The elasticity of the demand curve is represented graphically as the *slope* of the demand curve in *Figure 2*. The more inelastic the demand, the *steeper* the demand curve.

c. Cross-elasticity of demand [§601]

This measures the relation of demand for two *different* goods or services. Cross-elasticity is defined as "the percentage change in the quantity of the given product taken by buyers, divided by the percentage change in the price of *another* product."

---

e.g. **Example:** Suppose that widgets and spinners are interchangeable goods, that they both sell for $1.00, and that the number of widgets demanded at that price is 100. Then suppose that because of material shortages, the price of spinners rises to $1.10; some spinner buyers shift to widgets, raising widget demand to 105. The cross-elasticity between widgets and spinners is the percent change in widget demand (5%, from 100 to 105) divided by the percent change in the spinner price (10%, from $1.00 to $1.10)—5% ÷ 10%, or 1/2.

---

(1) Positive or negative cross-elasticity [§602]

The cross-elasticity of demand between two goods will be *positive* when the two goods are substituted for each other. (A good example of substitute products is butter and margarine.) The cross-elasticity of demand of two goods for each other will be *negative* when the two goods complement each other. (For example, automobiles and tires—where a decrease in the price of cars will probably cause an increase in the number of tires demanded.)

(2) Distinct products or markets [§603]

Cross-elasticity of demand is important in both economic and antitrust analysis in determining what is a distinct product or market. Two "products" with very high cross-elasticities of demand are apt to be considered such close substitutes as to be in fact the same "product" for all practical purposes.

---

e.g. **Example:** In **United States v. E. I. duPont,** *supra,* §146, the defendant manufactured cellophane wrapping material. The relevant market was held to be the market for flexible packaging material. The Court relied on the fact that there was a high cross-elasticity of demand between cellophane and other kinds of wrapping material.

(a) Criticism

In determining the relevant market, it must be remembered that cross-elasticities may and do *vary at different prices* for the product. At a given price, for example, the cross-elasticity of demand between cellophane and other wrapping material might be quite high; but at lower prices, the cross-elasticity could be quite low, indicating that the relevant market might in fact be just cellophane, instead of all flexible wrapping paper.

3. Cost Concepts

a. Opportunity cost [§604]

Accountants and economists define costs very differently. Typically, accounting defines cost on the basis of the original purchase price less depreciation over time. Economics employs the concept of "opportunity cost," which defines cost as equal to the value of resources if they were consumed in their best alternative use. Opportunity costs include the cost of capital invested by a firm, since the capital could have earned interest if it had been invested elsewhere.

Example: The owner of a building uses the space for her own clothing store business. However, the owner could rent the building to a store chain for $1,500—the highest rent that could be charged. Hence, the opportunity cost of the building is $1,500 a month.

---

(1) Comment

A major difficulty in using alternative cost in legal analysis is that it is very difficult to assess. Therefore, courts and enforcement agencies tend to use historical or accounting costs. Nevertheless, it may be a mistake in many instances simply to treat capital costs as "profit." [*See* **Borden Co.**, 1962 Trade Reg. Rptr. ¶16191]

b. Fixed and variable cost [§605]

It is traditional to divide the total costs necessary to produce any given amount of a good or service in a given period of time into two components: fixed costs and variable costs.

(1) Fixed costs [§606]

These are costs such as the investment in plant, equipment, top management personnel (who generally must be hired on long-term contracts), etc., that *cannot be varied* except over a long period and are relatively *independent of the amount of output* produced. Fixed costs are spread over the number of units produced, so that as output increases, the proportion of fixed cost per unit decreases. [*See* Average Fixed Cost ("AFC") curve in *Figure 3*]

(2) Variable costs [§607]

These represent the costs of materials used, ordinary labor hired, power utilized, etc., that *can be varied* in a relatively short period of time and hence are more or less a *direct function of the firm's output*. In the long run, of course, almost all costs are variable—*i.e.*, the firm can change plant size.

c. Average cost [§608]

Average cost is simply the total cost required to produce a given quantity of output divided by the quantity of output produced. *Average variable cost* ("AVC") and *average fixed cost* are the respective averages of total fixed cost and total variable cost. [*See Figure 3*]

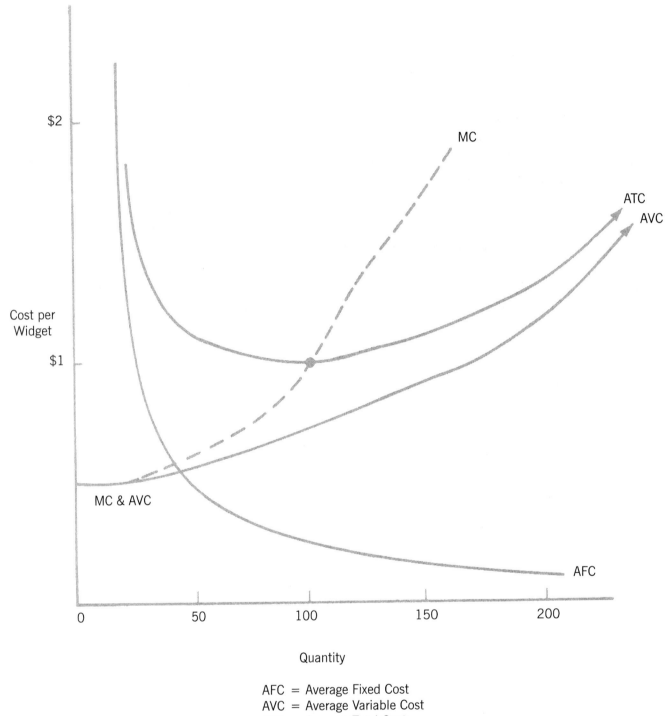

$2

Cost per
Widget

$1

MC

ATC
AVC

MC & AVC

AFC

0   50   100   150   200

Quantity

AFC = Average Fixed Cost
AVC = Average Variable Cost
ATC = Average Total Cost
MC = Marginal Cost

FIGURE 3—Widget Cost Curves

(1) *There are two average cost curves relevant to an individual firm:* the short-run average cost curve relates average costs to various levels of output, *given* the firm's scale of plant; the long-run average cost curve shows the relation between average cost and quantity of output over the long run, in which the firm can *vary* its plant size.

(2) *Short-run average cost curves are generally assumed to be U-shaped.* It is generally inefficient to produce a very small output with a large scale of plant; thus increasing one's output causes the average cost curve to fall to some point. After that point, the principle of diminishing returns may take effect; *i.e.,* when one input (the plant) is held constant, at some point the productivity of other inputs will begin to decrease.

(3) *The long-run average cost curve of most firms is also generally assumed to be U-shaped:* *i.e.,* larger scales of plant are, up to a point, more efficient (*economies of scale*); while beyond some point, a firm generally suffers administrative inefficiency and other size problems (*diseconomies of scale*).

(4) *Constant returns* to scale would occur where long-run average cost remains constant for all outputs. In this case, a firm is equally efficient at any size.

(5) *The optimal* (*i.e.,* most efficient) *level of output* from a social standpoint would be to have all firms operating at the lowest point on their long-run average cost curve. [*See Figure 3*]

d. Marginal cost [§609]

Marginal cost ("MC") is the change in a firm's total costs for each unit change in output. For example, if the total cost of producing 50 widgets is $56 and the cost of producing 51 widgets is $56.55, the marginal cost of widgets is $.55 at that output. *Note:* Depending upon the AVC curve, the marginal cost of an additional unit may be greater, less than, or the same as that for the preceding unit. [*See Figure 3*]

4. Revenue Concepts

a. Total revenue [§610]

The total revenue derived from a product is equal to the price of the product multiplied by the amount sold (assuming that all of the output is sold at a constant cost).

b. Average revenue [§611]

This is simply total revenue divided by the number of units sold. Thus, average revenue equals price, and the average revenue curve for a firm is the same as the firm's demand curve.

c. Marginal revenue [§612]

This is the change in total revenues obtained by selling one additional unit of output. If the firm faces a perfectly elastic demand curve, it can sell its product at one and only one price—because of perfect competition. [*See Figure 5*] In that case, the marginal revenue curve is identical to the average revenue curve. If the demand curve facing the firm is downward sloping, however, marginal revenue is less than average revenue because, in order to sell *one more* unit of output, the firm has to decrease its price on *all* units of output. [*See Figure 4*]

> **Example:** In *Figure 4*, Widget Co. can sell 50 widgets at $1.50 each, for a total revenue of $75.00. If Widget Co. wants to sell a 51st widget, it must cut its price to $1.49—not only on the 51st widget but also on the 50 preceding units. Total revenue for 51 widgets is 51 × $1.49, or $75.99. Thus, the marginal revenue from the 51st widget is $.99, or $75.99 less $75.00.

> **Example:** In *Figure 5*, on the other hand, Spinner Co. can sell any number of spinners for $1.00. Since the sale of an additional spinner does not require a reduction in price, marginal revenue is $1.00 (the same as the price).

B. Market Structures

1. In General [§613]

The *structure* of a market is a function of three characteristics: (i) the number of buyers and sellers; (ii) the degree of product differentiation (*i.e.*, whether the products of firms in the industry are basically similar or different); and (iii) entry conditions (*i.e.*, how difficult is it to enter the industry as a new enterprise).

2. Monopoly [§614]

A monopoly is a market with only one, or with one large, dominant seller of a product with no very close substitutes. Monopoly can ordinarily exist over a significant period of time only if there are *barriers to the entry* of other firms in the market. Barriers to entry may be either:

a. *"Legal" barriers*—patents, franchises, etc.; or

b. *"Natural" barriers*—*i.e.*, there may be large economies of scale, so that a new firm would need to capture a large share of the market in order to minimize production costs and compete with existing firms (*scale economy barriers to entry*), or the amount of initial capital necessary to begin production may be prohibitive (*absolute cost barriers*).

3. Perfect Competition [§615]

This requires a very large number of sellers. The crucial factor in such a market is that the individual seller must take the market price as given—he can sell as much or

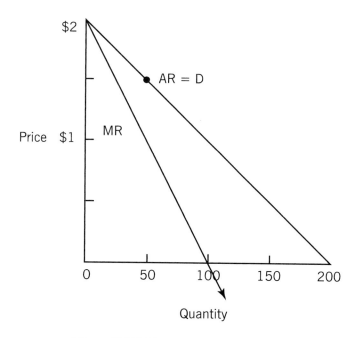

AR = AVERAGE REVENUE CURVE (Same as Demand)
MR = MARGINAL REVENUE CURVE

FIGURE 4—Widget Revenue Curves (Declining Demand)

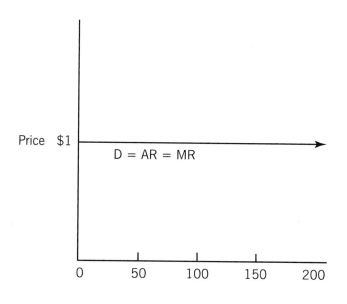

FIGURE 5—Spinner Revenue Curves (Constant Demand)

as little as he likes at that price without altering the price. If he raises his price *above* the market price, however, he will not be able to sell his goods. The necessary conditions for perfect competition are:

(i) *A sufficient number of sellers* (and buyers) so that no one seller (or buyer) can influence the price of what he buys or sells. (The actual number required for a given market depends on several economic factors.)

(ii) *No barriers to the entry of new firms* into the market.

(iii) *A uniform product* offered by all sellers.

(iv) *All buyers and sellers having perfect knowledge of market conditions* (*i.e.*, no buyer will pay more to buy from one seller than he would have had to pay another, out of ignorance).

a. Note

Perfect competition is a model of economic analysis. Although there is probably no real-life market or industry that can be classified as perfectly competitive, the model is nevertheless useful for assessing actual economic performance.

4. Oligopoly [§616]

This is a market with a small number of sellers—more than one, but few enough so that a single seller can influence the price of what she sells. For oligopoly to persist over time, there must be barriers to the entry of new firms. (*See supra*, §614.)

5. Monopolistic Competition [§617]

This involves a market similar to that for perfect competition except for one fact: The sellers in this market offer *differentiated products*. Because each seller's product is relatively distinct, buyers may prefer it over others. Thus, the seller retains *some* discretion to raise the price without losing all his customers.

6. Monopsony [§618]

This is simply a monopoly on the buyer's side of the market; *i.e.*, there is *only one buyer*. (An example might be the company in a "company town." It is the only buyer of labor.) Also, there can be an *oligopsony*—only a few buyers with some influence over price.

7. Cartels [§619]

A cartel results from an *agreement* of the firms in an industry to set an agreed price and/or to produce agreed quantities of output.

8. Bilateral Monopoly [§620]

This is a market in which a monopolistic seller faces a monopsonistic buyer.

C. Functioning of the Price System

1. Three Basic Functions of Price System

a. Rationing of available goods [§621]
In the very short run, when the supply of goods and services is fixed, the price system serves to allocate this supply among consumers and over time, much like an auction. The market clearing price will be determined by the "forces of supply and demand."

b. Assigning society's limited resources to production of goods and services most desired by consumers [§622]
If consumers desire a certain product, they will bid up the price for it. This, in turn, increases the profitability of producing the product, causing more resources to be devoted to such production. The desirable end result is that it becomes equally profitable to make all goods and services in the economy; if one product is more profitable to make than another, more resources will be devoted to that product.

c. Distributing scarce economic goods and services among members of society [§623]
The price system determines how much income people will receive through the prices paid to factors of production, *i.e.*, labor, land, and capital. The price system also determines how much that money income will purchase in consumer markets. The concept of equity implies that prices paid by consumers to producers should just cover the costs of producing economic goods and services. If prices are too high—if they exceed costs—the effect is to transfer income from consumers to producers.

2. Effect of Market Structure on Functioning of the Price System [§624]
Under all market structures, the first basic function of the price system (rationing available goods) is achieved equally well. For the second and third functions, however, market structure becomes crucial. (*Note:* A basic assumption of economic analysis of the price system is that all individual firms will seek to maximize their profits in determining what amount they will produce.)

a. Under perfect competition [§625]
If perfect competition prevails throughout the economy, society's resources will be optimally allocated, and prices will comply with the economic standards of equity.

(1) Profits [§626]
Any firm will maximize its profits by producing that quantity at which *marginal cost equals the marginal revenue*. Since the marginal cost is usually rising, a firm will produce up to—but not beyond—the point where producing an extra unit adds more (or at least as much) to revenue than it adds to cost.

(2) Output [§627]

Since a firm under perfect competition can sell as much or as little of its product as desired at the given market price (*i.e.*, marginal revenue equals price), the firm will produce the output at which marginal cost equals the price. In *Figure 6*, Widget Co. can sell as many widgets as it likes at $1.00 each. It will sell 100, because at that point the marginal cost of producing the 100th widget exactly equals the marginal revenue from the 100th widget. To sell less would be to forego revenue in excess of costs; to sell more would result in costs which exceed revenue.

(3) New firms [§628]

If firms in the industry are making a profit (*i.e.*, if the price exceeds average cost), then other firms will be induced to enter (the allocating function of the price system). This will increase the amount sellers are willing to supply and drive the market price **down** to the point where price equals average cost.

(4) Optimal resource allocation [§629]

Society's resources are said to be optimally allocated in this case because the value of the goods (the price) will equal the marginal cost of the goods. Society would not be better off by devoting more resources to the production of the goods, since the cost of producing another unit (the marginal cost) would exceed the value (the price).

(5) Result [§630]

In a competitive equilibrium, firms in an industry are charging prices exactly equal to the cost of production, including a normal or "fair" rate of profit. Hence, consumers are paying no more for the goods than they are worth. This concept of economic equity or fairness is based upon a price theory of value.

b. Under monopoly [§631]

If some of society's goods are produced under monopoly conditions, resources will **not** be optimally allocated. With an unchecked monopoly, too few of society's resources will be devoted to producing that particular good. In *Figure 7*, Widget Co. as a monopolist will produce only up to point Z, rather than up to point X (as it would under perfect competition). At the same time, society will be paying more for the widgets that are produced.

(1) Restricted output [§632]

The monopolist restricts output because he faces a falling marginal revenue curve: To sell more output, he must drop his price to all buyers in the market. Therefore, the monopolist restricts output to only 75 widgets (point Z in *Figure 7*), whereas a competitive widget industry would produce at a lower price and sell a large quantity of output (point X).

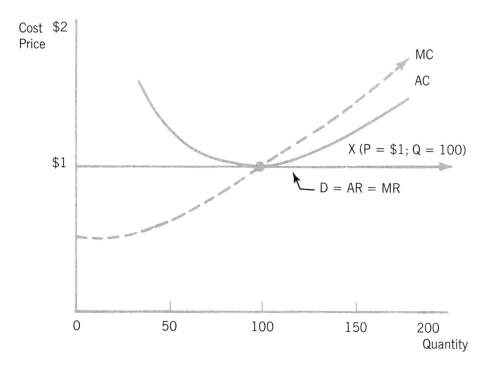

FIGURE 6—Widget Co. Facing Perfect Competition

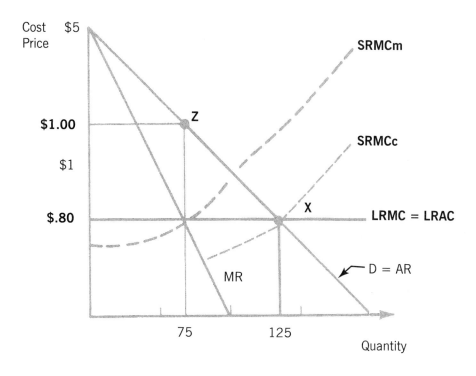

FIGURE 7—Widgets: Monopoly and Competition Compared

(2) Profits [§633]

The monopolist maximizes profit by selling that quantity at which marginal cost is exactly equal to marginal revenue (SRMCm = MR). If the monopolist sold less, the marginal revenue from selling one more unit would be greater than the marginal cost of producing that extra unit. But if the monopolist was selling more than 75 widgets, the extra revenues obtained from one more unit would be less than the additional cost of producing that unit.

(3) Pricing [§634]

For any given quantity, the price is determined by the demand, or average revenue curve. In *Figure 7*, the market-clearing price for 75 widgets is $1.00, so that is what the monopolist will charge. (Assuming a constant long-run cost curve, as in *Figure 7*, a competitive industry would produce at the point where the marginal cost curve intersects the demand curve (point X, SRMCc = AR), and charge a price of $.80.)

(4) Poor resource allocation [§635]

Society's scarce resources are not optimally allocated in this case, because the price of the good exceeds the marginal cost of producing it. Society would be better off if it devoted more resources to the production of the good, up to the optimal point X, which is the competitive result. In effect, the monopolist harms society in two ways: by charging prices that are too high, and producing too little output.

(5) Result [§636]

Because the monopoly profit-maximizing price ($1.00) is greater than the long-run average cost of production ($.80), the monopolist earns excess profits, thereby effectively transferring income from consumers of the product to the producer. In the competitive result, the price is equal to the average cost, so that firms in the industry earn only a normal rate of profit, and consumers pay only what the product is worth.

c. Under cartels [§637]

Depending on the terms of agreement among firms in the cartel, a cartelized industry can behave just like a monopolist in restricting output and misallocating resources. In some respects, a monopoly may actually be preferable to a cartel: *i.e.*, a monopoly can at least take advantage of economies of scale.

(1) But note

The members of a cartel have an incentive to ***cheat*** by cutting their prices and expanding output. If only one member of a cartel cheats, it can capture a greater share of the market while still maintaining a price above the competitive level. Of course, if all of the cartel members cheat by expanding output, the industry price will fall toward the competitive price.

d. Under oligopoly [§638]

The behavior of firms in an oligopoly cannot be analyzed *even in theory* by referring solely to demand for the industry's product and costs for the firms. This is because each firm, in considering the consequences of a proposed action (such as increasing price), must take into account the *reactions* of other firms in the industry. In general, however, it is thought that oligopoly tends to result in restricted output (though to a lesser extent than in a monopoly situation).

(1) Price rigidity [§639]

One possible assumption about the behavior of oligopolists is that a firm's competitors will immediately meet any price cut by that firm but will *not* necessarily follow a price increase. If so, the oligopolist faces a "kinked" demand curve. The principal characteristic of oligopolistic behavior under this assumption is price rigidity: firms are hesitant to lower or raise prices, and even increases or decreases in cost may not result in a change in price. Price rigidity has been confirmed empirically in many oligopolistic industries.

(2) Price leadership [§640]

Another assumption about the behavior of oligopolists is price leadership. Under this theory, the firms in the industry will tacitly (*i.e.*, without any agreement to do so) follow the price movements of the leader firm (which is usually the largest firm in the industry). This assumption is also frequently borne out in the actual behavior of certain oligopolistic industries (such as steel).

(3) Result [§641]

Oligopolists who sell differentiated products tend to compete on the basis of product changes, improvements, and advertising, rather than on price. As a consequence of this *nonprice competition*, consumers may have to pay higher prices, to cover the costs of excessive advertising, style changes, etc.

e. Under monopsony [§642]

Monopsony generally occurs where one firm producing a final product is the sole buyer of an item used in the manufacture of the final product. In this case, the monopsony will result in *underutilization* of the monopsonized input and a corresponding restriction of output in the final product.

(1) Inputs [§643]

The monopsonist cannot buy as much of the input as she desires at a constant price because she faces the entire supply curve for the product (which is rising); *i.e.*, the more of the input she buys, the higher the price she must pay for all inputs.

(2) Profits [§644]

The monopsonist will maximize her profit by using the monopsonized input up to the point where the marginal cost of the input equals the marginal revenue product of that input.

(a) Note

"Marginal revenue product" is a function of the productivity of the input in producing the final output and the value of that output (*i.e.*, the price, if the monopsonist sells competitively; or the marginal revenue, if she sells monopolistically).

(3) Result [§645]

The monopsonized input is underutilized because the price of the input is *less* than its value in producing the final product (the marginal revenue product). Monopsony thus results in underutilization of the monopsonized input, overutilization of other inputs, and restriction of output of the final product.

(4) Comment [§646]

One important type of monopsony power is that of employers in the market for labor since in many localities there is only one or a few major employers. Labor unions have been exempted from the antitrust laws (*see supra*, §§568 *et seq.*), so that workers can organize to bargain collectively with their employer, creating a form of *countervailing* market power.

D. Summary—Competition as an Ideal

1. Efficiency [§647]

The chief economic value of competition is that it allows the optimal allocation of society's resources according to consumer demand. Competition is also considered a stimulus to efficiency. Competition and its attendant characteristic—a large number of economic units—is likewise favored by many for noneconomic values, such as individual liberty and local control of business, which could be usurped (some would argue) by concentrated industries and huge corporations.

2. Innovation and Stability [§648]

Other economic values worth considering are *innovation* and *stability*. The relationship of competition to innovation is *not* agreed upon by economists. Many have argued that some degree of monopoly is more conducive to innovation than competition. (The patent laws adopt this theory.) Economists agree even less about the effects of competition on economic stability, business cycles, and the like.

3. Equity and Fairness [§649]

An important motivation for the passage and enforcement of the antitrust laws is the concern for equity and fairness. The ideal of a market economy is that consumers can purchase goods and services at prices equal to the cost of their production, that the quality and quantity of products offered for sale will reflect consumers' preferences, and that people will have economic opportunities to enter an industry if they choose. These ideals are achieved in an economic system where power is diffused among many producers and consumers.

Review Questions
and Answers

Review Questions

1. Determine whether each of the following statements is true or false:

    a. At early common law, one party could properly agree with another never to engage in a particular trade or profession.

    _____

    b. Under modern American common law, an agreement not to compete may sometimes be implied against a seller who transfers the goodwill of his business to another.

    _____

    c. In some states, an agreement by an employee not to accept competitive employment is unenforceable.

    _____

    d. If Amy agrees with Beth for valuable consideration not to compete with Beth, the contract is enforceable against Amy according to the law of most states.

    _____

    e. The "reasonableness" of the geographic area covered by a covenant not to compete depends upon the probable future area of business, as well as its present area of activity.

    _____

    f. If an agreement not to compete is unduly broad or long, courts will never reform it to conform to "reasonable" coverage.

    _____

    g. Where state statutes governing covenants not to compete have been enacted, they generally tend to be somewhat less restrictive than the common law rules.

    _____

2. The 10 firms that comprise the widget industry agree among themselves to restrict output to a specified amount per firm. Would this agreement be valid at common law?

    _____

3. Where the Sherman Act uses common law terms such as "restraint of trade," the courts are bound by judicial interpretations of such terms made prior to the Act. True or false?

    _____

4. Does the Federal Trade Commission have broader authority than the courts in enforcing the antitrust laws?

    _____

5. Paintco and Colorco are competitive paint manufacturers who operate solely within Colorado. If the two agree to charge the same price, their actions cannot be challenged under the Sherman Act. True or false?

    _____

6. Widget International does business outside the United States. In certain nations, Widget International is required by local authorities to meet with its competitors and allocate territories. Can this be challenged under the federal antitrust laws? _____

7. Widget International, which does business outside the United States, agrees with several of its American competitors to fix prices in various United States markets. Is this a criminal act? _____

   a. Would the result be the same if Widget International entered into tying arrangements with its customers, in violation of the Clayton Act? _____

   b. Assuming Widget International has violated a penal provision of the antitrust laws, are individual officers or directors of the company subject to criminal sanctions? _____

8. If a company is found to have monopolized trade in the relevant market, a federal court has the power to break up the company and create competing entities from its assets. True or false? _____

9. Larry, Moe, Curly, and Shemp compete in the market for aged oak barrels. Larry files a private antitrust action, alleging that Moe, Curly, and Shemp have formed a cartel and agreed to raise prices and restrict output. Does Larry have standing to assert such a claim? _____

10. The government sues Apex Corporation for various violations of the antitrust laws. Mosaic Company, a competitor of Apex, claims to have been injured by the violations and moves to intervene in the case. Should Mosaic's motion be granted? _____

    a. Assume Mosaic seeks treble damages from Apex, alleging that Apex's anticompetitive conduct foreclosed a market that Mosaic intended to enter. Is this a proper basis for recovering damages? _____

    b. Suppose Mosaic shows that it lost profits as a result of Apex's activities. Apex objects to admission of evidence on the amount of such damages, contending that it is "mere speculation." Should the evidence be admitted? _____

11. To recover treble damages, a private plaintiff must show that its injury was the direct result of the defendant's unlawful conduct. True or false? _____

12. If the defendant in a private antitrust action can establish that the plaintiff also violated the antitrust laws, recovery will probably be denied. True or false? _____

13. Plaintiff files a treble damages action against Defendant in 2005, alleging damages sustained in 2000 as a result of antitrust violations by Defendant. Can Defendant have the suit dismissed? _____

    a. Would the result be different if government proceedings had been commenced against Defendant in 2003? _____

14. Protégée Company is the only firm operating in the relevant market. Does this indicate a violation of Sherman Act section 2? _____

    a. Suppose Protégée Company has several competitors in the relevant market. Can it still be guilty of monopolizing trade and commerce? _____

15. Makit Company is charged by the government with monopolizing the regional market for widgets. In its defense, Makit Company asserts that the relevant geographic market is nationwide (there being many other widget makers in the country). Would the freight charges on widgets be significant in determining this issue? _____

    a. Makit Company also contends that the relevant product market includes items other than widgets, and introduces a consumer-preference survey showing that widgets and certain other products tend to be used interchangeably. Will this support a finding that the market is broader than widgets? _____

16. A relevant antitrust market can sometimes be defined as the market for a single firm's products. True or false? _____

17. If a company possesses 100% of the market at the time an antitrust suit is filed, it necessarily has power in that market. True or false? _____

18. Blimpo Corporation is charged with monopolizing trade in the relevant market. Must it be shown that Blimpo intended to monopolize in order to prove a section 2 violation? _____

    a. If Blimpco can demonstrate that its market position was acquired because of unique production techniques and facilities, will it have a successful defense? _____

19. Tone, a start-up company providing local telephone service, seeks access to the existing telephone lines of its established competitor, Bell. Bell refuses to allow Tone to interconnect to its lines, even though Tone is willing to pay the same rate as other companies. Is Tone entitled to demand access to Bell's lines? _____

20. After the product and geographic markets are properly defined, Versacorp Company is determined to have a 40% share of the relevant market. Is Versacorp Company guilty of monopolization under section 2 of the Sherman Act? (Assume that Versacorp Company has engaged in "anticompetitive conduct.") _____

21. Jambo Enterprises is charged with an attempt to monopolize under section 2. If it is shown that Jambo's conduct resulted in a dangerous probability of monopolization in the relevant market, and no defense is offered, the violation will be established. True or false? _____

22. While the terms of Sherman Act section 1 prohibit every combination in restraint of trade, the courts have read the statute as condemning only *unreasonable* restraints. True or false? _____

23. Kramer, Benes, and Costanza, competing appliance manufacturers, agree that each will produce no more than 1,000 electric can openers in any given year. No mention is made of the price for this appliance. Are the three guilty of price fixing? _____

    a. Can these firms defend on the grounds that the level of output set was reasonable and that the three were too small in the aggregate to influence the market price for can openers? _____

    b. Would the results above be different if the three firms had agreed to allocate markets among them? _____

24. Suppose Kramer, Benes, and Costanza agree that they will not sell to any retailer who carries manually operated can openers. Is this a per se violation of Sherman Act section 1? _____

    a. Would the result be different if the three had agreed to sell only to buyers who complied with applicable provisions of the Civil Rights Act regarding employment of minorities? _____

25. Ten competitors in the aluminum industry form a jointly managed company to conduct very expensive exploration for undersea ore deposits. Does this violate Sherman Act section 1? _____

    a. Would the result be different if the new company also allocates all raw materials to the 10 joint venturers in fixed proportions? _____

26. A trade association of widget manufacturers circulates among its members a monthly "sales sheet" detailing price data on sales by each member during the preceding month. Is it relevant to the legality of this activity whether the manufacturers' customers are identified on the sheet? _____

    a. Could the widget trade association use membership dues to lobby for a special congressional exemption permitting widget manufacturers to fix prices and allocate output in various geographic markets? _____

27. Toolco, a large machine tool manufacturer, publicly announces that in the future it will sell only at delivered prices, using Baltimore and San Francisco as basing points. Subsequently, most other firms in the industry adopt the same policy, and uniform prices result. Have the firms violated Sherman Act section 1? _____

    a. Would the result be different if the firms were challenged under section 5 of the FTC Act? _____

28. HC, a large conglomerate, agrees with two of its subsidiaries not to sell raw materials produced by the subsidiaries to competitors of a third HC subsidiary. When a section 1 lawsuit is filed by one of the competitors, HC moves for summary judgment in its favor. Should the motion be granted? _____

29. Penny Washington, a noted banker, is a director of Peerless Paper Company. If Washington also serves as director of a large timber and pulp company, is her position actionable under the antitrust laws?

30. A manufacturer may not set minimum retail prices for his products but he can set maximum prices, so as to limit a retailer's power to charge more to the consumer. True or false?

31. Frizzy Company manufactures hair dryers, which it sells through independent retail outlets. Can Frizzy place its dryers with retailers on consignment, setting the retail price and paying the dealer a percentage commission on each sale?

    a.   Suppose Frizzy publishes suggested retail prices for its dryers, and follows a policy of terminating dealers who refuse to adhere to the list price. Does this conduct violate Sherman Act section 1?

32. Mulcher, a manufacturer of electric lawn mowers, signs an agreement making Marcup its exclusive distributor in New Jersey. If the agreement eliminates intrabrand competition for Mulcher mowers in New Jersey, does it violate the Sherman Act?

    a.   Suppose the Mulcher-Marcup agreement also contains covenants by Marcup that he will not resell the mowers outside New Jersey or to more than one retailer in any given county within the state. Does this violate the Sherman Act?

33. A seller may validly "tie" sales of two or more of her products, so long as she does not have a formalized agreement with the buyer. True or false?

34. Daffy Drink Company agrees to sell its patented soft drink dispenser only if the buyer also agrees to use Daffy's fountain syrups exclusively in the machine. Does this arrangement violate the Clayton Act?

    a.   Suppose that Daffy has no patent on the dispenser, but is a very large manufacturer of fountain syrups. If Daffy offers to sell its dispenser at very low prices provided the buyer agrees to purchase only its fountain syrups, is there a Clayton Act violation?

    b.   Assuming either of the above arrangements is otherwise illegal, could Daffy successfully argue that its actions were justified on the ground that use of Daffy's syrups was necessary to insure proper operation of the dispenser and protection of Daffy's goodwill in both markets?

    c.   If Daffy supplied consulting services rather than dispensers to fountain operators, would the arrangement in a. (above) be illegal?

35. Slick Oil Company obtains contracts from all of its independent gasoline dealers, whereby each dealer agrees to purchase all its gas from Slick. These contracts involve approximately $75 million in sales, but Slick has only 5% of the market. Is the arrangement illegal? _____

36. As a general rule, judicial scrutiny of possible anticompetitive effects in a Clayton Act section 7 case is more rigorous than in Sherman Act cases. True or false? _____

37. The Department of Justice "Merger Guidelines" are binding on a court resolving a section 7 lawsuit. True or false? _____

38. Audio Company manufactures radio components. Baratone Company, a radio manufacturer, acquires the assets of Audio Company. Neither has more than a 6% share of its respective market. Is the Justice Department likely to challenge the merger under section 7? _____

39. There are eight firms in the produce industry. Apple has 28% of the market, Blueberry has 28%, Cherry has 13%, Date has 10%, Eggplant has 7%, Fig has 7%, Guava has 5%, and Horseradish has 2%. If Fig acquires Guava, is the Department of Justice likely to challenge this merger? _____

   a. Would the result be different if the first four firms had these market shares: Apple = 20%, Blueberry = 20%, Cherry = 20%, and Date = 19%? _____

   b. If the merger is subject to challenge in either of the above situations, could a showing of improved efficiency as a result of the merger justify the acquisition? _____

40. Where a conglomerate merger is involved, will the merger be challenged if a potential entrant into one of the two markets is involved? _____

41. If a seller has market power and faces an inelastic demand for the product, she can discriminate in price as a matter of economics. True or false? _____

42. Bristow Company uses a "zone" pricing system, whereby all purchasers within a given zone are charged the same delivery price. Could one customer within the zone bring a successful claim under the Robinson-Patman Act if she showed that transportation costs in fact varied? _____

   a. Would the result be the same if Bristow Company leased rather than sold its products? _____

43. Daily Dairy sells vanilla ice cream under the "Daily" brand for 50¢ less per quart than it sells the same ice cream under the "Gourmet" brand. Is there a possible Robinson-Patman violation? _____

44. If Daily Dairy's "Gourmet" brand ice cream contained pure vanilla extract (costing an extra 2¢ per quart), whereas the "Daily" brand used artificial flavoring, would the result be different?

_____

45. Daily Dairy sells its cottage cheese in River City for 20¢ per quart less than the normal market price and 25¢ less than Daily's price in other locations. Two small River City dairies are forced to discontinue sales of cottage cheese. Is there a possible Robinson-Patman violation?

_____

46. Daily Dairy lowers its milk price by 2¢ per quart to one retail grocer for a 24-hour period. Can competitors of the grocer obtain damages under the Robinson-Patman Act?

_____

47. Super Soap Company establishes a substantial quantity discount on sales of more than $50,000. When charged with price discrimination, Super Soap argues that the discount is warranted by packing and freight savings, and offers supporting evidence. Is this a defense to the Robinson-Patman claim?

_____

    a. Could Super Soap establish an average discount for stores in a large grocery chain?

_____

48. Goodparts Company sells flywheels used in the manufacture of electric motors. Colonel Motors, a customer, tells Goodparts that it can get a better price on flywheels from Flywheels Unlimited. May Goodparts lower its price to Colonel Motors without violating the Robinson-Patman Act?

_____

    a. Would it make a difference whether Flywheels Unlimited's flywheel was inferior in quality to Goodparts's product?

_____

49. Under the FTC Act section 5, the Federal Trade Commission can issue cease and desist orders for conduct that violates neither the letter nor the spirit of the Sherman or Clayton Acts. True or false?

_____

50. Luz Company obtains a patent on an electrical wiring design and licenses the patent to Yipee Electronics, an electronics manufacturer, on a percentage royalty basis. Yipee defaults on its royalty payments, whereupon Luz sues to enforce the licensing agreement. Can Yipee avoid any payment by proving that the patent is invalid?

_____

    a. Would Yipee have a successful defense if it showed that Luz conditioned its license on the purchase by Yipee of all electronic components from Luz?

_____

51. Expando Corporation patents a new razor blade that costs much less, and lasts much longer, than any other blade on the market. If Expando subsequently acquires a monopoly of the razor blade market through sales of the new blade, is there a Sherman Act section 2 violation?

_____

52. Sally Pulp patents a new method for finishing paper, and licenses her patent to various paper companies throughout the country. Can Pulp properly require a licensee to agree on the price for which its finished paper can be sold?   _____

    a. Can the licensing agreements extend beyond the expiration date of Pulp's patent?   _____

    b. Could Pulp require her licensees to contract for patents on other paper production techniques as a condition of obtaining the paper finishing patent?   _____

    c. Suppose that Stock and Ream also obtain patents for a paper finishing process, whereupon Pulp, Stock, and Ream enter an agreement to pool their patents and divide all royalties from the licensing thereof. Can the three proceed with the arrangement without violating the antitrust laws?   _____

53. Under the Capper-Volstead Act, a meat packer could join with cattle ranchers to form a sales association without violating the antitrust laws. True or false?   _____

54. If a proposed bank merger is shown to have an anticompetitive effect, it will not be approved if some alternative and less restrictive means will serve the community in question. True or false?   _____

55. A mail order insurance company may well be subject to the federal antitrust laws. True or false?   _____

56. All labor union activities are exempt from the antitrust laws, so long as they further the interests of union members. True or false?   _____

57. Concerned about possible competition from a new barber shop, Alcutt, an established barber, persuades the city council to pass an ordinance prohibiting any new barbers from opening a shop within the city limits. Barbieri, another barber, sues, and offers evidence that Alcutt convinced the city council members to vote for the ordinance by paying them a percentage of his shop's profits as campaign contributions. Has Alcutt violated the antitrust laws?   _____

Answers to Review Questions

1.a. **FALSE**   The earliest common law cases held any covenant not to practice a lawful calling void per se, and later cases relaxing the rule still required that any such restraint be partial, rather than total. [§§1-3]

 b. **TRUE**   Some courts will imply a covenant in this situation (whether or not there is an express agreement). Others are contra, or hold only that the seller cannot solicit his former customers. [§9]

 c. **TRUE**   Virtually all states hold such covenants illegal unless they meet an overarching requirement of reasonableness. [§12]

 d. **FALSE**   A restraint that is not incidental to the sale of a business (including goodwill) or other property is generally not upheld. [§13]

 e. **TRUE**   And as a result, very broad restraints may be enforceable where the business sold is expanding nationwide. [§§17-19]

 f. **FALSE**   Some state courts will reform ("blue pencil") the restraint. However, other courts refuse to "rewrite the contract" for the parties and simply hold the restraint (and possibly the sales contract as well) invalid. [§23]

 g. **FALSE**   Statutes generally tend to be *more* restrictive—although covenants in connection with sales of a business are usually permitted. [§§24-26]

2. **PROBABLY NOT**   Regulating output among all firms in an industry can clearly affect prices and tends to create a monopoly. (A few courts might find an exception if this were a "distress industry.") [§§32, 41-42]

3. **FALSE**   The Sherman Act is a new body of law, giving federal courts the opportunity to develop a "new common law" interpreting its language. [§§49-51]

4. **PROBABLY**   The FTC has concurrent jurisdiction with the courts to enforce the Clayton Act; but it has exclusive jurisdiction to enforce FTC Act section 5 (which encompasses the broadest possible range of anticompetitive or unfair conduct). The FTC has no specific authority to enforce the Sherman Act, but, in civil actions, can probably reach most activities included therein under FTC Act section 5. [§§56-61]

5. **FALSE**   If the business of Paintco and Colorco has a substantial *effect* on interstate commerce (as where their pricing affects paint sales by out-of-state manufacturers), the Sherman Act applies even though the business is purely intrastate. [§§67-70]

6.	**NO**	Where particular activities are *required* by foreign law, they cannot be condemned under American antitrust laws. [§81]
7.	**YES**	Violations of Sherman Act section 1 are crimes, and price fixing violates section 1. [§§84, 251]
a.	**NO**	There are no criminal sanctions for Clayton Act violations. [§86]
b.	**YES**	Those who authorized or committed the criminal acts are guilty of misdemeanors. [§88]
8.	**TRUE**	Among other forms of injunctive relief available, the court may require a defendant to "spin off" assets to create new competitors. [§94]
9.	**NO**	Because Larry is a direct competitor, he stands only to benefit from any supra-competitive pricing engaged in by his competitors. Because he will benefit, it has not suffered "antitrust injury," and so lacks standing to file suit. [§§110-111] *Note:* Larry could file suit if he could show that Moe, Curly, and Shemp had conspired to deprive it of access to an essential facility, or otherwise injure it competitively. [§§98, 178]
10.	**PROBABLY NOT**	Private parties are generally not allowed to intervene in government antitrust suits. Unless Mosaic could show exceptional circumstances (*e.g.*, that it was uniquely damaged by Apex's conduct), the motion would probably be denied. [§§134-135]
a.	**DEPENDS**	If Mosaic was *prepared* to enter the market, damages may be recoverable. But a mere intent to compete in the future is not a sufficient "injury to business." [§104]
b.	**PROBABLY**	As long as Mosaic has proved the *fact* of injury, a "just and reasonable estimate" of damages can be made by the jury. The amount of damages in private antitrust cases is generally speculative, to a greater or lesser extent. [§121]
11.	**TRUE**	However, courts have held that this "proximate cause" requirement is satisfied by showing that plaintiff was within the "target area" at which defendant's conduct was aimed or alternatively, within the relevant market affected. [§§98, 107-109]
12.	**FALSE**	While the "in pari delicto" defense was recognized at one time, this is no longer a bar to recovery by the plaintiff. (Of course, where defendant can show that *plaintiff's* conduct injured *him*, he may have a valid counterclaim.) [§124]
13.	**PROBABLY**	The statute of limitations on private damage actions is four years, so Plaintiff's claims would be barred unless she can show fraudulent concealment by Defendant of the facts constituting the violation. [§§125-127]

a. **YES**   The filing of such actions (including FTC proceedings) *tolls* the four-year limitations period. Plaintiff's suit is timely if brought within one year after conclusion of the government proceedings. [§128]

14. **NO**   Section 2 prohibits the *act of monopolizing*—not monopolies per se. Protégée Company must therefore have taken some *deliberate act* to acquire or maintain its monopoly power. [§§142-143]

a. **YES**   "Monopoly power" is the power to control prices or exclude competition in the market; Protégée Company could have such power despite the presence of other firms (*i.e.*, Protégée Company may choose not to exercise its power to exclude all competitors). [§§153, 168]

15. **YES**   Transportation costs are likely to limit the size of the relevant geographic market. If widgets are expensive to ship, manufacturers in other regions are not likely to be effective competitors of Makit. [§§149, 151]

a. **PROBABLY**   The relevant product market is largely determined by consumer preferences, as reflected in cross-elasticity of demand and functional interchangeability with other items. If Makit's survey accurately measures these indicia, the broader market is appropriate. [§§145-148]

16. **TRUE**   Where customers have purchased expensive durable goods (such as a high-speed photocopier), they are "locked in" to using that item for the foreseeable future. The relevant market for replacement parts is limited to those parts that will work with the item they have purchased. [§148]

17. **FALSE**   While a 100% market share is certainly indicative of market power, courts must also look to other factors, such as the ease of entry by competitors and likely future market shares. Where the company's market share declines rapidly after the suit is filed, courts are less willing to find market power. [§§161, 165-166]

18. **NO**   "Deliberate and purposeful" conduct sufficient to violate section 2 does not require proof that Blimpo specifically intended to monopolize. [§171]

a. **PROBABLY**   Where monopoly power is acquired solely by reason of superior skill, foresight, and industry, that mere acquisition does not violate section 2. (Note, however, that innocently acquired monopoly power can result in such a violation if it is subsequently *used* in a predatory manner, etc.) [§§189-191]

19. **PROBABLY**   Bell's local telephone lines most likely constitute an "essential facility," to which Bell must provide access on nondiscriminatory terms. [§178] *But note:* In some states, government utility regulation prevents Tone from competing with the monopoly telephone company. [§574]

20. **PROBABLY NOT**   While courts are not unanimous in their evaluation of market share, most courts would conclude that a 40% market share was insufficient for a finding of market power. Other factors relevant to the determination of market power include the existence and size of barriers to entry and the likelihood of potential competition. [§§163-167] *Note:* Versacorp Company might be guilty of *attempted* monopolization if Versacorp is found to have acted with the requisite intent. [§§192-194]

21. **FALSE**   In addition to the "dangerous probability" requirement, it must be shown that Jambo *specifically intended* to monopolize *and* used *unfair means* to achieve this goal. [§§193-195]

22. **TRUE**   However, certain kinds of business agreements are considered unreasonable as a matter of law (*i.e.*, "per se" violations). [§§202, 205] Other restraints are judged by the "rule of reason" analysis of behavior and effects of the restraint in each case. [§§201-202]

23. **YES**   Agreements on production ceilings constitute price fixing in violation of section 1 even though the parties fix no specific price. [§220]

   a. **NO**   Price fixing is a per se violation of section 1, and no defenses are recognized. [§§211-212] Nor is it necessary to show that the parties had sufficient market power to set or influence prices. [§215]

   b. **NO**   Division of markets among competitors is also a per se violation of section 1, and no justifications are recognized. [§§225-226]

24. **POSSIBLY**   This would almost certainly be held a horizontal group boycott (concerted refusal to deal), which some courts hold is a per se violation of section 1. [§§230, 232] However, other courts treat such conduct under the rule of reason. [§§233-234]

   a. **POSSIBLY**   If a court were to conclude that this restriction was politically rather than economically motivated, it might characterize the agreement as something other than a boycott. [§237]

25. **PROBABLY NOT**   Exploration for ore is presumably a lawful purpose for a joint venture, and the effort may enable exploration not otherwise possible for any single firm (due to the expense involved). Under the rule of reason, therefore, the venture would probably be permitted absent some significant anticompetitive effect, and provided there are no less restrictive alternatives. [§§238-241]

   a. **POSSIBLY**   Allocation of raw materials creates the possibility of regulating production and price. If this is the *purpose* of the venture, it would be illegal per se. And in all events, if its *effect* is to regulate production and price, it would be illegal under the rule of reason. [§§239-241]

26. **YES**   Circulation of price information is always suspect, but the courts have been especially quick to find a section 1 violation (either per se price fixing or an unreasonable restraint) where customers are identified by name. [§249]

   a. **YES**   The Supreme Court has approved concerted lobbying activities even where designed to promote anticompetitive statutes or regulations—provided the activity does not constitute pure harassment of a competitor (*Noerr-Pennington* doctrine). [§§582-585]

27. **NOT NECES- SARILY**   The primary question is whether any tacit or express **agreement** among the firms can be shown. If not, and if adherence to the basing point system by each firm could be justified on the basis of independent business judgment, there is probably no section 1 violation. [§§251-256, 258]

   a. **PROBABLY**   Section 5 prohibits "unfair methods of competition," and does not require a contract, combination, or conspiracy (*i.e.*, an agreement). Basing point systems that induce price uniformity have previously been held to violate section 5. [§257]

28. **PROBABLY**   If the two subsidiaries were **wholly owned** by HC, then no conspiracy exists within the antitrust laws. [§262]

29. **POSSIBLY**   Assuming both of the companies have capital aggregating more than $10 million, Washington's dual position may violate Clayton Act section 8 under the government stance that interlocking directorates involving **related** businesses are proscribed by that statute. [§263]

30. **DEPENDS**   Although agreements on **maximum** prices used to be per se illegal, they are now evaluated under the **rule of reason**. Agreements with anticompetitive effects, such as being tacitly used to set agreed minimum prices, will be invalidated. [§§272-273]

31. **PROBABLY NOT**   In light of the *Simpson* case, such consignment arrangements with retailers are probably illegal price fixing. [§274]

   a. **NO**   Technically, Frizzy's refusal to deal comes within the conduct upheld in *Colgate*. However, if there is any pressure on dealers to adhere (beyond the stated policy and refusal to deal), or reinstatement provisions, a violation probably exists. [§§275-278]

32. **PROBABLY NOT**   Unless there is no **interbrand** competition (*i.e.*, Mulcher is the only producer of power mowers), the exclusive distributorship is probably valid. [§§281-284]

   a. **DEPENDS**   Under the former law, legality might hinge on whether the mowers were sold or consigned by Mulcher to Marcup. Now, however, the restriction would be evaluated under the rule of reason. [§§285-287]

33.	**FALSE**	If the tying arrangement has the requisite effect on competition, it is a violation of Clayton Act section 3 regardless whether it is formalized or not. [§299]
34.	**DEPENDS**	Since Daffy has a legal monopoly in the "tying" product (the patented dispenser), some decisions suggest that its attempt to extend its power in fountain-syrup sales (the "tied" product) is illegal per se under Clayton Act section 3. [§§304, 307] However, more recent cases require the plaintiff to prove market power in the tying product; one cannot presume it by virtue of the patent. [§308]
a.	**DEPENDS**	An exclusive dealing arrangement is judged under the rule of reason with focus on the size of the market affected. [§§315-319] Here, Daffy may be guilty of *predatory pricing* under the Sherman Act, if the price charged is below some measure of cost and if Daffy can recoup its losses. [§§174-176]
b.	**PROBABLY NOT**	The "quality control" defense is recognized only where specifications for a substitute (syrup) would be so detailed that they could not feasibly be supplied. Thus, the defense rarely succeeds. [§313]
c.	**DEPENDS**	If consulting services are a significant part of the fountain business, and if Daffy has market power in that area, the arrangement may well violate Sherman Act section 1. (It does *not* violate Clayton Act section 3 because the consulting services are not "commodities.") [§298]
35.	**PROBABLY NOT**	Under the *Standard Oil* doctrine, the contracts would probably be held to violate Clayton Act section 3 (because of the substantial business volume involved). However, Slick might well prevail under the *Tampa Electric* "market share" test, which is the currently prevailing test of exclusive dealing arrangements. [§§315-317]
36.	**TRUE**	Section 7 has been held to have a "prophylactic purpose"—*i.e.*, to prevent and not merely correct anticompetitive effects. Hence, probable effects may condemn a merger; and market definitions may be narrower than under the Sherman Act. [§§320-325]
37.	**FALSE**	The Guidelines are not binding on the courts and differ in several important ways from the approaches most courts use to evaluate mergers. [§371]
38.	**PROBABLY NOT**	Under the Merger Guidelines, the Justice Department probably would not challenge a merger involving such small market shares unless it increased barriers to entry in an already concentrated market. [§380]
39.	**UNCLEAR**	This merger produces a post-merger HHI of 2034 ($28^2 + 28^2 + 13^2 + 10^2 + 7^2 + 12^2$ [post-merger share of Fig and Guava] $+ 2^2 = 784 + 784 + 169 + 100 + 49 + 144 + 4 = 2034$). In this concentration range the Department of Justice will challenge a merger that increases the HHI by 100 or more points. However, the merger of Fig and Guava increases the HHI (*i.e.*, post-merger compared to

pre-merger total) by only 70 points (7 × 5 × 2 = 70), and in this range the Department of Justice will consider other factors before deciding whether to challenge the merger. [§§380-381]

a. **YES** By changing the shares of the four largest firms, the post-merger HHI falls to 1758 points. In this range, the Department of Justice will not challenge the merger unless the increase in HHI is more than 100 points. The merger of Fig and Guava produce an HHI increase of only 70 points. [§377]

b. **POSSIBLY** The 1992 Horizontal Merger Guidelines list efficiencies related to economics of scale, lower costs, etc., as factors the government will consider in evaluating mergers. [§378]

40. **NOT NECES-SARILY** Although the Merger Guidelines pay lip service to the potential entrant theories, in practice the Department of Justice has all but ignored conglomerate mergers. [§384]

41. **FALSE** While those two conditions are necessary, they are not sufficient to permit discrimination; the seller must *also* be able to separate buyers according to their elasticities of demand. [§§388-389]

42. **YES** If actual freight charges vary to different customers within the zone, this may well constitute "discrimination in price." [§§400-404]

a. **NO** The "discrimination" must involve a *purchase*; leases are not covered by Robinson-Patman. [§397]

43. **YES** Differences in brand name or label are not enough to make the products "of different grade and quality." [§410]

44. **PROBABLY** Any physical difference in the products that affects their acceptability to buyers precludes their being of the requisite "like grade and quality." [§410]

45. **YES** Daily's actions have all the earmarks of primary line price discrimination. [§§411-413]

46. **PROBABLY NOT** Ordinarily, such discrimination among competitor-purchasers might establish a secondary line injury. However, the temporary duration of the price differential makes recovery unlikely in this case. [§§414-415]

47. **YES** However, to prevail, Super Soap must show that cost savings on such sales justify the entire discount *and* that the discount is not "unduly discriminatory." [§§419-421]

a. **PROBABLY NOT** If some stores could not have earned the discount if considered individually, the classification is probably improper. [§422]

48. **DEPENDS** Goodparts must have facts that would lead a reasonable and prudent person to believe that its lower price was meeting the price of a competitor. Merely relying on a customer's word may not be enough. [§§424-425]

   a. **YES** A seller cannot grant a price break to meet the price of a lower quality product. [§428]

49. **TRUE** If the FTC finds that such conduct is an "unfair method of competition," it can enjoin the activity. [§456]

50. **NOT NECESSARILY** While a licensee can defend an action for royalties on the ground that the patent is invalid, the court may still require *some* compensation for use of the (unpatented) idea. [§482]

   a. **DEPENDS** Such attempts to "tie" unpatented items to the design would constitute misuse of the patent by Luz if the tied product is a staple good and if Luz had market power in the tying product. [§§483, 487]

51. **NO** Assuming that Expando has simply exploited the cost and quality advantages of the patented blade, it has a defense to any section 2 charge of monopolizing. [§502]

52. **NO** Resale price restrictions on an unpatented product manufactured through a patented process are illegal per se. [§512] However, if the product itself had been patented, the outcome might be different under the *General Electric* case. [§511]

   a. **NO** Such agreements are unlawful. [§521]

   b. **NO** Such an arrangement would constitute illegal "block-booking." [§523]

   c. **DEPENDS** Pooling arrangements are not illegal per se, but if used to restrain competition, they may run afoul of the antitrust laws (as where selective licensing to "freeze out" competitors of pool members is employed). Pooling arrangements are encouraged as a means of settling patent disputes. [§§525-526]

53. **FALSE** The Capper-Volstead agricultural exemption does *not* extend to "mixed" associations of producers and nonproducers (such as packing houses). [§546]

54. **TRUE** This reflects the narrow interpretation the Supreme Court has given the bank merger exemption from the Sherman and Clayton Acts. [§§559-560]

55. **TRUE** A company doing mail order business in a state where it is *not* licensed would be subject to federal law. [§563]

56. **FALSE** Unions cannot aid nonlabor groups (employers, etc.) in monopolizing or restraining competition, even if their members also benefit thereby. [§570]

57. **NO**   The "state action" exemption shields Alcutt from liability for restrictions on competition imposed by states and most local governments. There is no exception to the state action doctrine for state actors who conspire with private individuals. [§577]

Exam Questions
and Answers

QUESTION I

In the late 1970s, Atari Corporation pioneered video games. Atari sold video game machines ("consoles"), known as the "Atari 2600" model, along with compatible cartridges ("games") to play games on television sets. For the first time, this allowed consumers (largely teenage boys) to play interactive games on their television sets. By spending $200 on a console, the consumer could then purchase a wide selection of games at $40 each. Games for the Atari system were sold through retail stores both by Atari and by third parties who designed games ("game developers"). Atari's system was "open" in the sense that Atari would provide game developers with the technical information necessary to program their games to play on the Atari console. Atari sold some 20 million consoles from 1978 through 1982, facing only minor competition from others selling their own consoles and cartridges ("systems"), which were incompatible with the Atari system (*i.e.*, a cartridge from one system would not play on a console from another system). Sales of games, and especially consoles, crashed after 1982, however, and the market was essentially dormant in 1983 and 1984. Many commentators at that time felt that a lack of interesting new games, along with saturation of the target population of teenage boys, offered little future for the video game category. Furthermore, an increasing number of consumers were buying personal computers, which offered their own games ("computer games").

In mid-1985, the Japanese firm Nintendo (which originally sold playing cards) began selling its own video game system in the United States. Nintendo entered the market with its "Nintendo Entertainment System" ("NES"), consisting of a Nintendo console and some 15 games developed by Nintendo itself. Nintendo's system was an "8-bit" system, as opposed to Atari's "4-bit" system, and offered far more realistic visual displays. For example, the Nintendo system offered fairly realistic human figures, rather than the Atari system's stick figures. By late 1985, a number of very popular games developed by third-party game developers became available on the Nintendo system, in addition to the initial group of Nintendo's own games. Industry experts all agree that the key to selling consoles is to have popular games that can play on the console; Nintendo's success was built on the "hit" games available for play on the NES. The typical pattern was for a hit game to first achieve success as a video arcade game in Japan, after which it would be converted for play on home consoles.

Nintendo's policies with respect to third-party game developers were sharply different from Atari's policies. To begin with, Nintendo charged each third-party developer a royalty fee for all games sold to play on Nintendo consoles. For example, if Capcom, a third-party game developer, charged retailers $20 per cartridge for its game "Zordon" designed to play on the Nintendo machine, Capcom would be required to pay a 20% royalty back to Nintendo, or $4 per cartridge. Nintendo makes 80% of its profits from software. Nintendo enforced this policy through licensing contracts signed with game developers, backed up by Nintendo's copyrights and trade secrets, which prevented game developers from writing games to play on the Nintendo system without Nintendo's approval.

In addition, Nintendo imposed an exclusivity requirement on game developers. Specifically, in the example above, a clause in the licensing agreement between Nintendo and Capcom for Zordon prevented Capcom from making a version of Zordon for any other video game system for two years after the first sale of Zordon by Capcom. By 1992, several hundred games, including many hit games, were available on the Nintendo system.

The Nintendo system was an instant success, surpassing the Atari system in sales by early 1986. By all accounts, Nintendo's enormous success was due to good timing (a new crop of teenage boys was ready to buy a system), a clearly superior system, exciting games including Super Mario Brothers (Mario effectively being the Nintendo mascot), and excellent marketing. Over the 1985-1992 time period, Nintendo sold some 30 million consoles; over 150 million cartridges were sold to play on the Nintendo system, with about 50 million of these being games developed in-house by Nintendo and 100 million being games developed by third-party game developers. In any given year, the bulk of the sales of cartridges were made by a handful of hit games, although there were over 100 titles available on the Nintendo system by 1987. Typically, a hit game would make the vast bulk of its sales within the first year or two after its release.

Atari did not abandon the market after 1982; quite the contrary. Atari continued to offer its 4-bit Atari 2600 system for sale, and developed its own 8-bit system, the Atari 7800, which it introduced in 1986. The Atari 7800 was technically comparable to the NES, but it never achieved more than about 5% of the sales of 8-bit (or "second-generation") console sales. A third firm, the Japanese firm Sega, also entered the market with their own 8-bit system. Nonetheless, from 1987 through 1991, Nintendo achieved 85% to 90% of video game console sales.

Atari had sought to make versions of popular games available for its own Atari 7800 system but was rebuffed both by Nintendo itself and by third-party game developers who were either under exclusive contract with Nintendo, or were unwilling to forgo the Nintendo market by dealing with Atari. According to Atari, no developer of a hit game would make a version of that game for the Atari 7800, as this would prevent the game developer from selling to the Nintendo installed base of machines, which was at all times far larger than the installed base of Atari 7800 machines. Atari noted that in the computer industry, programmers typically make versions of their programs (including computer games) for a variety of computer platforms, *e.g.*, for both IBM and Apple computers. Atari also complained that Nintendo refused to license its own hit games, such as Super Mario Brothers, to play on the Atari system.

Atari seeks your advice concerning whether it has viable antitrust claims that can be asserted against Nintendo. Please identify and evaluate Atari's antitrust claims. Also, discuss how you expect Nintendo to defend against such antitrust claims. Finally, how do you evaluate Atari's prospects for antitrust relief?

QUESTION II

Your client, the National Association of Widget Retailers, approaches you to evaluate its antitrust exposure following its recent annual convention in New Orleans. The association president tells you that, following a somewhat extended cocktail hour, a general session of the delegates may have gotten a bit out of hand. The executive director had just made a speech describing the growth of discount catalog widget vendors, when a large, red-faced delegate from Illinois got up and started haranguing the group to "take a stand against this threat to our livelihood." This was followed by a roar of what might have been approval and a number of similar remarks, capped by another red-faced delegate's call to stop dealing with widget makers who dealt with these catalog vendors. This prompted an even bigger roar.

You ask for more information. Your investigation reveals the following:

(a)   The executive director painted a dark picture of the threat to traditional retailers and described the suppliers selling to the catalogs as cannibalizing their long-term interests in maintaining the traditional, full-service sector.

(b)   The only motion passed at the meeting asked the executive director to write to the widget makers to convey the view that the makers, in dealing with catalogs, were acting contrary to their own long-term interests, and such a letter was sent after review by the executive committee. The letter also noted that "if this situation continues, many of our members are likely to find it impossible as a matter of simple economics to continue carrying your products, because they are incurring the costs of maintaining a trained sales staff to educate consumers about your products, but consumers are using these services and then ordering from the catalogs." All members were sent copies of the letters.

(c)   After receiving the letter from the Association and after receiving individual phone calls from some member retailers, some of the widget makers have cut off the catalog vendors.

(d)   Thirty-five percent of the widget retailers in the country belong to the Association.

How do you assess antitrust exposure for the Association and its members?

QUESTION III

Recently, American Corporation and Pierre's, Inc. agreed to merge. American is a large corporation with several divisions. It ranks in the top 100 in *Fortune's* Directory of the 500 Largest U.S. Industrial Corporations. One of American's divisions, Ms. Zee Desserts, is a major producer of dessert products. While Ms. Zee Desserts is an industry leader in such sales as cheese cake and coffee cake, controlling 95% of the former market and 70% of the latter market, the company's sales of frozen dessert pies have been conspicuously unimpressive. Indeed, Ms. Zee's frozen pie sales declined from over $7 million in 2000-01 to about $4.5 million in 2003-04, despite an expanding market during that period.

Pierre's, Inc. is a corporation that produces a wide variety of frozen dessert pies and markets them with considerably greater success than does Ms. Zee. Pierre's total frozen pie sales in 2004 exceeded $36 million.

The frozen dessert pie business is divided into two distinct categories: retail pie sales and institutional pie sales. Retail pies are generally sold through supermarkets and grocery stores to consumers for home use. Most retail frozen dessert pies are eight inches in diameter, and their packaging is design-oriented in order to attract the consumer's attention. Institutional pies, on the other hand, are sold through food distributors to restaurants, hospitals, schools, etc., to be consumed by the slice on the premises. These pies typically are 10 inches in diameter, and they are packaged in plain boxes. Retail frozen pies are also more expensive than institutional pies, especially on an ounce-for-ounce basis. There are specialized vendors for retail frozen pies. Many food brokers, acting as sales agents for manufacturers, specialize in the sale of retail pies, and those that sell both retail and institutional maintain separate staffs for each. Finally, retail pies and institutional pies are sold to distinctly different groups of consumers. There is little substitutability between the two types of frozen pies.

Pie eaters are a peculiarly loyal group and will not switch to other dessert products unless the price of pies were to rise significantly. Moreover, fresh pies are not a significant competitive factor in the frozen pie business.

Ms. Zee's sales are exclusively retail. Ms. Zee's $4.5 million volume placed it 11th among 13 major retail frozen dessert pie producers in 2004, with 3.1% of the retail market.

Pierre's, by contrast, leads the field of institutional frozen dessert pie manufacturers. Pierre's $25 million in sales amounted to 40% of the institutional frozen pie business in 2004. In addition, the company does a respectable retail trade as well. Its $10,248,000 in sales makes Pierre's the fourth-ranked producer, with 7% of the retail market.

The relevant geographical market is the United States. In 2004, total sales of retail frozen dessert pies in the United States were $144,546,000. This figure consists of the sum of individual sales by the following 13 producers:

Company	Sales	Percent
Mrs. Smith's	$59,137,000	40.9
Morton's	15,814,000	10.9
Ward	10,490,000	7.3
Pierre's	10,248,000	7.1
Harriss	9,606,000	6.6
Banquet	9,400,000	6.5
Pet	7,334,000	5.1

Fasano	5,195,000	3.6
Quality	5,120,000	3.5*
Edwards	4,636,000	3.2
Ms. Zee	4,498,000	3.1
Table Talk	1,980,000	1.4*
Fields	1,088,000	.8*

*These companies were recent de novo entries into the market.

Although Ms. Zee has not lost money, it has experienced a steady and precipitous rate of decline in retail frozen pie sales over the past several years. Measured by dollar volume, the company's sales reached their high point at $7,535,000 in 2001-02. At the end of fiscal year 2003-04, this figure had fallen to $4,525,000. Furthermore, the company was forced to eliminate several varieties of pie due to poor sales results. Distribution of Ms. Zee pies has become very "spotty." Some outlets have discontinued Ms. Zee pies altogether, while others will carry only one or two varieties, such as apple, and possibly pumpkin in season.

The president of American attributes Ms. Zee's lack of success in the retail pie market to its inability to match other manufacturers in either quality or price. Ms. Zee has had technological problems and presently produces its pies with equipment that is widely regarded as obsolete.

Ms. Zee's lack of success in the retail business and the company's persistent inability to solve its technological problems have caused it to refrain from entering the frozen institutional pie trade. Indeed, Ms. Zee actually made one attempt at de novo entry into the frozen institutional pie trade but failed miserably.

American has been informed that the Antitrust Division of the Department of Justice is about to file suit to enjoin the merger of American and Pierre's, Inc. What legal theories or lines of attack will the government most likely advance? What are the strongest arguments and defenses American can make in support of the merger? Is the government likely to prevail?

QUESTION IV

Tucked away in the California hills near Stanford University is a thriving community for retired adults called Paradise. Today, Paradise has a population of 9,000 residents (10,000 on weekends, when the children and grandchildren come to visit). All of the residents live in housing cooperatives or condominiums built by Paradise Corp., the sole developer and builder of Paradise. Paradise began with 1,000 units in 1990 and has added 200-300 new units each year thereafter. Present plans call for a continuation of this pattern of growth until 2020.

When Paradise first opened its doors in 1990, new housing units were sold without carpeting. The home purchaser was responsible for the selection, purchase, and installation of carpeting or other floor covering. Most purchasers turned to carpet retailers located in the Palo Alto-Menlo Park area (a 15- to 20-minute drive from Paradise), although several purchased their carpeting from retailers located further away.

Acme Carpets is located in Menlo Park. Acme has been installing carpeting in Paradise homes since 1990. Acme's Paradise business has included both installing carpeting in newly built homes and installing replacement or additional carpeting in older homes.

Acme has reached the Paradise residents by advertising in the Yellow Pages, the local newspapers, and until 2005, in the *Paradise Gazette*. The *Gazette* is a weekly community newspaper published by Paradise Corp. and distributed without charge to the residents of Paradise. On January 1, 2005, Paradise Corp. opened a wholly-owned subsidiary named Quality Carpet Corp., with a sales office in the small commercial area of Paradise. Paradise Corp. and Quality have separate management staffs. Immediately after Quality began its business in Paradise, the *Gazette* refused to accept advertising from Acme or any other retail carpeting company.

In addition, from January 1, 2005, to the present, all new housing units in Paradise have included installed carpeting within the purchase price of the home. Not surprisingly, all carpeting is installed by Quality. The purchaser is permitted to select color. If a higher grade of carpet is desired, an additional fee is added to the purchase price of the home.

Between 1990 and 2004, Acme installed carpeting in approximately 20% of Paradise's new housing units. This amounted to 4% of Acme's total annual carpet sales to all customers. When Paradise Corp. changed its carpeting policy to include installed carpeting in the purchase price of its new homes, Acme's share of that market, of course, dropped to zero.

By 2004, Acme was also installing approximately 20% of all replacement or new carpeting added in older units. Such sales comprised 4% of Acme's total annual carpet sales to all customers. After January 1, 2005, Acme's share of this market dropped to 10% annually.

In light of the above facts, the owner of Acme would like an opinion and advice concerning potential antitrust claims Acme may have against Paradise Corp. or Quality Carpet Corp. Draft a comprehensive memorandum to the owner of Acme discussing the following items:

(1) The antitrust claims that might reasonably be asserted against Paradise Corp. or Quality Carpet Corp.;

(2) The problems (if any) anticipated in proving such claims, giving attention to any defenses that might be raised; and

(3) An evaluation of the likelihood of success on the merits with respect to each claim.

Please assume that all interstate commerce jurisdictional requirements are established in this case.

QUESTION V

The following amendment has been proposed to section 2 of the Sherman Act:

Proposed section 2A

I. *Purpose*

Sherman Act section 2A would permit the government to institute an expedited proceeding seeking structural (or other) relief where substantial, persistent monopoly power is not justified by patents or efficiencies of scale.

II. *Nature of Proceedings*
   A. Proceedings could be instituted only by designated federal agencies.
   B. The proceedings would be equitable in nature.
   C. Neither criminal sanctions nor civil penalties would be appropriate as remedies.

III. *Liability*

To establish that a firm has substantial, persistent monopoly power, the government would have to demonstrate that:
   A. The firm has had monopoly power in a properly defined relevant market for the five years preceding the filing of the complaint; and
   B. Sales in the relevant market exceeded $500 million in the year immediately preceding the filing of the complaint.

IV. *Remedy*
   A. After a finding of substantial, persistent monopoly power, the ordinary remedy would be structural relief sufficient to create as much competition as is feasible without substantial loss of efficiencies of scale. . . .

You are employed by a senator who wants help in analyzing the "Liability" portion of the proposed amendment. Please draft a memorandum to the Senator addressing the following questions, being careful to explain fully your reasoning and analysis:

(1) Does the proposed amendment make any significant change in monopoly law?

(2) What arguments do you expect will be made in favor of the proposed amendment?

(3) On balance, do you regard the proposed amendment as an improvement in the antitrust laws?

Note: The following answers have been adapted from actual student answers written under exam conditions.

ANSWER TO QUESTION I

Section 2 of the Sherman Act condemns "[e]very person who shall monopolize, or attempt to monopolize . . . any part of . . . trade or commerce. . . ." The Supreme Court defined the offense of monopolization as consisting of two elements: (1) the possession of monopoly power in the relevant market, and (2) the willful acquisition or maintenance of that power, as distinguished from growth or development as a consequence of a superior product, business acumen, or historic accident. [**United States v. Grinnell Corp.**] Here, while Nintendo has monopoly power, under a rule of reason analysis, it has several strong arguments against Atari's antitrust claim. For this reason, Atari is unlikely to prevail in its claim.

A. Nintendo's Monopoly Power

To be convicted of monopolization, a firm must have monopoly power in a relevant market. The relevant market is one for which both elasticity of demand and supply are low. To determine the relevant market, we look to the relevant *product* market and the relevant *geographic* market to gauge Nintendo's monopoly power.

The relevant product market is largely determined by consumer preferences and the extent to which products are reasonably interchangeable. Atari will argue for a narrow product market, confining it to 8-bit system video game consoles. Nintendo will argue that the product market should be viewed broadly; for example, to include computer games and arcade games. In this larger market, Nintendo's share of the market will be considerably lower than that which it currently enjoys in video game consoles.

There is evidence that computer games compete with video game consoles. Part of the stagnation in the market from 1982 to 1984 was due to the fact that more consumers were acquiring home computers with games. However, video game consoles are distinct in that they require only a television set to function. A typical consumer will not view computer games (for which the consumer will have to buy an expensive computer) nor arcade games (for which the consumer will have to leave home) as reasonable substitutes for the convenient, realistic 8-bit systems which can be hooked up to a home television set. Thus, it is likely that a court will side with Atari in confining the relevant product market to the 8-bit systems.

The geographic market is generally defined by the area in which the defendant and its competitors sell the product. As to the relevant geographic market here, both Atari and Nintendo compete nationwide. Because the 8-bit systems currently at issue are imported, consumers are unable to turn outside of the area for substitutes, and producers outside the area are not likely to quickly flood the area with their own versions.

Thus, the relevant market should be defined as 8-bit systems sold nationwide. In this market, from 1987 to 1991, Nintendo achieved 85% to 90% of video game console sales. Courts find market shares of 85% to 90% (and higher) to be sufficient to conclude that the defendant is a monopolist. Hence, Nintendo has monopoly power in the relevant market.

B.   Nintendo's Conduct

In addition to proof of monopoly power, however, the offense of monopolization requires proof that the defendant engaged in some purposeful and intentional action to increase the amount or duration of its monopoly. Monopolization cases are governed by the rule of reason. [**Standard Oil Co. v. United States**] The rule of reason distinguishes between efficient or competitive exclusionary conduct and inefficient or anticompetitive exclusionary conduct.

1.   Nintendo's exclusivity arrangements: Exclusive dealing may be analyzed under section 1 of the Sherman Act as well as section 3 of the Clayton Act. Exclusive dealing arrangements are condemned because they might foreclose a market so that it is completely inaccessible to other participants. This is especially likely if one level of the market is controlled by a monopolist. Thus, courts will evaluate exclusivity arrangements by focusing on whether a substantial amount of competition in a line of commerce is foreclosed. "Substantiality" is analyzed in terms of substantial dollar volume of the market or substantial percentage of the market foreclosed by the arrangement. If the foreclosure is substantial, the court will apply the rule of reason to look at other factors such as the degree to which the contracts actually appear to be hindering new entry and the number of other firms in the market who are also relying on exclusive dealing.

Here, Nintendo imposed an exclusivity requirement on game developers. This clause in the licensing agreement prevented game developers from making a version of their game for any other video game system for two years after the first sale. Since typically a hit game would make the vast bulk of its sales within the first year or two after its release, Nintendo effectively foreclosed Atari from profiting from these popular games. Moreover, Nintendo's exclusivity arrangements were effective. Atari had sought to make versions of popular games available for its own Atari 7800 system, but was rebuffed both by Nintendo itself and by third-party game developers who were either under exclusive contract with Nintendo, or were unwilling to forgo the Nintendo market by dealing with Atari. It appears, therefore, while exact figures are not stated in the facts here, that Nintendo successfully foreclosed a substantial amount of the market with its exclusivity arrangements. Thus, a court considering Atari's claim would proceed to evaluate the efficiencies promoted by the arrangement.

Nintendo will argue that its exclusive dealing arrangement enables both buyers and suppliers to avoid many of the uncertainties that accompany use of the market. When risks are reduced, so the argument goes, costs are reduced, and eventually consumers will reap the benefits. Moreover, the exclusivity arrangement is for two years only. While it is true that this is the most lucrative period in game sales, it still does not completely shut out Atari and other competitors.

In addition, Nintendo will argue that the reason that Atari has lost its market share is not because of Nintendo's exclusivity arrangements. Rather, it is because Atari's product had become stale and irrelevant to the target consumer—namely, teenage boys. Indeed, before Nintendo even entered the market in mid-1985, the market had already crashed. Subsequent to the crash of 1982, the market remained dormant in 1983 and 1984.

Nintendo was able to garner high sales because it was innovative, introducing the 8-bit system, a move welcomed by consumers. It was Nintendo's clearly superior system, exciting games, and excellent marketing that led to its high market shares; anticompetitive behavior was not the cause. Since the Sherman Act is not meant to punish growth that arises as a "consequence of a superior product, business acumen, or historic accident," Nintendo has a strong rule of reason argument against Atari's antitrust accusations.

2.   **Tying arrangements:** Atari might also try to argue that Nintendo is guilty of a tying scheme similar to that in **Eastman Kodak v. Image Technical Services**. In this case, Nintendo consoles are meant to operate specifically with Nintendo-compatible games. Atari could argue that Nintendo is using its dominance in the game market to dominate the console market. Indeed, Nintendo gets most of its money from the sale of games (80%). However, this argument will probably fail because Atari's games, likewise, only worked on Atari's machines. It is the nature of the product that they are console-specific. Since Atari's products are also "tied" in this manner, Atari will have difficulty proving that this arrangement was injurious.

3.   **Nintendo's refusal to license its hit games to play on the Atari system:** Atari may argue that Nintendo's refusal to license its games to Nintendo was a violation of antitrust law. However, here too, as a general rule, no firm has a duty to deal with a competitor. [**United States v. Colgate**] Likewise, there is no obligation to license a patent to a competitor. To overcome these general rules, Atari would have to show that Nintendo had no justification for its refusal other than to maintain its monopoly. [**Aspen Skiing Co. v. Aspen Highlands**] Atari could offer the fact that it successfully maintained an open system and provided game developers with technical information without charging a fee. However, Nintendo could point out that the strategy obviously did not save Atari from becoming obsolete. By maintaining strict control over the games produced for its system, Nintendo can argue that it is ensuring the integrity of the games that operate on its machines.

In sum, while Nintendo has monopoly power, Atari's prospects for antitrust relief are not good. Under a rule of reason analysis, Nintendo can offer several valid justifications for its behavior and thus, probably will not be vulnerable to Atari's antitrust claims.

ANSWER TO QUESTION II

Generally, a firm may refuse to deal with a competitor. [**United States v. Colgate**] However, under the *Colgate* rule, the decision must be unilateral. Concerted refusals to deal may be illegal. Concerted refusals to deal involve an agreement between two or more persons or firms that they will not deal with someone else. Here, the letter sent by the Association constituted a thinly veiled refusal to deal. As such, it makes the Association vulnerable to antitrust claims.

A concerted refusal to deal used to enforce a naked price fixing agreement would be characterized as illegal per se. [**Federal Trade Commission v. Superior Court Trial Lawyers Association**] Where there is no plausible argument that a concerted refusal produces economies, and where the only apparent purpose is facilitation of cartelization or protection from new entry, application of the per se rule is appropriate. Here, a catalog vendor might argue that the Association's refusal to deal with manufacturers who sold to catalog dealers was designed solely to eliminate competition. As such, it should be per se illegal. However, if plausible arguments for efficiencies can be made, the court may use a rule of reason approach. Also, since this case involves the actions of a trade association, a form of cooperation not quite at the level of a cartel, the court probably will use the rule of reason approach.

A.   The Relevant Market and Market Power

The first step in a rule of reason analysis is to define the relevant market. Here, that is already defined as the national market for widgets. As to market power, of the widget retailers nationwide, 35% belong to the Association. For horizontal mergers, the Court in *Philadelphia National Bank* held that 30% of the relevant market is sufficient to raise antitrust concerns. Thus, applying that logic to horizontal agreements, 35% seems sufficiently high to prompt a rule of reason analysis of the Association's activities.

B.   The Alleged Restraint of Trade

Section 1 of the Sherman Act requires an "agreement" among the firms. However, the agreement may be established by circumstantial evidence. For example, in **Eastern States Retail Lumber Dealers Association v. United States,** a lumber trade association circulated among members lists of wholesalers who sold directly to consumers. The Supreme Court said there could be "but one purpose" in circulating such information—to blacklist the wholesale dealers. The Court held that an agreement may be inferred from the act of mailing the list.

In this case, all members of the National Association of Widget Retailers were sent a letter, which had been reviewed by the executive committee and drafted by the executive director, suggesting that its members would be unwilling to deal with widget makers who deal with catalogs. The executive director, a person with clear authority to speak for the Association, described the suppliers as threatening their long-term interests in maintaining the traditional full-service sector. This may be interpreted as a move by the Association to take up the gauntlet against manufacturers who deal with catalog vendors.

The agreement to this proposal by the membership, likewise, can be inferred. After the speech, the members of the Association roared their approval when a delegate called for members to stop dealing with widget makers who dealt with these catalog vendors. The Association may argue that this dialogue occurred in the heat of the moment, after an extended cocktail party, and several members might have been drunk, as evidenced by their red faces. However, there is no indication that the executive director was drunk, and the letter that frames the agreement was sent after review by the executive committee. It appears to be part of a carefully reasoned strategy by the Association. Subsequent to the meeting the letter was sent and some member retailers made phone calls to widget manufacturers. Thus, there is a plausible argument to be made that an agreement in restraint of trade was made at the convention.

C. Evidence of Harm

After receiving the letter and individual phone calls from some members, some of the widget makers have cut off the catalog vendors. This is similar to the conduct described in **Klors Inc. v. Broadway-Hale Stores**. In that case, a retailer demanded that manufacturers of well-known brands of appliances not deal with a discount operation. The Court declared that demand to be a violation of the Sherman Act. If one party (here, the Association members) calls another party (the widget makers), and soon thereafter, the widget makers cut off the competitor, the court is likely to find this a conspiracy in restraint of trade. If the catalog vendors proved that the Association members were complaining about the catalog vendors' low prices, then the catalog vendors might have a case for proving a price restraint, a per se illegal agreement.

Apart from this possibility, the conduct of the Association members in calling the manufacturers raises several antitrust concerns. The Court in *Klors* said that if it allowed the retailers' conduct to go unpunished, "a group of powerful businessmen may act in concert to deprive a single merchant . . . of the goods he needs to compete effectively. . . ." In this case, if the widget manufacturers are allowed to cut off the catalog vendors, the court may find direct harm. Beyond the effect on competitors, this type of behavior will leave fewer and fewer choices open to consumers.

Even under the stricter standards set out by the Court in **Monsanto Co. v. Spray-Rite**, a plaintiff has a good chance of prevailing. In *Monsanto*, several dealers complained to the supplier about another dealer and the supplier terminated its relationship with the wayward dealer. The Court found a meeting of the minds, from which a jury could conclude an agreement had been made. The situation here is similar.

In response, the Association may argue the efficiencies of its conduct. The burden of proof would thus shift to the defendant, our client, to prove under the rule of reason that its conduct was warranted. The Association will argue that it was worried over the "free rider" problem. The letter sent to widget makers read, in part, "many of our members are likely to find it impossible as a matter of simple economics to continue carrying your products, because they are incurring the costs of maintaining a trained sales staff to educate consumers about your products, but consumers are using these services and then ordering from catalogs." By free riding on the services offered by Association members, the catalog dealers' behavior threatened to drive full-service merchants out of business.

This ultimately would harm consumers because they would no longer have a well-educated sales staff to answer their widget-related questions.

On the other hand, the catalog vendors might argue that many customers do not require the services offered by Association members. They are well-informed and would not be affected by the loss of the full-service sector. In contrast, if forced to pay the higher prices of Association members, they would be harmed.

Indeed, the court may inquire whether there was a better way to handle the free riding problem than calling for Association members to discontinue carrying the products of manufacturers who dealt with catalog vendors. However, under the less drastic means analysis, the alternative would have had to be obvious at the time this letter was written and be a substantially better way to deal with the free rider problem.

Ultimately, while the Association has a good argument in the free rider dilemma it faced, the actions of the executive director and executive committee in sending the letter, a thinly veiled refusal to deal, raises antitrust concerns. The subsequent phone calls by members to manufacturers, and the response of manufacturers in cutting off the catalog vendors, constitute a tough case against the Association.

ANSWER TO QUESTION III

The government will invoke section 7 of the Clayton Act and attack this merger under two theories: (i) that there is a *horizontal merger* resulting in a competitor in the retail pie market with an undue market share and in a significant increase in concentration, and (ii) that there is a *conglomerate or product extension merger* which eliminates potential competition in the institutional pie market. The government's case on the first point appears strong, but its case on the second point is weak.

Horizontal merger: Under the *Philadelphia National Bank* test, a horizontal merger is presumed illegal if it creates an undue market share and a significant increase in market concentration. Evaluation of either of these criteria requires an analysis of the relevant market. From the facts presented, the geographic market clearly appears to be the United States. The product market is more of a problem to define. While all pies would appear interchangeable, the facts indicate that industrial and retail pies are in fact in separate markets, or at least in separate submarkets. Under the *Cellophane* test (*Alcoa*), markets are defined by analyzing cross-elasticity of demand between a product and its competitors. Demand elasticity looks at "reasonable interchangeability." At first blush, this definition might suggest that all pies—institutional and retail, frozen and fresh—and all other dessert products should be lumped into one market, since as the price increases a consumer would reasonably switch from one dessert to another. However, the facts indicate a high consumer resistance to switching from pies to other desserts and further indicate that fresh pies do not compete with frozen. Thus, on the basis of actual interchangeability, frozen pies are a distinct market or submarket. (A court might arrive at frozen pies as a distinct market by either determining product market in terms of actual elasticity or by determining a broad dessert market based on theoretical elasticity and then separating out frozen pies as a submarket because of consumer preference. The latter technique is suggested by the *Brown Shoe* decision.)

The government will argue, and the facts tend to indicate, that a further grouping of frozen institutional pies and frozen retail pies into submarkets should be made. Again, the two are theoretical substitutes, but consumers are unlikely to make such substitution. First, consumers are not given the opportunity to substitute these products because of the separate distribution lines. Second, each group of consumers is likely to consider the other group's product inferior. The smaller size of retail pies would make per piece sales difficult for institutional users, and the plain packaging would make institutional pies unattractive to retail buyers. American Corporation might argue that retail buyers would pay for the less attractive product because of lower price, but if this were true, it seems that some current competitors would be trying to sell institutional pies retail. Further, the possible desires of retail buyers are thwarted by the different distribution chains. It is also significant that the industry recognizes two separate markets by having separate distribution chains and by the fact that some companies do not compete in both markets. (*See Brown Shoe*.)

Having defined the relevant submarket in which American and Pierre's compete (*i.e.*, frozen pies), the government's prima facie case then turns on market share and market concentration analysis. A merger of the two will result in a company with 10.2% of the market (the third largest producer) and will result in an increase in the three-firm concentration ratio from 59.1% to 62% and the four-firm ratio from 66.2% to 69.3%. Whether these figures demonstrate a "significant" increase in concentration or an "undue" market share is not an easy question to resolve. Figures of this magnitude were found to be a violation in *Von's* (although there was a clear trend in that case toward concentration) and in *General Dynamics* (where the Court indicated that such figures would have constituted a violation if the defendant had not successfully rebutted plaintiff's prima facie case by showing that the merger had no anticompetitive effect). Thus, the government should be able to establish its prima facie case on the facts here.

American might attempt several possible defenses to this prima facie case. First, under *General Dynamics* it may be able to prove that there is no anticompetitive effect. The defendants may attempt to demonstrate the possibility of supply substitutability, *i.e.*, the possibility that institutional pie producers may readily enter the market. (This is properly the subject of rebuttal, since the Supreme Court test of markets does not appear to require a plaintiff to address supply substitutability as part of plaintiff's market definition.) Furthermore, there do not appear to be substantial barriers to entry between the two submarkets, since the institutional pie makers or de novo entrants might enter the retail market at any time. Thus, the defendants will argue that such potential entry will restrict retail pie manufacturers from charging excessive prices. One flaw with this argument, however, is that some of the institutional producers may already be producing retail pies (like Pierre's). If this is true, then the pro-competitive influence exerted by institutional producers could be minimal.

Second, American can argue that Ms. Zee was a failing company and merger with Pierre's was necessary to save it. This defense probably cannot be established. First, Ms. Zee is a division of a healthy company, and as such may be prevented from using the failing company defense. Moreover, Ms. Zee seems only to be faltering, not failing as *Citizens Publishing* requires. Ms. Zee has no history of losses. Its business arguably might be turned around by use of new techniques or technologies. Finally, it is not clear that American considered other less powerful merger partners, as required by *Citizens Publishing*.

Thus, the merger would seem to be **presumptively illegal** under the *Philadelphia National Bank* test, and American appears unable to rebut that presumption.

Conglomerate-Product Extension Merger: The government may also try to attack the merger because of its effect in the institutional pie market, but this attack will probably be unsuccessful.

First, **Federal Trade Commission v. Procter & Gamble Co.** indicates a concern with the disruptive effects to competition when a very large firm merges with an industry leader (here, Pierre's). Such an increase in market power (as American has) can entrench Pierre's as the market leader. There may be barriers to entry created by the merger: advertising efficiencies, a greater potential for predatory pricing (American has a deeper pocket), and the size may simply scare competitors from "rocking the boat." Additionally, this new strength may allow Pierre's to emerge as a price leader. Even if these concerns are not found to be sufficient in themselves to condemn the merger, they may make a court more willing to condemn a merger on potential competition grounds, discussed next.

There are two branches of potential competition theory, neither of which is convincingly established by the facts of this merger. For there to be a **"wings effect"** limiting the behavior of current competitors in a concentrated market, a corporation must be perceived as a potential entrant. It is unlikely that current institutional producers perceive Ms. Zee as a potential entrant. It has tried entry before and has failed, and it is an ineffective and faltering competitor even within its own market.

For there to be a **potential deconcentration effect**, the Supreme Court has indicated in *Marine Bancorporation* that the potential entrant (i) must have a feasible means of making a de novo or toe-hold entry, **and** (ii) that such entry would have a more competitive effect on the market than the proposed merger. This is an extremely difficult burden for the plaintiff to prove, especially the second element, although the *BOC* case (following *Marine Bancorporation*) indicates that the second element might be inferred from proof of the first element. Here, Ms. Zee's failure in the past suggests that it lacks the means for such entry. If the government could prove that Ms. Zee had the means to enter, the court might then presume entry would have a pro-competitive effect by shaking up a concentrated market. However, American might be able to rebut that presumption with proof of Ms. Zee's inferior product and production.

Thus, although the question is a close one, the government is unlikely to prevail on this second theory of conglomerate merger. The fear of concentration will not be sufficient to establish illegality because there is no additional proof of reduced potential competition.

Note: *The above student answer was written before the introduction of the 1992 Merger Guidelines. It still accurately reflects case law standards for merger enforcement. However, a good exam answer today would also take account of the differences that might result under the 1992 Merger Guidelines. Thus, one might add:*

The 1992 Merger Guidelines use a somewhat different approach to market definition. They take the product of the merging firms as the beginning point to establish a "provisional" product market. The Guidelines then seek to determine whether buyers would respond to a 5% price increase by shifting to other products within one year. If so, the provisional market would be expanded to include those products. The process of expansion will continue until a hypothetical firm that was the only present and future seller of the products in the market could raise prices profitably. In other words, the Department of Justice would define a provisional market, create an imaginary monopolist in that market, and ask whether that imaginary monopolist could increase its profits by increasing its price 5%. As long as the imaginary monopolist could not earn supracompetitive profits because buyers would buy substitute products, then those products would be included in a new and broader provisional market. Once the relevant product has been identified, the Guidelines would then seek to identify the firms that produce or could produce that product. The Guidelines would include firms that have "existing productive and distributive facilities that could easily and economically be used to produce and sell the relevant product within six months in a response to a . . . price increase of 5%." In other words, the Guidelines define the relevant market by counting firms not currently producing the relevant product, but which could easily do so by "production substitution." Once the product market is defined and the product producers or potential producers are identified, the Guidelines then turn to geographic market definition and apply a similar approach to identify the firms that produce or could produce the relevant product at relevant locations.

In view of the limited amount of information available in this question, it is difficult to apply the Guidelines' market definition approach to the retail frozen pie industry. This "evidentiary" difficulty, however, is likely to occur in real-life cases as well, and, accordingly, represents a deficiency in the Guidelines' approach. An effort to determine what would happen in the face of a 5% price increase will probably require extensive economic and industry expert testimony as well as whatever available historic evidence might exist. The point at which the Guidelines' approach might differ with the suggested traditional analysis has to do with estimates of "production substitutability." If a 5% price increase in the retail frozen pie market would induce institutional frozen pie makers to shift production, then the provisional market is likely to be expanded to include both products. In that event, the market shares of the merging firms would not likely be substantial enough to merit challenge.

However, if a similar retail frozen pie market were to be defined under the Guidelines' approach, yet another difference in analysis would occur. The Guidelines reject a four-firm concentration ratio approach and instead endorse a Herfindahl-Hirschman Index ("HHI") to measure concentration and increases in concentration. The post-merger HHI for this industry is approximately 2,083. While this is clearly in the highly concentrated area under the Guidelines, the *increase* in the HHI brought about by the merger of Pierre's and Ms. Zee is only 42 points, obviously below the 50-point level at which the Department of Justice begins expressing concern. Thus, it would appear that a challenge to this merger by the Justice Department would be unlikely under the 1992 Guidelines.

With respect to a "potential competition" challenge to the merger, the 1992 Guidelines are probably tighter than the case law discussed under the traditional analysis. Therefore, a challenge on this theory is unlikely by the Department of Justice.

ANSWER TO QUESTION IV

There are a number of claims that Acme might reasonably bring against Paradise Corp. or Quality Carpet Corp. The potential theories for recovery include: tie-in, boycott, exclusive dealing, attempt to monopolize, and monopolization.

There are essentially two separate series of actions by Paradise, Quality Carpet, and the *Gazette* that might give rise to liability under the antitrust laws. The first is the refusal by the *Gazette* to carry Acme advertising. The second is the sale of carpeted housing in Paradise. Each will be discussed below.

Boycott: At first glance, the *Gazette's* conduct looks like a boycott, since it involves a refusal to deal which deprives Acme of a valuable business relationship. It is not a classic boycott, however, because it involves a vertical, rather than horizontal, agreement. Quality Carpet did not agree with its **competitors** to deprive Acme of access to the *Gazette*; rather, it agreed with its "customer," Paradise. It is possible to read the *Klors* case as prohibiting such boycotts, even though they involve vertical relationships. On the other hand, a careful reading of *Klors* indicates that a horizontal agreement among the suppliers of *Klors* was involved. If *Klors* nevertheless is read to prohibit boycotts based on vertical agreements, then the "agreement" between Paradise and the *Gazette* to refuse to sell advertising to Acme would be treated as per se illegal.

However, the defendants will argue that no "agreement" exists, since the defendants are not separate entities, but merely one corporation. It is clear from *Copperweld Corp.* that an agreement between a corporation and its wholly-owned subsidiaries does not constitute a section 1 violation. Therefore, a boycott claim is likely to fail on these facts.

Tie-in: Paradise's sale of carpeted homes might be regarded as a tying arrangement, where the home is the tying product and the carpeting is the tied product. If there is sufficient power in the tying product and restraint of a not-insubstantial amount of commerce, then the tying arrangement will be found per se illegal.

Power in the tying product can be established by copyright or patent, market dominance, or the uniqueness of the tying product. Here, the question is one of market dominance or uniqueness of the product. These are difficult questions to answer.

On the one hand, Paradise homes are arguably not unique; that is, they are like other homes available in the area surrounding Paradise. Likewise, it is arguable that Paradise does not have market dominance because the relevant market is housing in the broad geographical area that includes—but is not limited to—the community of Paradise. On the other hand, housing in a retirement community may be viewed as a distinct type of housing by consumers who show a strong preference for living in an adult community away from children. For these people, the product may indeed be regarded as unique. Furthermore, if there are no other retirement communities in the area, Paradise might be regarded as a separate submarket for housing in which it would clearly have a dominant market share.

As indicated above, on the facts in this case the question appears to be a close one. Assuming that a unique product or market dominance is found, plaintiff will probably be able also to establish that a not insubstantial amount of commerce was restrained, since all carpet installers, other than Quality Carpet, are foreclosed from the Paradise new-housing market. This foreclosure amounted to a 4% loss in Acme's total annual carpet sales to all customers. The percentage lost to other carpet installers is not indicated by the facts, but together the foreclosure would appear to meet the minimal requirements of the tie-in test.

If the prerequisites of power and commerce are established, then per se analysis follows. However, it should be noted that even if the prerequisites are not established, the conduct should be analyzed under the rule of reason to determine if it nevertheless should be condemned as an unreasonable restraint on trade.

As defenses, Paradise might attempt to argue that its carpeting and housing should be treated as one product, rather than two, thereby precluding a tie-in claim. This defense will probably not succeed, since the products were previously marketed separately, and there appears to be no clear efficiency justification for now marketing them together. Reliance upon a "new entrant" defense would probably also be unsuccessful in this case, since Paradise is not a new entrant into the housing market. Even if it were, the tying arrangement might still be found illegal under a rule of reason analysis (*Jerrold Electronics*).

Exclusive Dealing: If Paradise and Quality Carpet were viewed as separate entities, Acme might claim a section 1 violation on the ground that Paradise entered into an exclusive dealing arrangement with Quality Carpet, whereby Quality Carpet agreed to supply all of Paradise's carpet needs, thus foreclosing Quality Carpet's competitors from that market. The test applied is that of rule of reason. The test is more liberal than the test applied in tie-in analysis, because exclusive dealing arrangements have the potential of aiding buyers as well as sellers and thus may be viewed as an efficiency-creating relationship. A violation may be found under section 1 of the Sherman Act if plaintiff is able to prove that the exclusive dealing arrangement forecloses a substantial amount of competition in a line of commerce. In *Standard Oil*, "substantiality" appeared to be analyzed in terms of the dollar amount involved in the foreclosure. In *Tampa Electric*, substantiality was measured by the market share foreclosed, which of course required a full market definition and analysis. Since approximately 300-400 homes are involved per year in the Paradise case, the dollar amount involved may not be viewed as a "substantial" enough foreclosure to warrant a finding of illegality. Application of the *Tampa Electric* test requires market definition, which on the facts in the Paradise case would seem to be the area in and about Paradise where carpet installers typically travel to install their carpeting. The market would seem to be substantially greater than the Paradise community itself. Since a broad market definition may be quite realistic in this case, "substantial" foreclosure may not be found under this test either. A final determination of reasonableness or unreasonableness would depend upon all of the various factors that must be analyzed by the trial court under a rule of reason analysis. However, as stated above, Paradise and Quality Carpet are not separate entities, and, as such, cannot violate section 1.

Attempt to Monopolize: The refusal of the *Gazette* to carry Acme's advertising and/or the conduct of Paradise and Quality Carpet in foreclosing Acme from competing for new carpet installation in Paradise may form the basis for an attempted monopolization claim by Acme. Proof of exclusionary or predatory practices by a firm may be sufficient to constitute attempted monopoly under section 2 of the Sherman Act if the plaintiff is able to prove that (i) the defendant had a specific intent to monopolize, and (ii) there was a "dangerous probability" of success. In this traditional formulation of the attempted monopolization test, "dangerous probability" generally requires proof by the plaintiff of defendant's power in a relevant market.

In the case of Paradise, Acme may be able to make a prima facie case of specific intent to monopolize by demonstrating that Paradise's conduct prohibiting advertising in the *Gazette* and foreclosing Acme from the new carpet market is sufficiently exclusionary and unfair to permit an inference of specific intent to monopolize. The difficulty, however, will be in establishing Paradise's power in a relevant market. If a broad market definition, including the geographical area extending beyond the community of Paradise, is adopted, then it will be difficult to demonstrate Paradise's market power.

Although the Ninth Circuit at one time applied a more liberal approach to the attempted monopolization analysis, the Supreme Court specifically struck down the Ninth Circuit approach in *Spectrum Sports*. Therefore, the venue of this case will not affect its outcome on the attempted monopolization claim.

ANSWER TO QUESTION V

This memorandum answers the three questions posed concerning the proposed amendment to section 2 of the Sherman Act.

(1) **Changes in monopoly law:** The proposed amendment will make a significant change in monopoly law. For the particular firms covered, the amendment effectively eliminates the necessity of proving exclusionary acts or conduct. While some have suggested that the *Alcoa* decision can be read broadly to eliminate the necessity of proving conduct, most

courts have continued to require that bad conduct be proved, even though the conduct has at times been quite minimal. [*See, e.g., Alcoa, Grinnell*] The minimal exclusionary conduct requirement usually means that the firm must have been presented with a choice of options and chose that which had a greater exclusionary effect on competition. As indicated above, under the proposed amendment, even such a minimal conduct test is eliminated.

Furthermore, the proposed amendment appears to place greater limitations upon the defenses available to one charged with monopolizing. Under *Alcoa* and *Grinnell*, a defendant might prove that its market power was based on superior product, superior business skill, foresight, and industry. These defenses are arguably broader than the "patents or efficiencies of scale" defenses allowed in the proposed amendment. Thus, the proposed statutory amendment casts an even wider net of illegality than does a broad reading of the *Alcoa* test. However, it should be noted that the five-year and $500 million requirements of the proposed amendment are limitations not found in *Alcoa* or other monopoly tests, and thus create a safe harbor for monopolies under those limits. Such monopolies must still be tested by traditional standards.

(2) **Arguments for the amendment:** There are a number of arguments that will be made in favor of the proposed amendment. First, it will be argued that the harms of monopoly—uncompetitive pricing, reduced output, lack of innovation—are harms that result from size alone, regardless of how the size was obtained. Society is therefore harmed by the size and power of the monopolist, regardless of how the power was achieved or the conduct of the monopolist. Therefore, conduct should not be an element of the offense of monopolization. Second, the amendment strives to avoid any negative consequences flowing from condemnation of market power and size, by excluding treble damages and criminal penalties as remedies. The remedy provided may only be sought by the government. Furthermore, the structural relief permitted by the remedy is limited to that which is "feasible without substantial loss of efficiencies of scale"—*i.e.*, size will not be condemned if defendants can prove related efficiencies. Thus, consistent with scale economies, competitors are encouraged to increase their size and market share and will not be penalized. Third, the amended statute would provide businesses with a greater sense of certainty concerning legal standards for liability. This "bright line" effect should permit businesses to better plan for the future. Fourth, the proposed amendment will be considerably easier to administer in the courts, since proof of conduct will no longer be an element of the government's case.

(3) **Opinion of amendment:** While there are several arguments that can be advanced against this proposed amendment, on balance the amendment should be passed. [*Note:* Since this is a question asking for student evaluation and opinion, you certainly could come to the opposite conclusion advanced in this sample answer. Any conclusion is acceptable if it is argued well.] The arguments for the proposed amendment are stated above. The arguments in opposition to the proposed amendment are: the amendment essentially punishes good conduct and successful firms, and thereby will be a disincentive to compete effectively in the marketplace; the amendment fails to define "substantial, persistent monopoly power," "a properly defined relevant market," or "efficiencies of

scale"; the amendment is arbitrary in that it singles out only certain firms for special treatment; and present legal standards have been working well enough and have properly singled out only those firms that have market power *and* have engaged in abuse of that power or other reprehensible conduct.

Although the question is a close one, on balance the amendment should be passed, since society's interest in being free from the effects of monopoly outweighs the cost imposed on certain businesses in possession of monopoly power. In recognition, however, of the arguments that will be made in opposition to the proposed amendment, it might be suggested that the proposed amendment include a mandatory five- or 10-year termination date, after which period of time the Department of Justice should be instructed to gather data and make a report concerning the efficacy of the amendment and make recommendations to Congress concerning whether or not it should be relegislated.

Table of Cases

Table of
Cases

F

F. C. Russell Co. v. Consumers Insulation - **§517**

FTC v. - *see name of party*

Falls City Industries v. Vanco Beverage, Inc. - **§§429, 430**

Falstaff Brewing Corp., United States v. - **§349**

Fashion Originators' Guild v. FTC - **§235**

Federal Baseball Clubs v. National League - **§572**

Federal Maritime Commission v. Pacific Maritime Association - **§549**

Federal Maritime Commission v. Seatrain Lines, Inc. - **§§539, 549**

Feist Publications, Inc. v. Rural Telephone Service Co. - **§492**

Fineman v. Armstrong World Industries, Inc. - **§§162, 183**

First Comics, Inc. v. World Color Press, Inc. - **§408**

Flintkote Co. v. Lysfjord - **§121**

Flood v. Kuhn - **§572**

Ford Motor Co. v. United States - **§361**

Fred Meyer, Inc., FTC v. - **§§396, 435, 439**

G

Gaste v. Kaiserman - **§498**

General Dynamics Corp., United States v. - **§§166, 340, 342, 357, 358, 378**

General Electric, United States v. (1973) - **§§274, 511**

General Electric, United States v. (1949) - **§185**

General Electric, United States v. (1926) - **§§274, 511, 512**

General Leaseways v. National Truck Leasing - **§227**

General Motors Corp., *In re* - **§246**

General Motors Corp., United States v. - **§232**

General Talking Pictures Corp. v. Western Electric - **§513**

Getz Bros. & Co. v. Federal Salt Co. - **§30**

Glaxo Group, Ltd., United States v. - **§§94, 505**

Goldfarb v. Virginia State Bar - **§§217, 588**

Gordon v. New York Stock Exchange - **§567**

Graham v. John Deere Co. - **§472**

Grand Union Co. v. FTC - **§§442, 455**

Great Atlantic & Pacific Tea Co. v. FTC - **§§425, 441**

Greater Buffalo Press, Inc., United States v. - **§327**

Griffith, United States v. - **§188**

Grinnel Corp., United States v. - **§§143, 157, 160, 170**

Group Life & Health Insurance Co. v. Royal Drug Co. - **§564**

Gulf Oil Corp. v. Copp Paving Co. - **§§77, 78, 396**

H

H. A. Artists & Associates, Inc. v. Actors' Equity Association - **§570**

Hallie, Town of v. City of Eau Claire - **§576**

Handgards, Inc. v. Ethicon, Inc. - **§530**

Hanover Shoe, Inc. v. United Shoe Machinery Corp. - **§§116, 123**

Harrison v. Glucose Sugar Refining - **§18**

Hartford-Empire Co. v. United States - **§§220, 322**

Hartford Fire Insurance Co. v. California - **§§81, 235, 565, 566**

Hartley & Parker, Inc. v. Florida Beverage Corp. - **§410**

Hayden Publishing Co. v. Cox Broadcasting Corp. - **§162**

Haywood v. National Basketball Association - **§573**

Heater v. FTC - **§141**

Heatransfer Corp. v. Volkswagenwerk, A. G. - **§160**

Henry Broch, FTC v. - **§433**

Herriman v. Menzies - **§39**

Hertz Corp. v. City of New York - **§578**

Hiland Dairy, Inc. v. Kroger Co. - **§109**

Hinote, United States v. - **§545**

Holloway v. Bristol-Myers Corp. - **§58**

Hoopes v. Union Oil - **§107**

Hoover v. Ronwin - **§576**

Horizons, International v. Baldridge - **§556**

Hospital Building Co. v. Trustees of Rex Hospital - **§72**

I

Ideal Plumbing Co. v. Benco, Inc. - **§407**

Illinois Brick Co. v. Illinois - **§§114, 117, 118, 119**

Illinois Corporate Travel v. American Airlines - **§274**

Image Technical Services, Inc. v. Eastman Kodak - **§507**

Imperial Chemical Industries, United States v. - **§80**

In re - *see name of party*

Independent Service Organizations Antitrust Litigation ("Xerox") - **§507**

Indian Coffee Corp. v. Procter & Gamble Co. - **§411**

Indiana Federation of Dentists, FTC v. - **§§209, 234, 586**

Inglis & Sons Baking, Inc. v. ITT Continental Baking Co. - **§176**

Intergraph Corp. v. Intel Corp. - **§524**

International Boxing Club v. United States - **§147**

International Logistics Group v. Chrysler Corp. - **§152**

International Raw Materials, Ltd. v. Stauffer Chemical Co. - **§554**

International Salt Co. v. United States - **§§307, 309, 518**

International Shoe Co. v. FTC - **§338**

Interstate Circuit, Inc. v. United States - **§§253, 254, 255**

J

J. Truett Payne v. Chrysler Motor Corp. - **§§121, 447**

Jefferson County Pharmaceutical Association v. Abbott - **§444**

Jefferson Parish Hospital District No. 2 v. Hyde - **§§304, 306, 308**

Jerrold Electronics, United States v. - **§312**

U

V

WX

Y

Z

Index

Index

heavily regulated industries, **§236**

industry self-regulation, **§235**

per se rule, **§232**

political boycotts, **§237**

quick look analysis, **§234**

refusals to deal by group, **§230**

rule of reason, **§233**

BROKERAGE, §433

See also Price discrimination

BURDEN OF PROOF

commerce requirement, **§78**

failing company doctrine, **§339**

horizontal mergers, **§357**

predatory pricing, **§175**

BUYING POWER

See Monopsony

C

CAPPER-VOLSTEAD ACT, §§542, 548

CARRIERS, COMMON

See Common carriers

CARTELS, §§45, 619, 637

CAUSATION, §§107-112

See also Damages

CEASE AND DESIST ORDER

See also Federal Trade Commission; Remedies

Capper-Volstead Act, **§548**

FTC remedy, **§136**

CELLER-KEFAUVER ACT, §§64, 323-325

See also Mergers

CHARACTERIZATION

boycotts, **§§231-234**

horizontal mergers, **§347**

horizontal restraints, **§§206-210, 224**

joint ventures, **§§239-241**

mergers, **§347**

price fixing, **§§211-213**

vertical restraints, **§269**

CIVIL INVESTIGATORY DEMANDS, §§65, 90

CIVIL SUITS, §§92-106

by FTC, **§§58, 136-141, 447**

CLAYTON ACT

See also Robinson-Patman Act

amendments to, **§§62-65**

Celler-Kefauver Act, **§64**

Hart-Scott-Rodino Antitrust Improvements Act, **§65**

Robinson-Patman Act, **§63**

enforced by FTC and Justice Department

concurrent power, **§§59, 136, 451**

gaps in Act, **§455**

potential violations, **§454**

remedies, **§§137-141, 461**. *See also* Remedies

exemptions, **§§55, 541, 558, 568**. *See also* Exemptions

interlocking directorates, **§§263-266**

interstate commerce requirement, **§§55, 75-77**

joint ventures, **§§370-371**

mergers and acquisitions, **§§320-369**. *See also* Mergers

patents as assets, **§504**

provisions of, **§55**

treble damages, **§§55, 98**

tying arrangements, **§§55, 297-300, 302**. *See also* Tying arrangements

vertical restraints, **§268**. *See also* Vertical restraints

who may sue, **§§93, 98-119**

COMBINATION IN RESTRAINT OF TRADE

See also Common law monopoly; Horizontal restraints

common law, **§§32-42**

defined, **§32**

rule of reason, **§§39-42**

Sherman Act, **§§251, 259**

COMMERCE

See Foreign commerce; Interstate commerce

COMMODITIES, §§297, 406-410

price discrimination, **§§406-410**

tying arrangements, **§297**

COMMON CARRIERS, §§550-551

COMMON LAW

and Sherman Act, **§§49-52**

ineffectiveness of, **§§46-48**

monopoly. *See* Common law monopoly

restraint of trade, **§§1-23**. *See also* Restraint of trade

COMMON LAW MONOPOLY, §§31-42

combinations in restraint of trade, **§32**

criminal conspiracy, **§38**

defined, **§31**

distress industries, **§43**

local guilds, **§34**

middleman offenses, **§33**

private monopolies, **§§37-38**

rule of reason, **§§39-42**

Statute of Monopolies, **§36**

COMMON LAW RESTRAINT OF TRADE, §§1-23

See also Restraint of trade

COMPETITION

as an ideal, **§§647-649**

Clayton Act, **§56**

economic analysis, **§§591-612**

cost concepts, **§§604-609**

demand concepts, **§§592-603**

revenue concepts, **§§610-612**

FTC Act, **§57**

COMPETITIVE BIDDING, §§203, 222, 589

Engineers' Ethical Code, **§589**

price fixing, **§222**

CONCURRENT AUTHORITY, §§136, 451

bright line rules, **§344**

burden of proof, **§358**

characterization, **§347**

defenses, **§§326-332**

defined, **§343**

Department of Justice Guidelines, **§§359, 375-378**

market structure analysis, **§345**

presumptive illegality test, **§§353-356**

    increased concentration, **§355**

    mitigating factors, **§346**

    relevant market, **§354**

    totality of circumstances, **§356**

    when presumed, **§357**

totality of circumstances, **§§344, 356**

HORIZONTAL RESTRAINTS, §§199-266

See also Boycotts; Division of markets; Joint ventures;
                Price fixing; Rule of reason

agreements, combinations, or conspiracies, **§§251-266**

    agreement critical, **§251**

    combination, expanding concept, **§259**

    conscious parallelism, **§§251-258**

        circumstantial evidence of agreement, **§§251,
            254**

        defined, **§252**

        direct evidence, **§251**

        FTC Act, illegal under, **§257**

        indirect proof of conspiracy, **§258**

        inferences of agreement, **§§251, 253**

        parallel conduct alone insufficient, **§255**

        plus factors, **§256**

        proof of conspiracy, **§258**

    inter-corporate conspiracy, **§§261-266**

        interlocking directorates, **§§263-266**

            bank exemption, **§266**

            Clayton Act prohibition, **§§262-264**

            enforcement, **§266**

            obvious competitive danger, **§265**

        partially-owned subsidiary, **§262**

    intra-corporate conspiracy, **§260**

    Sherman Act, **§§251, 262**

boycotts, **§§230-237**. *See also* Boycotts

characterization of conduct, **§§206-210, 224**

    effect of, **§210**

    in price fixing, **§224**

    per se conduct, **§§207, 210**

    procedure, **§208**

    "quick look" rule of reason, **§209**

    rule of reason, **§208**

competitors agreement necessary, **§200**

defined, **§199**

division of markets, **§§225-229**. *See also* Division of
                markets

information exchange, **§§248-250**

joint ventures, **§§238-247**. *See also* Joint ventures

per se violations, **§§205-209**

    characterization as, **§207**

effect, **§§205, 210**

    intermediate analysis, **§209**

    vs. rule of reason, **§208**

political boycotts, **§237**

price fixing, **§§211-224**. *See also* Price fixing

refusals to deal, **§§230-237**. *See also* Boycotts

rule of reason test, **§§202-204**. *See also* Rule of reason

self-regulation by trade groups, **§§235-236**

Sherman Act provision, **§251**

I

IMPORTS, §§80-81

IN PARI DELICTO DEFENSE, §124

INCREASED ECONOMIES

See Mergers

INDICTMENTS, §91

INDIRECT PRICE CONCESSIONS, §§399, 432-438

See also Price discrimination

INDUSTRY STRUCTURE, §246

See also Joint ventures

INFORMATION, §91

INFORMATION EXCHANGE, §§248-250

nonprice data, **§250**

prices, **§249**

INJUNCTION, §§93, 97, 139-140

INJURY, §§107-114

See also Damages

INNOCENTLY ACQUIRED MONOPOLY, §§189-190

INSURANCE, §§561-566

INTELLECTUAL PROPERTY RIGHTS

See also Copyrights; Patents

antitrust laws, **§§502-535**

as legal monopoly, **§§502-506**

compulsory licensing remedy, **§505**

copyrights, **§§489-501**. *See also* Copyrights

Department of Justice Guidelines, **§§532-535**

    market definition, **§533**

    rule of reason, **§535**

economic justifications, **§§462-463**

enforcement of rights, **§§528-531**

    anticompetitive litigation, **§530**

    antitrust petitioning immunity doctrine, **§531**

    fraudulent procurement, **§529**

exclusive licensing, **§506**

limitations, **§§464-467**

    duration, **§467**

    rights granted, **§465**

    scope of protection, **§466**

patents, **§§468-488**. *See also* Patents

refusal to deal, **§507**

restraints of trade, **§§508-527**. *See also* Patents,
                restraints of trade

sham infringement suits, §§530-531

tying arrangements, §§518-520

INTENT

attempt to monopolize, §194

criminal, §85

INTERBRAND COMPETITION, §§281-284

INTER-CORPORATE CONSPIRACIES, §§261-267

INTERDEPENDENCE, §253

See also Conscious parallelism

INTERFERENCES

See Patents

INTERLOCKING DIRECTORATES, §§55, 263-267

INTERSTATE COMMERCE, §§67-78

See also Jurisdiction

Clayton Act, §§75, 77

instrumentalities, §77

Robinson-Patman Act, §§76-77

Sherman Act, §§67-74

   de minimis exception, §72

INTERSTATE FORMULA, §§253-254

See also Conscious parallelism

INTERVENTION, §134

INTRA-CORPORATE CONSPIRACIES, §260

JK

JOINT VENTURES, §§238-247, 370-371

See also Horizontal restraints

defined, §238

joint research ventures, §§242, 247

National Cooperative Research Act, §247

per se violation, §239

rule of reason, §§240-245

structure of industry, §246

treated as mergers, §§370-371. *See also* Mergers

unlawful purpose, §239

JUDGMENT, EFFECT OF, §§129-130

See also Remedies

JURISDICTION, §§67-82

See also Antitrust laws, in general; Foreign commerce; Interstate commerce

L

LABOR UNIONS, §§55, 106, 568-571

See also Exemptions

LEARNED PROFESSIONS, §§587-590

LICENSE

common law monopoly, §31

patents, §94. *See also* Patents

LIMITATION OF ACTIONS, §§125-128

LIST PRICES, §214

LOBBYING, §§582-586

antitrust immunity, §582

conspiracy with foreign agent exception, §586

harassment or sham limitation, §586

Noerr-Pennington right of petition, §§582-584

   governmental bodies only, §§583-584

M

MARGINAL COST, §609

MARGINAL REVENUE, §612

MARKET DIVISION

See Division of markets

MARKET POWER

See also Monopolization

customer and territorial restraints, §284

defined, §154

economic analysis, §§154-157

exclusive distributors, §284

horizontal mergers, §§344-358. *See also* Horizontal mergers

in competitive market, §158

in imperfect market, §159

intellectual property, §519

measured by market share, §§158-163

   insufficient share, §162

   prime measure, §159

   sufficient share, §§160-161

price discrimination, §387

tying arrangements, §§293, 519

vertical nonprice restraints, §284

MARKET SHARE

and market power, §§158-163

exclusive dealing, §317

horizontal mergers. *See* Horizontal mergers

MARKET STRUCTURES, §§613-620

See also Economic analysis

bilateral monopoly, §620

cartels, §§619, 637. *See also* Cartels

monopolistic competition, §617

monopoly, §§614, 631-636. *See also* Monopoly

monopsony, §§618, 642-646. *See also* Monopsony

oligopoly, §§616, 638-641. *See also* Oligopoly

perfect competition, §§615, 625-630

MAXIMUM PRICE, §§218, 273

See also Price fixing; Resale price maintenance

McCARRAN-FERGUSON ACT, §561

McGUIRE ACT REPEALED, §§279-280

MEETING COMPETITION, §§424-431

See also Price discrimination

MERGERS, §§320-386

special per se rule, §305
price discrimination, §294
requirements, §292
separation of tying and tied products, §306
Sherman Act, §§301-302
types of, §291

U

UNCLEAN HANDS, §124

UNFAIR COMPETITION, §§448-450, 455-458
See also Federal Trade Commission; Federal Trade
Commission Act
FTC authority, §§136, 451-453

UNFAIR OR DECEPTIVE ACTS, §57
See also Federal Trade Commission; Federal Trade
Commission Act
attempt to monopolize, §195

UNFAIRNESS STANDARDS, §457

UNIFORM DELIVERED PRICE, §401
See also Freight charges

UNITED STATES TERRITORIES, §82

UNREASONABLE RESTRAINTS
See Restraint of trade

USE RESTRICTIONS
See Patents

V

VARIABLE COST, §607

VERTICAL MERGERS, §§360-363, 379-383
See also Mergers
Brown Shoe test, §361
Clayton Act, §361
de minimis foreclosure test, §§361-362
defenses, §362
defined, §360
Department of Justice Guidelines, §§379-383
factors evaluated, §361
modern test—significant anticompetitive effect, §362

VERTICAL RESTRAINTS, §§267-319
defined, §262
exclusive dealing, §§315-319
    de facto, §319
    market share test, §317

quantitative substantiality test, §316
    rule of reason, §318
nonprice restraints, §§281-289
    customer and territorial restrictions, §§285-289
        formerly illegal per se, §286
        rule of reason, §§287-289
    exclusive distributors, §§281-284
        market power required, §284
        rule of reason, §281
relevant statutes, §§268, 318
requirements contracts, §§315-319
resale price maintenance, §§270-280
    maximum prices, §§272-273
        difficult standing rules, §272
        rule of reason applies, §272
    per se exceptions, §§274-280
        consignments, §274
        state fair trade laws, §§279-280
        unilateral refusals to deal, §§275-278
    per se violations, §§270-273, 280
        economic analysis, §271
        minimum prices, §270
        trademarked goods, §280
rule of reason vs. per se rule, §269
state fair trade laws, §§279-280
tying arrangement, §§290-313. *See also* Tying
    arrangements

WXY

WATER CARRIERS, §549

WEBB-POMERENE EXPORT TRADE ASSOCIATIONS ACT, §§552-554
See also Exemptions

WHOLESALERS, §405
See also Price discrimination

WHOLLY OWNED SUBSIDIARIES, §261

WILSON TARIFF ACT, §66

WINGS EFFECT, §§349-351
See also Horizontal mergers

Z

ZONE PRICING, §403
See also Price discrimination

Notes

Notes

Notes

Notes

Notes

Notes

Notes

Notes

Notes

Notes